Islamic Monuments in Cairo

*A Practical Guide to Islamic
Monuments in Cairo* by Richard
Parker and Robin Sabin was first
published in 1974, and was published
in a second, revised edition in 1981.
The third edition, revised and
enlarged by Caroline Williams, was
published as *Islamic Monuments in
Cairo: A Practical Guide* in 1985.

Islamic Monuments in Cairo

A Practical Guide

Fourth Edition

by

Caroline Williams

The American University in Cairo Press

Illustration credits:

Figure 8: *The Minarets of Cairo*, Doris Behrens-Abouseif. The American University in Cairo Press, 1985.

Figure 9: Marston Morgan.

Pages 40, 80, 92, 95, 135, 168, 220, 232, 234, 240, 253: Richard B Parker.

Pages 39, 85, 112, 140, 189, 192, 196, 200, 243, 247, 261: Marian Precht.

Page 12: *The Mosques of Egypt*, The Survey of Egypt, 1949.

Page 133: K.A.C. Creswell. Courtesy of the Rare Books and Special Collections Library of the American University in Cairo.

Pages xii, 8, 37, 54, 74, 76, 125, 129, 145, 172, 179, 187, 191, 198, 207, 227, 238, 251, 257, 265: Caroline Williams.

113 Sharia Kasr el Aini
Cairo, Egypt

Second printing 1999

Dar el Kutub No. 2232/93
ISBN 977 424 310 2

Printed in Egypt by the American University in Cairo Press

Contents

Figures

Illustrations

$\mathcal{M}$aps

Foreword

When the first edition of this guide was published in 1974, it was a modest effort, the principal virtues of which were simplicity and clarity. It was intended as a practical handbook to the Islamic monuments of Cairo for the person with more interest than the average tourist. (I had originally wanted to call it 'The Practical Diplomat's Guide to the Islamic Monuments of Cairo,' because that was the sort of person I had in mind when I began writing it, but that seemed too precious.)

Seven years later the American University in Cairo Press brought out a second edition for which demand was gratifying and constant, but there was also a demand for more information about more monuments.

The third edition, therefore, was completely rewritten by Caroline Williams. She put enormous energy and enthusiasm into the task and produced a book which had the same general organization and retained some of our original language, but was essentially a new text. She described over two hundred monuments, as opposed to one hundred and fourteen in the second edition, and added substantial new information about many of those described earlier. While we tried to maintain clarity and simplicity, this was a much more ambitious and more informative book than the earlier editions. The fourth edition is her enlargement and revision of the third.

I had much help with the first and second editions—first of all from my collaborator Robin Sabin and also from the Egyptian Department of Antiquities and many friends in Cairo. This edition, like the third, is almost entirely the work of Caroline Williams.

Richard B. Parker

Acknowledgments

My own early explorations of Cairo's Islamic art and architecture owed much to Richard Parker's first edition of this book, which as congenial guide and as practical walking companion served well the distances of time and space. It is for me therefore a great pleasure to expand and update subsequent editions, and to continue the original purpose of practical guiding for those who would do their own wandering and their own searching.

For the information presented in this book my debt is to many sources: to the scholarly works of Max van Berchem, Gaston Wiet, and K.A.C. Creswell; to mentors such as J.M. Rogers, Christel Kessler, J.A. Williams, and Laila 'Aly Ibrahim; to the research of colleagues at the American University in Cairo such as Doris Behrens-Abouseif, Elizabeth Higashi, Shahira Mehrez, Eleanor Fernandez, Nelly Boulos Hanna, William Lyster; to individual and community enthusiasts such as John Rodenbeck and the Society for the Preservation of the Architectural Resources of Egypt (SPARE); to the comprehensive library collections at the French Institute of Archaeology in Cairo and the Creswell Collection at the AUC; to the staff at the Center for Middle East Studies at the University of Texas in Austin who typed the manuscript; to Marian Precht for her handsome photographs; to Marston Morgan for his architectural drawings; to J.A. Williams for his translations of the Quranic passages; and lastly to the city of Cairo, whose monuments are sources of history and beauty in neighborhoods full of life and diversity.

Caroline Williams

Bayn al-Qasrayn

How to Use This Book

Two introductory chapters on historical background and architecture are followed by thirteen chapters describing the various monuments, each with a detailed sketch map showing the monuments described therein. The tours in these chapters move from the south to the north, starting with the Island of Roda and ending with Bulaq. Those monuments that are outstanding are marked with asterisks. Three asterisks indicate a monument of prime importance, two mean that it definitely merits a visit, one that it is interesting.

The other monuments are all worth seeing if you have the time. A few now in ruins have been included because their fragments indicate the richness that once was.

For the tourist in a hurry we recommend the following itineraries:

I. For the really pressed: Mosque of Ibn Tulun with the adjoining Gayer-Anderson Museum (see Chapter 4) and Sultan Hasan Madrasa (Chapter 5). Total time: one and a half hours (minimum).

II. Itinerary I, plus the Qalawun complex, which is convenient to the souvenir shopping area of Khan al-Khalili (Chapter 11). Total time: two and a half hours.

III. Itinerary I, plus a walk from al-Azhar to Bab al-Futuh (Chapter 11), including Qalawun's complex listed in II. This itinerary contains most of the three-starred monuments. Total time: four hours (minimum).

IV. For the person who wants to see the chef d'oeuvre of Mamluk art, the complex of Qaytbay in the Northern Cemetery:

hard to find but worth the effort (Chapter 13). A close runner-up is the Mosque of Qajmas al-Ishaqi (Chapter 6). Total time: one and a half hours.

The person with ample time can start with Chapter 3 and work northward, chapter by chapter. In hot weather one chapter will suffice for a morning or afternoon. In the winter the vigorous may be able to cover two chapters in a morning, although it is not recommended. Chapter 11 will take an entire morning in any weather.

The numbers given in the text with the names of the monuments are those of the green and white plaques that mark them and show that they are historic. A blue and white plaque that appears on some monuments gives the number of the *waqf* (foundation) deed. Sometimes the monument has a date in Arabic numerals engraved in its façade. This corresponds to the date it was restored by the Comité de la conservation de l'art arabe, active between 1882 and 1952. In this book, dates of monuments are given first according to the Western calendar, then the Islamic.

A few words of general advice

1. The accessibility of the different monuments varies and some are hard to find. If you are hardy, speak Arabic, have a sense of direction, and have a car, you can drive to (or at least close to) most of them. If you cannot speak Arabic, you can still get around but may have difficulty finding some places. A car is a practical way to cover large distances quickly and comfortably, but it cannot be used all the time because streets are narrow and crowded, and walking is half the fun. If you are a stranger to the city, you will save time by hiring a guide to lead you to the monuments. It is advisable always to have plenty of change for entrance fees and tips.

2. Remember that many of these monuments are still used as places of worship. The major mosques tend to be open from 8 or 9 A.M. until 8 P.M., whereas some of the small neighborhood mosques are often closed between the dawn and the noon prayer. The times of prayer vary according to the position of the sun, but are generally at dawn, noon (summer, ca. 1 P.M.; winter, 12 noon), mid-afternoon (summer, 4:30; winter 3:30),

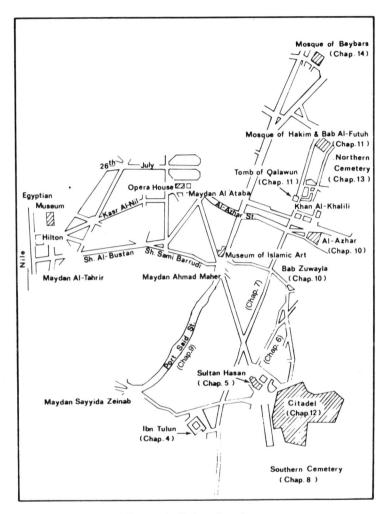

Figure 1: Cairo sketch map

dusk, and mid-evening. Friday in Islam is not a day of rest; the streets are crowded and full of life. It is a good day for touring, but all sightseeing is best done before the noon prayer, which is the most important one of the week. On Sundays the bazaars are closed and the medieval city tends to be deserted. This is a good day to photograph monuments.

Remember also that the important monuments are located in that part of Cairo that is by nature most conservative. It is important to be culturally sensitive. Women should wear a skirt or pants and walking shoes, and may find a headscarf useful. Shorts, miniskirts, tank tops are not considered proper or appropriate. Men should wear trousers and tops with sleeves. Take off your shoes at the entrance to those mosques that are still in use, and do not try to enter areas of buildings when the custodian tells you not to. At mosques frequented by tourists, such as Sultan Hasan, canvas overshoes are provided. For other visits, women may wish to carry socks as protection against cold floors and the dust of centuries. Another point worth noting is that except for the facilities mentioned in Chapter 11, restrooms are not usually available, nor are Western-style places in which to eat, so it is best to plan accordingly.

3. Those monuments that are restored usually have a caretaker and a fixed admission fee. Entrance fees vary from a tip to the man at the door, to several Egyptian pounds. If you pay a fee be sure to get a receipt in the form of a ticket.

4. Finally, these monuments are best approached in a leisurely fashion, with plenty of time for contemplation and the resting of feet. We have described those of major importance or interest, deviating here and there to say something about minor monuments that the resident may be curious about. The maps occasionally show lesser monuments that are not described in the text. This is usually done to give a landmark or to identify a frequently-passed minor monument.

On October 12, 1992, a severe earthquake occurred thirty kilometers south of Cairo. Many of the Islamic monuments of the capital were structurally weakened by the tremors and a number of minarets lost their finials. The overall damage is still being assessed. Thus visitors may find a monument wrapped in scaffolding or temporarily closed.

In the text the monuments are arranged geographically. In

the index, in addition to the alphabetical listing, there is also an attempt to present the material chronologically and typologically.

Note on the transliteration

In the interests of clarity and brevity we have transliterated Arabic words as simply as possible: emphatic letters and long vowels are not marked, and the *hamza* or glottal stop has been omitted. The letter *'ayn* is indicated by an apostrophe. While we have tried to be as true to the original Arabic lettering as possible some inconsistencies derived from earlier transliterative systems, foreign renderings, or popular usage remain. For the monuments themselves, with a few exceptions, the *Index to Mohammedan Monuments* by the Survey of Egypt, 1951, has provided a base. Arabic words not explained in the text will be found in the glossary.

1 ◊ Historical Summary and Chronology

The traveler is commonly pleased to find a dozen buildings from the Middle ages in a single European city. Cairo has them by the score. It is an unequaled treasure house of Islamic architecture—a treasure house that most visitors pass by in ignorance.

Medieval Cairo was one of the cities of the Thousand-and-one-Nights. It was in the narrow streets of Bayn al-Qasrayn and Darb al-Ahmar that many of the characters of those tales were supposed to have lived. If they were imaginary creatures, there were enough real heroes, rogues, and clowns who did in fact live there to people another set of a thousand tales, and to build a city that, unlike Baghdad and Damascus, was spared the devastation of the Mongol invasions. Many of its medieval structures are still standing. One has to search them out, but they will repay the effort. Unfortunately, Cairo's architectural treasures are being threatened today as never before. The *Index to Mohammedan Monuments in Cairo*, published by the Survey of Egypt in 1951, lists 622 different monuments or fragments of historic interest. Of these, the great majority are Mamluk and Turkish. Since 1951, due to pressures from the ever-expanding population, commercial interests, and general indifference to the problem, many of these buildings have disappeared, while others are seriously threatened. In October 1992 an earthquake seriously damaged over 125 monuments. Time seems to be running out for Islamic Cairo, and for this magnificent architectural and urban heritage.

By Near Eastern standards, Cairo is young. At the time of the Arab conquest in 641, it was a provincial fortress town called Babylon, the nucleus of which is now occupied by the Coptic Museum, the Hanging Church, and related buildings in the medieval Coptic quarter of Old Cairo (Misr al-Qadima). The fortress of Babylon guarded the northernmost single crossing of the Nile. North of Cairo the Nile divided and one had to cross two or more channels to pass over it. To the desert Arabs Babylon, at the juncture of Upper and Lower Egypt and with its back to the desert, was a safer and more strategic site than the Greco–Roman capital of Alexandria, a city that lay on the unfamiliar sea with its back to a hinterland crossed by numerous canals and other impediments to the rapid movement of mounted Bedouin. The leader of the Arab troops, 'Amr ibn al-'As, therefore established a garrison town called al-Fustat, north and east of Babylon, as the first Muslim settlement in Egypt. Al-Fustat means 'the camp.' On the western or Nile edge of al-Fustat he built a simple mud-brick mosque, the first in Egypt.

Subsequent expansion under the Abbasids, Tulunids, and Fatimids was to the northeast, with the city finally centering around the area lying between the Citadel and Bab al-Futuh (figure 2), while outlying fringes reached the present northern limits of the City of the Dead or Northern Cemetery in the time of the Mamluks. The suburb of al-Fustat was burned and abandoned in 1168 to deny it to the Crusaders, and that portion of the city has never been resettled. The southern boundary of the medieval city was thus roughly the Mamluk aqueduct that still runs from the Nile to the east and then turns north toward the Citadel (figure 3). From that point on the Nile a canal once wound northward along the route of present-day Sharia Port Said to Azbakiya and eventually out to the Red Sea. Most of the Islamic monuments of interest lie in the area that is immediately east of central Cairo, i.e. the area of Sharia Port Said. The sketch map (figure 1) provides an idea of the location of major areas covered by this book in relation to Maydan al-Tahrir and the Nile Hilton Hotel.

In the nineteenth century the city of Cairo moved westward to the Nile, firstly as a series of palaces and gardens along its banks (whose memory survives in such names as Qasr al-'Aini

*View from Garden City toward the Citadel
and Muqattam hill*

and Qasr al-Dubara) and then radiating out from the new planned city that the Khedive Isma'il created as part of the impressive extravaganza organized around the opening of the Suez Canal. Maydan Isma'il, renamed Maydan al-Tahrir (Independence Square) after the Egyptian Revolution, is still the hub of Cairo's central business district.

To the person who is not a student of Arab or Islamic history, the procession of exotic names and dates following 'Amr ibn al-'As, the first Arab conqueror, is hard to keep straight. To appreciate the monuments, however, it helps to have some idea of the sequence of dynasties, to know when the monuments were built, and to know something about what distinguished one architectural style from another (e.g., to know a Fatimid pepper pot from a Mamluk jelly mold). The summary that follows will help.

The Rashidun (632–61). The four orthodox khalifs or successors of Muhammad are: Abu Bakr, 'Umar, 'Uthman, and 'Ali. There was general acquiescence in, if not agreement on, the claims to leadership of the first three, but a struggle over the succession began with the assassination of 'Uthman. When he died, the khalifate was contested by his relatives, the Umayyads, against 'Ali, the Prophet's son-in-law. In 661 'Ali was murdered and the Umayyads, who had already established themselves at Damascus, succeeded to the khalifate.

'Amr ibn al-'As conquered Egypt for the khalif 'Umar in 641, built his mosque, and established al-Fustat. From the period of the orthodox khalifs nothing identifiable remains in Cairo.

The Umayyad Khalifate (661–750). Al-Fustat was relatively unimportant during this period. The monuments of the Umayyads were built in Syria, Transjordan, and Palestine, and there are none from this period in Egypt.

Abbasids and Tulunids (750–935). In 750 the Abbasid branch of Muhammad's tribe put a bloody end to the Umayyads in Syria and succeeded to the khalifate. Under such figures as Mansur and Harun al-Rashid, they ruled the Arab world from an almost legendary Baghdad during one of the most splendid periods of Islamic civilization. Egypt was ruled by governors appointed by Baghdad, and one of them, Ahmad ibn Tulun, made himself independent of Baghdad and founded a short-lived dynasty (870–905). Three monuments date from this period: the Nilometer, the Mosque of Ibn Tulun, and the Aqueduct of Ibn Tulun ouside al-Fustat.

Ikhshidids (935–69). For the next thirty years control of Egypt passed once more to the Abbasid government in Baghdad, but soon another Turkish dynasty, like the Tulunids, seized power through the governorship. It left no monuments except the Mausoleum of the Sharif Tabataba, much altered, on the eastern edge of al-Fustat.

Fatimids (969–1171). The Fatimids were Shi'a (partisans of 'Ali) and believed in the principle of hereditary succession to the khalifate (as opposed to the Sunnis, who favored a succession by consensus based on their predominance in tribal society). They founded the only major Shi'i khalifate. Starting in Tunisia and claiming descent from the Prophet through his daughter Fatima (hence their name), they held Alexandria briefly in 914 and took control of Egypt in 969. Immediately after capturing al-Fustat they set to work to lay out a new quarter, which was called al-Qahira because Mars (al-Qahir or 'the conqueror') was in the ascendant at the time the foundations were begun. This is the present-day Arabic name of the city, which has become Cairo in English. The new city became the Fatimid capital in 973, and it remained the nucleus of the medieval and modern city until Cairo expanded westward in the nineteenth century. This medieval city was what the French referred to as *le grand Caire*. Under the Fatimids Cairo became the capital of a new Mediterranean Empire.

The Fatimid Empire reached its peak under its fifth khalif, Abu Mansur al-'Aziz (975–96), who built mosques, bridges, and palaces. Al-'Aziz's successor, al-Hakim bi-Amr Allah (literally 'Ruler by God's Command') was perhaps psychotic. A number of bizarre actions are charged to his record, including the destruction of the Church of the Holy Sepulchre in Jerusalem. The Fatimid dynasty lasted for another 139 years after al-Hakim but was in a steady decline for most of that period. This decline coincided with the establishment of the Crusader kingdom of Jerusalem, the expansion of Crusader power and influence, and

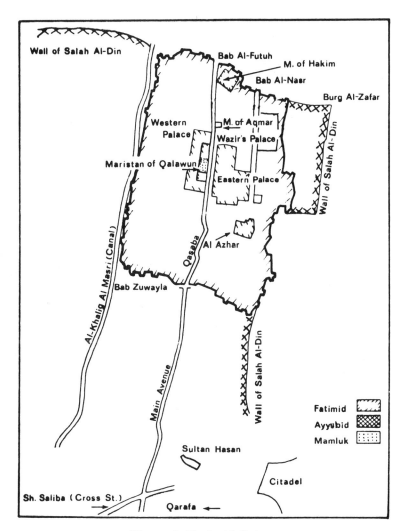

Figure 2: Fatimid Cairo

the resurgence of Sunni Islam under the Seljuq Turks and their successors in Iran, Iraq, and Syria.

There are numerous monuments from this period, the most important being the mosques of al-Azhar, al-Hakim, al-Aqmar, Salih Tala'i', al-Guyushi, the north walls and city gates (Bab al-Futuh, Bab al-Nasr, and Bab Zuwayla), and the mausolea in the Qarafa or Southern Cemetery.

Ayyubids (1171–1250). This was the dynasty of Salah al-Din Yusuf al-Ayyubi, the Saladin of the western chronicles. Salah al-Din was a Kurd from Syria who became wazir or prime minister of Fatimid Egypt in 1169 and whose immediate ambition was to convert Egypt from Shi'i back to Sunni Islam. He subsequently extended his control over Syria, Yemen, and the Hijaz. The last of the Fatimid khalifs expired in 1171 and in 1175 Salah al-Din had himself invested by the Abbasid khalif of Baghdad as ruler of Egypt, North Africa, Nubia, Western Arabia, and Syria. He subsequently defeated the Crusaders at the Horns of Hattin in Galilee in July 1187 and captured Jerusalem on 2 October of the same year. He died in 1193 and was buried at Damascus.

The empire Salah al-Din put together was split up among his sons and heirs at his death. In Egypt there was a succession of seven or eight Ayyubid sultans, depending on how one counts. (The term 'Ayyubid' means related to Ayyub, or Job, the father of Salah al-Din.) The sixth Ayyubid ruler was al-Salih Nagm al-Din, who introduced the practice of importing slave troops, the forerunners of the Mamluks. When he died in 1249, for a brief time his death was concealed. His Armenian concubine Queen Shagar al-Durr ('Tree of Pearls') assumed power, but the anomaly of a female ruling over men was so shocking that she was forced to marry Aybak, the commander of al-Salih's mamluk guard, and power passed to a new dynasty.

The most important monuments of the Ayyubid period are parts of the Citadel and city walls, the Tomb of the Imam al-Shafi'i, the Tomb of the Abbasid Khalifs, the Madrasa of al-Salih, and the Tomb of Shagar al-Durr.

Bahri Mamluks (1250–1382). Mamluk means 'one who is owned.' Non-Muslim children and adolescents, purchased or captured,

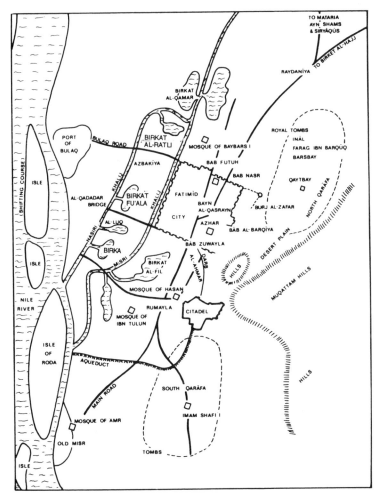

Figure 3: Mamluk Cairo

were brought to Egypt as slaves. After a long and careful training in military arts and in Islam they were formally freed. The lowest rank of Mamluk officer (or 'amir') commanded five household troops, next forty, then one hundred. An Amir Kabir, Grand Marshal, commanded one hundred high-ranking amirs, or an army of one thousand. Through ruthlessness, intelligence, or merit the young amir might hope to advance to the highest offices, even to the sultanate itself. As sultan he maintained himself by severity, prodigality, and the guard of highly trained soldiers with whom he surrounded himself. At the sultan's death rival amirs fought over the succession, often through the streets of Cairo, until the strongest, ablest ,or most cut-throat prevailed.

Mamluk rule is divided into two periods, the Bahri and the Burgi. The Bahris ruled from 1250 to 1383. Bahr means 'river,' and the Bahris were so called because their original barracks were on the Island of Roda in the Nile. The Bahri Mamluks were mostly Qipchacks from the steppes of the Volga river near the Caspian Sea. Most of the Bahri Sultans were descended from Sultan Qalawun, who established a dynasty that lasted a hundred years. The period of Bahri rule was relatively prosperous. Egypt, the wealthy crossroads of trade and commerce, provided the rulers with sums sufficient to support a crack army and subsidize learning and the arts. A succession of strong rulers maintained Egyptian control over Syria and eventually drove the Crusaders from the mainland. More importantly, they were successful in repelling four major invasions of the Mongols, thus sparing Egypt the crushing devastation that befell Iraq and Syria, and from which Iraq, at least, had still not recovered by the twentieth century.

Sultan al-Nasir Muhammad (1293–1340) ruled over medieval Cairo at its apogee. Ibn Battuta, the great medieval traveler, wrote in 1345: "I arrived at length at the city of Cairo, mother of cities, mistress of broad provinces and fruitful lands, boundless in the multitude of buildings, peerless in beauty and splendor. . . ." The *Index to Mohammedan Monuments in Cairo* lists one hundred monuments from the Bahri period. Of these the best known are the Complex of Sultan Qalawun, the monuments of al-Nasir Muhammad, the Mosque of Baybars, the Mosque of al-Maridani and the Madrasa of Sultan Hasan.

Others of historical importance and great beauty dot the medieval city.

Burgi or Circassian Mamluks (1382–1517). The Bahris were succeeded by the Burgi (or Burji) Mamluks, who were mostly Circassians from the Caucasus mountains and who took their name from the fact that they were quartered in the towers of the Citadel—*burg* means 'tower.'

Bahri rule was violent but Burgi was more so, and this was an unhappy era in Egyptian history—although worse was to come. The corrupt and arbitrary rule of the Circassians was the ruination of an economy that suffered further from natural catastrophes (such as plague and drought), from a breakdown of security in outlying areas, and from the discovery of a sea route to India by the Europeans. This bad luck was compounded by the invasion of Tamerlane, who got as far as Damascus, destroyed most of what he found, and routed an Egyptian army sent to stop him. Again, however, the Nile Valley itself was spared an invasion. The Mamluk period was brought to an end by the Ottoman Turks under Selim, who took Cairo and hanged the last Mamluk Sultan, Tumanbay, in 1517.

The money extorted from the economy by the Burgis was spent in part on architecture, and some fine monuments date from this period. The *Index* lists 133. A heaviness that had characterized some earlier Mamluk works was overcome, and the use of arabesque ornamentation in the carving of stone domes reached its apogee. Among the monuments that stand out are the tombs of Barquq and Qaytbay in the Northern Cemetery, the buildings of al-Ghuri around al-Azhar, and the Mosque of Qajmas al-Ishaqi near Bab Zuwayla.

The Ottoman Turks (1517–1798). Under Ottoman control Egypt reverted to the status of a pronince to be exploited by a distant power, and this period is generally regarded as decadent and inglorious. The Ottomans ruled Egypt through a series of viceroys, each of whom lasted an average of less than three years and delegated most of his authority to Mamluks who had survived the Turkish invasion. These were organized into a feudal order: they exercised powers and privileges in exchange for an obligation to provide troops for military service. They perpetuated their order by importing young slaves from the north.

As time went on, the power of the viceroys began to wane and that of the Mamluks grew; disorders and mutinies increased. What the Turks did not take, the Mamluks did. Famine and disease, together with the general lack of security, brought the population down to less than two million—compared to eight million in Roman times and just under sixty million today. This was the darkest period of Egyptian history.

The *Index* lists 216 monuments from the Turkish period. Although the most numerous, they are not the most exciting. Some are built in the Ottoman style (the mosques of Sulayman Pasha on the Citadel, of Malika Safiya, and of Sinan Pasha in Bulaq), but by and large the structures follow the styles of the preceding Mamluk period. Not as well built, many of them survive only in part. There is considerable charm, however, in the domestic architecture (Bayt al-Sihaymi) that survives and in the numerous sabil–kuttabs ('Abd al-Rahman Katkhuda) that dot the city. The sabil–kuttabs, combining public drinking fountains with Quranic schools, were a favorite civic charity and a type of monument unique to Cairo.

The Dynasty of Muhammad 'Ali (1805–1952). Napoleon invaded Egypt in 1798 and although he defeated the medieval army of the Mamluks at Imbaba in the so-called Battle of the Pyramids, he was not able to hold the country. Allied with English seapower the Ottomans drove him out and appointed Muhammad 'Ali, an Albanian mercenary and officer, as their viceroy in Egypt in 1805. In 1811 he massacred the leading Mamluks, ending forever an institution that had survived for over 550 years. He founded his own dynasty that lasted until 1952.

His reign was notable for the introduction of new Turkish styles and features. His mosque on the Citadel is a unique example of a Turkish imperial mosque and, by virtue of its dominating site, one of the most impressive structures of Cairo. Muhammad 'Ali's successors in the nineteenth and twentieth centuries continued the 'modernization' and 'westernization' of Cairo that he had begun. By confining it to new areas of the city such as the eastern and western banks of the Nile they did not obliterate the city's medieval heritage.

Chronology

639–641	Conquest of Egypt by 'Amr ibn al-'As
661–750	Umayyad khalifs rule from Damascus
750–870	Abbasid khalifs rule from Baghdad
870–905	Tulunid interregnum
905–935	Abbasid khalifs rule from Baghdad
935–969	Ikhshidid interregnum
969–1171	Fatimids
1171–1250	Ayyubids
1250–1517	Mamluks

Bahri Mamluk Sultans

Al-Mu'izz Aybak (husband of Shagar al-Durr)	1250–57
Al-Mansur 'Ali (son of Aybak)	1257–59
Al-Muzaffar Qutuz	1259–60
Al-Zahir Baybars (the Crossbowman)	1260–76
Al-Sa'id Baraka Khan (son of Baybars)	1277–79
Al-'Adil Salamish (son of Baybars)	1279
Al-Mansur Qalawun	1279–90
Al-Ashraf Khalil (son of Qalawun)	1290–93
Al-Nasir Muhammad (son of Qalawun)	1293–94
Al-Nasir Muhammad (again)	1299–1309
Al-Nasir Muhammad (again)	1310–1341
Al-'Adil Kitbugha ⎫ Mamluks of Qalawun	1294–96
Al-Mansur Lajin ⎬ and	1296–99
Al-Muzaffar Baybars ⎭ usurpers of al-Nasir	1309–10
(the Taster)	
Al-Mansur Abu Bakr ⎫	1341
Al-Ashraf Kuchuk	1341–42
Al-Nasir Ahmad	1342
Al-Salih Isma'il	1342–45
Al-Kamil Sha'ban ⎬ sons of al-Nasir	1345–46
Al-Muzaffar Hajji	1346–47
Al-Nasir Hasan	1347–51
(builder of the Madrasa)	
Al-Salih Salih	1351–54
Al-Nasir Hasan (again) ⎭	1354–61
Al-Mansur Muhammad (grandson of al-Nasir)	1361–63

Al-Ashraf Sha'ban (grandson of al-Nasir)	1363–77
Al-Mansur 'Ali (son of Sha'ban II)	1377–81
Al-Salih Hajji (son of Sha'ban II)	1381–82, 1389-90

Burgi Mamluk Sultans

Al-Zahir Barquq	1382–89, 1390–99
Al-Nasir Farag (son of Barquq)	1399–1405
Al-Mansur 'Abd al-Aziz (son of Barquq)	1405
Al-Nasir Farag (again)	1405–12
The Khalif al-'Adil al-Musta'in	1412
Al-Muayyad Shaykh	1412–21
Al-Muzaffar Ahmad (son of al-Muayyad)	1421
Al-Zahir Tatar	1421
Al-Salih Muhammad (son of Tatar)	1421–22
Al-Ashraf Barsbay	1422–38
Al-'Aziz Yusuf (son of Barsbay)	1438
Al-Zahir Gaqmaq	1438–53
Al-Mansur 'Uthman (son of Gaqmaq)	1453
Al-Ashraf Inal	1453–60
Al-Muayyad Ahmad (son of Inal)	1460–61
Al-Zahir Kushqadam	1461–67
Al-Zahir Yalbay	1467
Al-Zahir Timurbugha	1467
Al-Ashraf Qaytbay	1468–96
Al-Nasir Muhammad	1496–98
Al-Zahir Qansuh	1498–99
Al-Ashraf Ganbalat	1499–1501
Al-'Adil Tumanbay	1501
Al-Ashraf Qansuh al-Ghuri	1501–1516
Al-Ashraf Tumanbay	1516–17

1517	Ottoman Turks defeat Mamluks at Battle of Marj Dabiq, near Aleppo
1517	Ottoman rule of Egypt begins
1798–1801	Napoleon's invasion and occupation
1805–48	Muhammad 'Ali becomes viceroy of Egypt and Pasha
1811	Muhammad 'Ali massacres Mamluks

'Abbas (Pasha)	1848–54
Sa'id (Pasha)	1854–63
Isma'il (Khedive)	1863–79

1869   Opening of the Suez Canal

Tawfiq (Khedive)	1879–92

1882   British occupation begins

'Abbas Hilmi (Khedive)	1892–1912
Husayn Kamil (Sultan)	1914–17
Fuad I (King)	1917–36
Faruq (King)	1936–52

1952   Egyptian revolution under Gamal 'Abd al-Nasir
1954   Agreement ending British occupation

2 ◇ Architectural Summary

Most of the various monuments described here are religious, such as mosques and complexes; a few are secular—city walls, aqueducts, inns, houses. While there is a certain generic sameness to the religious structures—all minarets and domes look somewhat alike—they have distinct styles. The following may make their differences more understandable.

The Mosque. The only absolute requirement for a mosque is that it set off or demarcate a space in which people may gather for saying prayers while facing in the direction of Mecca. The first mosque was the courtyard of the Prophet's house in Medina, with no architectural refinements except a shaded area at one end. Early mosques built by the Arabs as their empire was expanding were as simple. From these beginnings developed the congregational or Friday mosque, whose essential features remain today more or less what they were 1,300 years ago—a large courtyard surrounded by arcaded porches, with more aisles or arcades on the side facing Mecca, the qibla side, than on the other sides (see figure 4).

Initially, the congregational mosque was the administrative and social as well as the religious center of the town, and in theory it should have been large enough to accommodate all the khalif's troops and subjects for the Friday sermon delivered by the local governor. The first congregational mosque in Egypt was that of 'Amr at al-Fustat, followed successively by those of Ibn Tulun, al-Azhar, and Baybars—reflecting the progressive northward shift of the administrative center of the town under

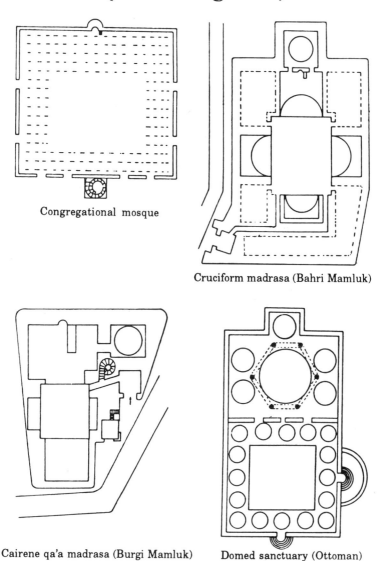

Congregational mosque

Cruciform madrasa (Bahri Mamluk)

Cairene qa'a madrasa (Burgi Mamluk)   Domed sanctuary (Ottoman)

Figure 4: Types of plans

different rulers. The principal congregational mosques in use today, other than al-Azhar, are Sayyidna al-Husayn (opposite al-Azhar) and Sayyida Zaynab, both normally closed to non-Muslims.

If we liken the congregational mosque to a cathedral then we can extend the parallel and compare smaller mosques to parish churches and chapels. Many of these follow the general plan of a courtyard with arcades, but some are simply rooms with a niche at one end marking the direction of Mecca. Some are very elaborate and some have special functions, such as the 'Umar Makram Mosque just off Tahrir Square, which is a favorite for the funerals of state officials.

The Madrasa. This is a school for law and theology. The students were trained for scholarly or administrative functions. The madrasa was introduced to Egypt by Salah al-Din as part of his effort to combat and suppress Fatimid Shi'ism. There are two special types that are of Cairene development. The first is the cruciform madrasa or theological college, the outstanding example being that of Sultan Hasan. Its basic form, that of four great vaulted halls or liwans that face each other across a central court, originated in Iran. There the liwans were connected by an open, double-storied arcade of rooms and cells. In Cairo, however, the dormitories and rooms were hidden behind the court façade, in an angle between the vaults. These madrasa buildings tend to rise vertically in a number of stories, as opposed to the flat parade-ground effect of the congregational mosque that provided space for a multitude on the same level. In the Mamluk period attachments of subsidiary units such as tomb chambers and sabil–kuttabs (see below) converted simple forms into large funerary complexes (see figure 4).

The second type of madrasa, the qa'a form, appeared at the end of the Mamluk period, a result both of the increasing complexity of the structure and of the fact that less urban land was available on which to build it. The basic cruciform madrasa plan was modified by shrinking the east and west vaults or liwans to vestigial proportions, and by reducing and covering the central courtyard with a wooden roof with a central lantern. This gave the madrasa unit a rectangular shape, about which were fitted the additional elements of the complex. This formula resulted in some of the most charming buildings in Cairo, with the mausoleum–madrasa of Qaytbay being perhaps the best example.

The Khanqah. This monastic residence for mystic, esoteric orders is another type of monument whose plan consists of a central court with surrounding lateral rooms. The earliest that survives is the Khanqah of Baybars II.

The Tomb or Mausoleum. In Arabic this is called a *qubba* (dome) or *turba*; usually it is a domed chamber holding one or more tombs, either freestanding or as part of a larger complex.

The Khan or Wikala. An inn for traveling merchants built around a courtyard, with stables and warehouses at ground level and living accommodation above. There is a well-restored example, Wikalat al-Ghuri, just down the street from al-Azhar.

The House. Cairene domestic architecture prior to the nineteenth century had considerable style and charm. Its controlling requirements were privacy, security, coolness, and a minimum of exterior ostentation. A number of attractive fragments remain, best known of which are the Gayer-Anderson Museum, next to the Mosque of Ibn Tulun, and the Bayt al-Sihaymi.

Fortifications and Aqueducts. These include the walls and gates of the Fatimid City, the Citadel, and the aqueduct that runs from the Nile to the Citadel.

The Sabil–Kuttab. In addition to those incorporated in Mamluk complexes there are a number of free-standing examples of these throughout the city. They are two-story buildings with a public fountain below and a Quranic school for boys above. They were a favorite charitable endowment of the Turkish period and some are still in use as schools, but the fountains have been supplanted by the municipal water system. The sabil–kuttabs are all in various stages of decay and the modernizers are stealthily sacrificing them to the bulldozer. Many of those that remain have much charm and beauty as, for example, those of 'Abd al-Rahman Katkhuda and Ruqayya Dudu.

Styles and Periods

The following is necessarily oversimplified, but it assembles in convenient form, without too much burdensome detail, an

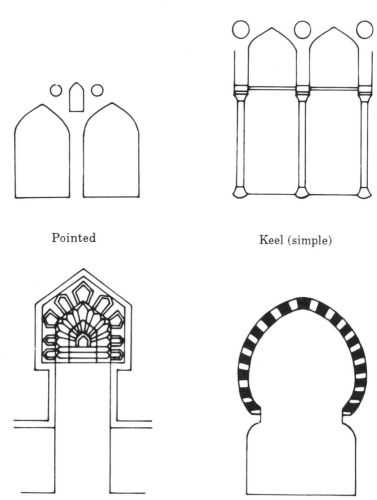

Pointed   Keel (simple)

Keel (ribbed, cusped)   Horseshoe

Figure 5. Types of Arches

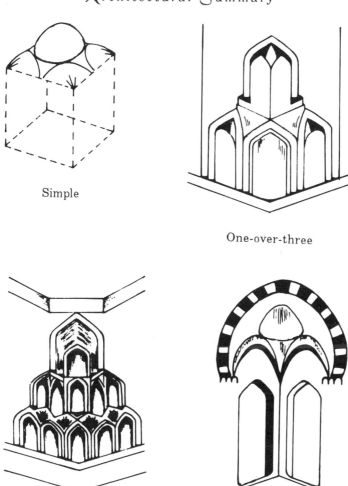

Simple

One-over-three

Stalactite

Window

Figure 6. Types of internal dome supports—squinches

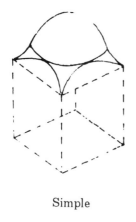

Simple

Fatima Khatun (see Ch. 8)

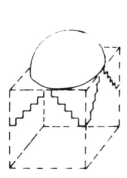

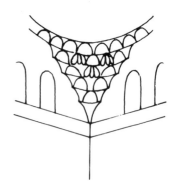

Stalactite

Figure 7. Types of internal dome supports—pendentives

overview of architectural periods. More detailed information appears in descriptions of individual monuments.

Early Islamic (750–969). A number of structures date from this period, but there is no uniform style. The outstanding monument of this era is the Mosque of Ibn Tulun, which is unique. Its inspiration came from Samarra, near Baghdad, the ninth-century capital of the Abbasids. It has brickwork piers, pointed arches, and a magnificent coating of carved stucco ornamentation. The brick piers were imitated in the Fatimid mosque of al-Hakim and the pointed arch and carved stucco became important features of Cairo architecture.

Fatimid–Ayyubid (969–1250). The first mosques of this period, al-Azhar and al-Hakim, were influenced by prototypes in Tunisia. The mosque of al-Aqmar, however, influenced by urban conditions in al-Qahira, offers a new plan and a new decorative scheme on its façade. The Fatimids continued the use of stucco, but preferred the keel arch, which they supported with Greco–Roman columns taken from older buildings and held together with iron rings and wooden tie beams. They carried the keel arch over as a frame for wall panels and windows, and filled the panels with stylized ornamentation: the results were happier at some times than at others. They also imposed the keel arch curve on the little domes they began putting on minarets, producing the Fatimid pepper-pot or shaker effect. An S-curve frame appears in windows, which later is incorporated into decorative niches of most minarets. A number of Fatimid tombs, such as that of Sayyida Ruqayya, have ribbed domes of North African inspiration.

The most important innovation of the Fatimid period was the introduction of stone masonry, starting with the stone walls and gates put up by the Armenian wazir, Badr al-Gamali. To the Fatimids also are due the earliest examples of domes now found in Cairo. They rested them on squinches, which developed into the elaborate stalactites that are a feature of Islamic buildings everywhere. Some of these are illustrated in figure 6.

The Ayyubids continued Fatimid styles with little innovation. They introduced a more flowing script, the Naskhi, which partially replaced the angular Kufic script in calligraphic ornamentation, and they introduced the madrasa or theological college, as well as the khanqah or sufi hostel.

Ayyubid / early Mamluk
(al-Salih Ayyub)

Bahri / mid-14th century
(al-Maridani)

Figure 8. Types of minarets

Burgi / late 15th century   Ottoman
       (Qaytbay)   (Sulayman Pasha)

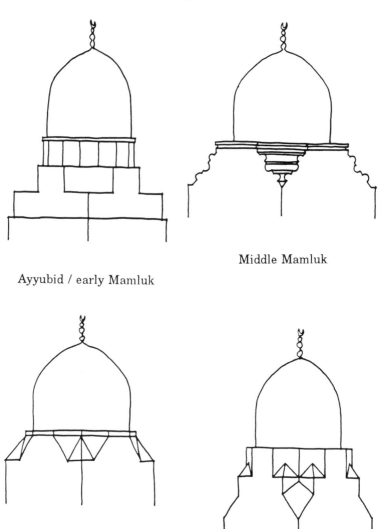

Figure 9. Types of external dome supports

partially replaced the angular Kufic script in calligraphic ornamentation, and they introduced the madrasa or theological college, as well as the khanqah or sufi hostel.

Early Mamluk (1250–1350). This is an era of transition and experimentation, with many innovations. It was during this period that the cruciform madrasa was developed. The domes of this period, in brick and plaster, were usually ribbed and followed a pointed arch curve as opposed to the keel arch curve of the Fatimids. The result resembles a jelly-mold.

Other innovations were the monumental doorway with stalactite decorations that became a characteristic feature of Mamluk architecture; the development of the minaret from a square, rather squat structure to a more slender shape with octagonal and round stages, approaching what has become the typical Cairo minaret (see figure 8); the gradual replacement of carved stucco with colored marble and mosaics; veneer joggling—the decoration of arches and entranceways with thin panels of marble, cut in jig-saw shapes and let into the stone; and, finally, the common use of ablaq or striped masonry, using alternating courses of different colored stone, often red and white.

Middle Mamluk (1350–1430). During this period, which spans the end of the Bahri and the beginning of the Burgi Mamluk periods, the use of stone for the domes of major structures became general. The stone dome begins to receive its first somewhat tentative decoration, as in the zig-zag lines on the domes of Barquq's desert mausoleum. This period produced a masterpiece of Mamluk art—the Madrasa of Sultan Hasan.

Late Mamluk (1430–1517). When town-founders such as 'Amr, Ibn Tulun, and the Fatimids built their mosques, they had ample land at their disposal. By the time of the Mamluks, however, the city of Cairo was well built-up and new buildings often had to be squeezed into the irregular spaces that remained between existing structures and streets. Early (i.e. Fatimid) mosques are almost uniformly rectangular, but later (i.e. Burgi Mamluk) buildings within the town are almost as uniformly irregular in ground plan, although considerable thought and effort was often given to making the building look

Windows

Fatimid   Ayyubid   Early Mamluk   Mid–late Mamluk

Cresting

Fatimid   Early Mamluk   Middle Mamluk

Late Mamluk

Figure 10: Types of windows and cresting

Simple Kufic

Foliate Kufic

Naskhi

Thuluth

"In the Name of God, the Merciful, the Compassionate"

Figure 11: Types of script

regular in shape. The search for regularity and rectangularity, even on irregular lots, became something of an obsession. The result was a number of jewel-like pieces, such as the beautifully restored Mosque of Qajmas near Bab Zuwayla, which is built on an irregular wedge of ground but still appears rectangular to the casual observer on the outside.

In the late Mamluk period, the crafts of decoration in marble and stone reached their peak. The delicate arabesques on the dome of Qaytbay's mausoleum are the finest example of this art. Other crafts, such as wood inlay and joining and metal sheathing, are also noteworty.

Toward the end of this period there begins a transition to Turkish styles, notably in the shapes of domes, which become flatter. There was a switch to less contrasting stone for ablaq (striped) masonry—a combination of white and soft yellow replaced the earlier red and white. There was also some experimenting with minarets, returning to the square of early Mamluk, with two or more finials on top. Good examples of these later minarets can be seen on the Mosque of al-Ghuri, as well as on al-Azhar.

Turkish Period (1517–nineteenth century). The late Turkish mosque is a variation of the congregational mosque plan, in which the sanctuary arcade is enclosed and covered by a large dome, and the lateral arcades around the courtyard are reduced to a simple portico. The Turkish minaret is pencil-shaped, thin, and tapered at the end. In this period it is secular monuments such as wikalas, houses, and sabil–kuttabs that predominate.

3 ◇ ᗞhe ᗅsland of ᖇoda
and ᖌld ᖘairo

Nilometer **
Mosque of Qaytbay
Manial Palace Museum **
Tomb of Sulayman Pasha al-Faransawi *
Mosque of 'Amr *
al-Fustat
Fortress of Babylon
Grand Hall in the Convent of St. George
Mu'allaqa Church
Coptic Museum **
Mamluk Aqueduct *

See map 1

Nilometer ** (No. 79) 861/247. Built after the Arab conquest, this is the oldest monument in Cairo that survives in its original form. It is situated on the southern tip of the island of Roda. The Nilometer is housed in the little building with a pointed roof, which is a recent reconstruction of a Turkish original. The pavilion on the west side is all that remains of the Palace of Hasan Pasha al-Monastirli, built c. 1830. It was part of the salamlik area and is now used as an exhibition center for local artists and crafts (closed Fridays). The gardens that once surrounded it have been replaced by a water treatment plant. The Nilometer is normally locked, but the custodian lives nearby.

As its name suggests, the main purpose of the Nilometer was to measure the river's annual August–September flood. It has been altered and repaired on numerous occasions, but the basic structure dates from 861, when it was built on the order of the Abbasid khalif al-Mutawakkil. It is a stone-lined pit that goes down well below the level of the Nile. Three tunnels lead into it from the river at different levels. In the center of the pit is a column graduated into sixteen cubits of about fifty-four centimeters each. When the water rose during the time of flood in August, it was possible to tell by the highest point it reached on the column whether it would be a year of too much, too little, or just enough water. When it reached sixteen cubits, this was the signal for cutting the dam that held the water back from the Khalig (the canal that once flowed through Cairo along the route of the present-day Sharia Port Said), a task that was performed with much ceremony during the Festival of the Opening of the Canal. In 1899 when the Khalig was filled in the festival ceased. The tunnels to the river are now blocked up, and the Nilometer no longer functions.

Enter and go down the steps to the level of the upper tunnel, the widest of the three levels. The pointed arches in the recesses are apparently from the original structure and thus antedate by some three hundred years the appearance of this arch in European architecture. As you go back up, notice the Quranic inscriptions in Kufic script that runs around the pit. These inscriptions are verses about rain, crops, abundance, etc. "And We sent down water as a blessing from heaven, causing thereby gardens to grow, and grain for harvest." (50:9) "Have you not seen how God sends down water from heaven, so that at morning the earth became green?" (22:63).

Originally this frieze ended with a short dedicatory inscription saying that the structure was built in 861. This was removed in 872 and replaced by more verses from the Quran, perhaps by Ibn Tulun as a way of asserting his independence from Abbasid Baghdad.

Mosque of Qaytbay (No. 519) 1481–90/886–96. Of the many medieval structures once found on the island of Roda, such as the palaces and barracks of the early Mamluk period, this mosque and the Nilometer are all that survive. Even so, the mosque, which has been restored several times, is perhaps only of interest to the dedicated art historian, since it is hard to find and rather disappointing. Approach the island from Cairo by the Qasr al-'Aini Bridge, and just past the Manial Palace turn left and left again.

Manial Palace Museum.** Because of one-way streets and traffic congestion, the best way to reach this is to cross to Roda

Mashrabiya windows at Manial Palace

from Giza on the University Bridge. The Palace Museum will be
on your right just before leaving the island.

Set in a garden surrounded by a great enclosure wall of
compact limestone, the complex was the residence of Prince
Muhammad 'Ali, 1875–1955, the younger son of the Khedive
Tawfiq and for a time the heir to King Faruq. It was constructed
between 1901 and 1929 and bequeathed to the Egyptian nation
as a museum at his death. The garden was once noted for its
fabulous collection of trees and plants from all over the world,
but today it is mostly the cactus and ornamental plants that
survive. The palace consists of several buildings:

1. The reception building through which one enters.

2. The mosque, built in 1933.

3. The game or hunting museum, opened in 1963, containing
ex-King Faruq's mounted game trophies and curios.

4. The residence of Prince Muhammad 'Ali. This building
affords an interesting look at the living arrangements and
furnishings of the upper class in Egypt before the revolution. As
one enters any of the downstairs reception rooms, the initial
impression is rather overpowering: marble floors and dadoes;
wood paneling on walls and ceilings, carved, painted, and
gilded; stained glass windows; tiled fireplaces; carpets and rich
coverings on floors and benches; wooden lattice screens; inlaid
furniture gleaming with mother-of-pearl. This is an example of
the fact that the main effect in a late Islamic room is achieved
by the massing of a variety of materials. The sleeping quarters
are upstairs.

5. The throne room of Muhammad 'Ali, a replica of the one
located on the Citadel, complete with original furniture and
portraits.

6. The museum. Prince Muhammad 'Ali was a great collec-
tor, and a special fourteen-room museum was built in the
southern part of the garden to house his collection. It contains
objects dating to two hundred years ago and the range is varied:
calligraphy, photographs of Istanbul, family portraits, furniture, textiles, glass, silver, costumes, porcelain, personal articles. It is well worth a visit.

Tomb of Sulayman Pasha al-Faransawi * d. 1859. Starting
with the Nilometer on the tip of Roda as a reference, head north

Tomb of Sulayman Pasha al-Faransawi

on the Nile corniche and turn right at the fourth side street. On the Nile bank on your left there will be a stand of date palms and mango trees; on your right by looking down the street you can see the tomb two short blocks away.

Sulayman Pasha was originally a French Colonel named Sevés, who, jobless at the end of the Napoleonic wars, was one of several thousand European advisers and technicians who came to Egypt in the reign of Muhammad 'Ali. Sevés became a Muslim and for over thirty-five years loyally served his adopted country. He had a wonderful mansion and garden on the Nile at this point. His great-great-granddaughter Nazli was the mother of King Faruq.

The tomb is a charming pavilion of cast iron, much in need of repair but well worth visiting. Nearby lies his widow (d. 1894), the Dame Maryam. Her tomb is unremarkable, but her story is romantic. She was a young Greek, and a great beauty. At the time of the Egyptian Expedition to Greece (1825–27), Sulayman rescued her from a boat that was to take her and other women to Alexandria, and married her himself.

Mosque of 'Amr * (No. 319) 827 and to 1977. To get there, at Malik al-Salih bridge, the southernmost of the bridges to Roda, turn east away from the river and go through the underpass below the Metro train track. Go one long block and turn right

Interior of the Mosque of 'Amr

on a wide but irregular street, Sharia Sidi Hasan al-Anwar. The Mosque of 'Amr is on the left-hand side of the street, 600 meters (about seven blocks) to the south. Or take the Metro (subway) to Mar Girgis (the Coptic Museum) and walk north. The entrance faces the street.

'Amr ibn al-'As was the Muslim general who conquered Egypt in A.D. 641. The building that bears his name has been much expanded and rebuilt. In the process nothing identifiable remains of the original, but the monument has interesting historical associations. In addition to being the site of the first mosque in Egypt and the starting point of the country's conversion to Islam, it was for centuries the religious and social center of the thriving and cosmopolitan city of al-Fustat.

The mosque has been enlarged and/or restored many times. The first restoration was made by 'Abdallah ibn Tahir, in 827/338, and thereafter by Salah al-Din after the Fustat fire of 1168, by the Amir Salar after the great earthquake of 1303, by Sultan Barquq in 1399, by Sultan Qaytbay in the fifteenth century, by Murad Bey in 1798 just before the Napoleonic invasion, by Muhammad 'Ali in 1845, and again in the 1930s and 1970s. The façade was rebuilt by the Department of the Awqaf in 1977. The minarets belong to Murad Bey's restorations. The present arrangement is not necessarily how it looked in the ninth or even in the eighteenth century, although the shape of the windows with colonnettes and carved wood in the south wall probably dates to the first enlargement of 827. The columns in the entrance and side arcades as well as the courtyard and fountain are twentieth-century, while the arrangement of the aisles perpendicular to the qibla wall is from the eighteenth century.

The dimensions of the mosque date to 827/200, when the original structure was doubled in size by order of the Arab governor. At this time the seven aisles were parallel with the qibla wall and the last column in each row was engaged to the wall by a wooden architrave carved with a late Hellenistic type of frieze. These, the oldest parts of the mosque, can still be seen along the right-hand wall of the sanctuary. The columns in the qibla arcade are reused from churches.

Perhaps the most interesting part of the mosque lies in the far corner of the left-hand side, the area that is used by women for prayer. Here is the tomb of 'Abdallah, the son of 'Amr ibn al-'As. He died in his house, and because house burial in early Islam was common, he was buried there. When the mosque was enlarged in 827, the house and tomb were incorporated into it.

Al-Fustat. The ruins lie in back (east) of the Mosque of 'Amr and the Fortress of Babylon. Take the first left south of the mosque. The pavements rapidly disappear and a dusty track leads to the little house.where the guardian of the excavation stays. A guard will show you the ruins, which date from many periods, with Fatimid predominant. Al-Fustat was a city far advanced over its European contemporaries, with a water supply and sanitation facilities then undreamed of in Europe. It was famous for its glassware and ceramics as well as for the wealth and variety of its markets. There are no monuments to be seen here, but there are some very interesting examples of domestic architecture and water supply.

Al-Fustat was the first city founded by the Muslims in Egypt. The name is derived from *fossatum*, meaning an entrenched encampment, and the site chosen was that upon which 'Amr had pitched his tent during the siege of Babylon.

In 1168 al-Fustat, one of the wealthiest cities of the world and with a population of 200,000, was threatened by an attack from a Crusader force led by Amaury, King of Jerusalem. Since the city was unfortified, the Fatimid wazir ordered it to be burned. For fifty-four days and nights the fire raged and most of the population fled or was killed. In later centuries attempts to rebuild al-Fustat were made, but it never recovered its former status. It has remained a vast mound of rubble and debris to the south of the medieval city.

Fortress of Babylon. From the Mosque of 'Amr continue southward along Sharia Sidi Hasan al-Anwar until it reaches the Coptic Museum on the left. One of the towers of the southern gate of the Fortress stands to the right at the garden entrance to the Museum. The other is visible as the foundation of the Church of St. George on the left.

The present fortress was rebuilt by the Emperor Trajan (A.D. 98–117) on the then east bank of the Nile to guard the canal that linked the Nile with the Red Sea. The name derives from Bab il-On, 'Gate of On,' the ancient sanctuary of the sun god at Heliopolis. The fortress has several interesting associations for Islamic Cairo. It was here that the Byzantine garrison was quartered that 'Amr ibn al-'As defeated before making Egypt an Islamic country. The use of polychrome masonry, which is almost a hallmark of Mamluk architecture, is derived from the roman tradition of building with alternating courses of brick and stone. This technique is visible in these towers in the layers of red brick and yellow limestone. Finally, although only two of the towers of the fortress are readily visible, the area it occupied is quite vast and most of the churches of Old Cairo are built on its foundations. There are two churches that contain interesting Islamic relics:

Grand Hall in the Convent of St. George 1021–94. Just next to the Greek Church of St. George are steps that lead down into the Coptic compound of Old Cairo. The door through which one passes and the narrow alley into which it leads are typical of medieval gates and streets. About ten yards along on the left is the entrance to the convent. Cross the courtyard with its citrus trees and enter the convent. Inside there is a vast qa'a, whose central section is higher than the two side sections. An enormously high door leads to the chapel of the convent, now housed in one of the arms of the qa'a. The sixty-six panels of the door belong to the Fatimid period. They are similar to panels in the Islamic Museum that depict court activities (drinking, hunting, dancing) against an arabesque background. This is most likely to be the remains of a Fatimid palace, possibly restored in the Ayyubid period, that was located along the river.

Mu'allaqa Church or the Hanging Church. This church is built above the east tower of the south gate of the Fortress of Babylon. It is the screens here that are of interest. That of the inconostasis and those of the sanctuary of St. Mark on the left date to the fifteenth and thirteenth centuries. Beautifully carved, the overall star pattern with its polychrome accents in bone and ivory is an example of the uniformity of the decorative arts of Egypt: the same careful craftsmanship and intricate patterns appear on similar objects whether they are intended for Christians or Muslims, for secular or religious uses.

Coptic Museum.∗∗ The museum was founded in 1910 by Marcus Simaika, and is the last of Cairo's major museums. The collection contains antiquities primarily of the Coptic period or of Christian usage. However, many of these artifacts are of interest to students of Islamic Cairo, because either they influenced the making of Islamic objects or they were themselves made under Muslim dynasties.

The main door of the museum is in a handsome limestone façade. Upon entering turn right, and continue past the limestone sculptures into a small garden courtyard. Climb the stairs at the eastern end for access to the old wing of the museum and its wonderful collection of wood furnishings: ceiling panels, mashrabiya screens, pieces of furniture, inlaid doors. Of special note is the sanctuary screen of sycamore wood from the Church of St. Barbara. The panels, with human and animal figures against a foliate arabesque background, are recognizable as having been crafted in the Fatimid period, eleventh or twelfth century.

One enters the new wing, built in 1947, by turning left at the entrance. The collection here is relevant because many styles and themes, such as geometric designs, acanthus and vine scrolls, inhabited friezes, rabbits, peacocks, etc., passed from the Greco–Roman–Byzantine–Coptic legacy into the Muslim artistic vocabulary. It is most likely that the niche in the Christian monk's cell that oriented him in prayer toward Jerusalem inspired the shape of the mihrab in an Egyptian mosque; and that the staired shape of the Egyptian minbar was derived from the pre-Islamic Coptic pulpit.

Mamluk Aqueduct.∗ Return to the Nile corniche and go north two blocks to the traffic circle, beside which there is a large hexagonal building of stone. This is Fumm al-Khalig, the mouth of the canal, from where a canal once wound along the route of Port Said Street and then all the way to the Red Sea. The hexagonal tower was the intake for an aqueduct built originally in the era of Sultan al-Nasir Muhammad about 1311/711 and subsequently extended to its present length by Sultan al-Ghuri in 1505/910. The intake tower housed huge waterwheels, of a type still used in Syria, which lifted water from the Nile up to the top of the tower, from where it flowed to the base of the

Citadel. The slots into which these wheels fitted can be seen on the west side of the tower. The aqueduct and the Khalig canal served as Cairo's principal water supply until 1872. The aqueduct can still be followed almost all the way to the Citadel. About one and a half kilometers from the Nile the section credited to al-Ghuri ends and that of al-Nasir begins. From about five hundred meters beyond the point where the aqueduct and the road turn northeast, the aqueduct is built on the city wall that dates from Salah al-Din's time (1176–93/572–89).

4 ◦ The Mosque of Ahmad ibn Tulun and Sharia Saliba

Mausoleum–Khanqah–Madrasa
of Salar and Sangar al-Gawli **
Madrasa of the Amir Sarghatmish *
Madrasa of Sultan Qaytbay
Mosque of Ahmad ibn Tulun ***
Bayt al-Kritliya (the Gayer-Anderson Museum) **
Mosque of Azbak al-Yusufi *
Mosque–Mausoleum of Hasan Pasha Tahir *
Mosque of Taghri Bardi *
Mosque–Khanqah of Amir Shaykhu **
Mosque of Qanibay al-Muhammadi
Sabil–Kuttab of Sultan Qaytbay **

See map 2

Up to the fourteenth century this area, which comprised both the former site of the Tulunid royal suburb known as al-Qata'i' and a large pond known as Birkat al-Fil, was dotted with waste and rubbish heaps, interspersed with cemeteries and individual estates or parks. The redevelopment of the Citadel under Sultan al-Nasir Muhammad in the fourteenth century was the central event that led to the transformation of this zone into an urban area. In the fourteenth century the area flourished when amirs built town houses and palaces along the shores of Birkat al-Fil and endowed madrasas and khanqahs along the main route that led to the Citadel. The route can be walked in either direction: the 'flow' of monuments seems better from the west, but parking is best at the eastern end of the street.

Sabil Ibrahim Bey al-Monastirli (No. 508) 1714/1126. This fountain is at the western end of Sharia Saliba, which starts as Sharia 'Abd al-Magid al-Labbana at the southeastern corner of Maydan Sayyida Zaynab. Fifty meters southeast of the maydan, on the right, are the remains of this early eighteenth-century

46

structure, originally with two façades, distinguishable by its decoration of tiles and almost random placement of rosettes and squares around the sabil grill. The top story is missing.

Façade of the Mosque of Sultan Gaqmaq (No. 217) 1449/853. One hundred and fifty meters eastward on the left, with the Ottoman cap to the lower story base of the Mamluk minaret, is the mosque built by the amir who was sultan from 1438 to 1453. His palace was in this area.

Sabil–Kuttab of Yusuf Bey (No. 219) 1634/1044. These remains are on the right.

Mausoleum–Khanqah–Madrasa of Salar and Sangar al-Gawli ** (No. 221) 1303–04/703. Tucked into an elbow of Sharia al-Khudari, as the street is called here, this double-domed complex contains the tombs of the Amir Sayf al-Din Salar (dome nearest the minaret) and that of his friend the Amir 'Alam al-Din Sangar al-Gawli. The Amir Salar played an important role in the agitated times that marked the beginning of the fourteenth century. With the Amir Baybars al-Gashankir he was involved in court intrigues during the second interregnum of Sultan al-Nasir Muhammad. In 1310 the Amir Salar was thrown into prison, where he died of starvation. The Amir Sangar was for a long time governor of Gaza, where he built many mosques, and also governor of Hama. He died peacefully in 1344/745. The names of both amirs are connected with restoration done on several mosques in the early fourteenth century.

The façade of this monument has several interesting features. The adjoining domes, although common in northern Syria, are unique in Cairo and attractively distinctive. They are brick with stucco ribs, which give them the appearance of jelly molds. The façades of the mausolea are related but differentiated. Each façade is divided into three panels, two narrow ones on either side of a broad one. The stalactite cornice that covers the broad panel in the first tomb is repeated over the narrow ones of the second tomb; the stalactite cornice over the side panels of the first tomb covers the broad panel in the second tomb.

In the evolution of Cairene minarets this one is important. It exhibits a marked elongation of the two top stories at the expense of the lower shaft, and the addition of a circular lantern supporting the mabkhara or domelet is a new feature, a move toward the colonnaded pavilion characteristic of later Mamluk minarets.

The complex stands on the northwest outcropping of the Muqattam known as Qal'at al-Kabsh, which means the Citadel of the Ram. This was the general site of the barracks of Ibn Tulun's al-Qata'i'. A flight of stairs leads up to the entrance, from which another flight ascends to the main level of the complex. At the top of the stairs there are two doors. That which is straight ahead leads to an open corridor that runs east–west and into a small tomb with a stone dome, perhaps the earliest one in Cairo. The cenotaph, in disrepair, offers no clue as to who is buried here. From the corridor, two doors on the right lead into the mausolea. The tomb of Sangar at the end is a small, plain chamber in which a plain marble centotaph lies in front of a plain mihrab. The only adornments are two bands of inscription. Salar's tomb, next door, is much more ornate. The decoration is concentrated in the marble inlay of the mihrab and the qibla wall, but is also present in the carefully carved wooden doors of the closets and panels of the cenotaph, and in the stalactite-squinch system.

One of the outstanding features of this building is the beautiful cut-stone screen that separates the corridor from the rear courtyard of the mosque. It is unique in Egypt. The panels on the left and in the center have a centralizing pattern of palmettes, while that on the right has a pattern of vine leaf motifs with bunches of grapes in the center. In the courtyard there is a fine band of stucco inscription along the wall and a small mihrab. One obtains from here a fine view of the domes and minaret, and of the trilobed merlons around the roof, which is a new form of cresting appearing at this time.

Placed obliquely across the corridor is a large room containing the madrasa and the khanqah or sufi dormitory. Entrance to them is through the door at the top of the stairs to the left. Inside on the left, raised one step, is a flat-roofed room with a liwan, a mihrab, and minbar—the madrasa. It was for one rite, the Shafi'i. The khanqah on the right was perhaps not originally roofed. The windows that look down from the second story illuminated the interior living units.

This monument was restored by the Comité in 1894/1312.

Madrasa of the Amir Sarghatmish * (No. 218) 1356/757. Two hundred meters east of Salar and Sangar on Sharia Saliba, attached to the northeast wall of the Mosque of Ibn Tulun, is the cruciform madrasa of the Amir Sarghatmish. This mamluk renowned for his beauty was acquired by Sultan al-Nasir Muhammad and grew up in the corps of jamdars or 'keepers of the wardrobe.' His prominence dates to the reigns of al-Nasir's minor sons, when Sarghatmish took an active part in the battles waged on their behalf. In 1354, supporting the Amir Shaykhu, he was one of the principal agents in the reelection of Sultan Hasan, and after Shaykhu's assassination he became the Amir Kabir, the Great Lord. He virtually ruled Egypt for Hasan, who, chafing at this, had Sarghatmish thrown into prison and murdered in 1358. He is buried in the domed-tomb chamber that projects into the street.

The red striping that is quite obvious in this monument was painted on in the nineteenth century, probably as part of the urban beautification and celebrations ordered by Muhammad 'Ali on the occasion of his son Ibrahim's victory in Greece in 1826. The dome is interesting in that it has a slight return to its curve, with a row of stalactite decoration at its base. This type of outline became characteristic of the domes of Central Asia at the beginning of the fifteenth century.

The minaret and the portal are at the other end of the façade. The minaret is a good example of the form to which the minaret of Salar and Sangar was leading. At the bottom the square shaft or story has been reduced to just a base set on inclined or prismatic triangles; at the top there is a colonnade pavilion with a crowning ovoid finial. Enter the complex through the portal on the main façade. The triangular hood above a mantle of stalactites and the carved arabesque patterns in the spandrels of the arch are typical of the early fourteenth century.

Inside, the twisting corridor leads to a square central court-yard with a marble floor inlaid in a bold pattern of black and white. In its middle is a fountain kiosk that has lost its dome, and around it are four vaulted halls, or liwans. Perhaps the best

view of this plan is from the minaret of Ibn Tulun, which
overlooks it. In the angles of the cross that this figure makes are
the dependencies: halls, libraries, cells for the professors, students, and servants. This madrasa is a good example of the kind
founded in the mid-fourteenth century by Mamluk amirs in
support of higher studies of the Quran, Prophetic traditions,
and jurisprudence—this one devoted to the Hanafi school. One
senior and three junior professors were appointed. Sixty students were enrolled, who were to devote themselves exclusively
to research in the Hanafi rite. There was also an orphanage
school, which was established as an annex. It accommodated
forty children and was directed by a teacher and an assistant
who taught them the Quran, calligraphy, and arithmetic.

The dome over the mihrab was restored in concrete in 1940
with unfortunate results. On the left side of the mihrab is a
panel of white marble with a medallion in the center and four
quarter medallions in the corners. Hidden among the leaf and
stem forms of the arabesque design are six birds and five hands.
The minbar dates to 1706/1118. Although the interior has been
stripped of its decorations it has a spaciousness of plan that is
pleasant. On leaving the building one notices the bank of
mashrabiya windows on the north corner of the façade. This is
a modern annex of the Egyptian Antiquities Organization,
Islamic Section, in which their collection of prints and nega-
tives is kept.

Madrasa of Sultan Qaytbay (No. 231) 1475/480. Proceed up
the southeast side of Sarghatmish (along the wall of the tomb
chamber) and the northwest side of Ibn Tulun. Take the first
turn to the right (opposite Ibn Tulun's wall) which is Darb al-
Talawni. Follow it until it intersects with Sharia Qal'at al-
Kabsh. Turn right. About ten meters further the street will
fork. (The right fork leads to the back entrance of the complex
of Salar and Sangar.) Take the left fork, following it until it runs
into Sharia al-Rahaba. Turn right and you will walk into an
open area in which the mosque stands. The main entrance is
under the minaret on the southwest façade, but the 'working'
entrance is on the northeast façade. To the left are the remains
of the *hod* or drinking trough Qaytbay attached to his madrasa.
Although it is no longer in use, a public pump nearby serves the

neighborhood, so the spirit of the deed is still evident. The façade is quite plain for a late fifteenth-century 'royal' construction, but the portal is not. Note the deeply carved lines of the double-chevron ablaq hood and the cut-out designs of the stalactites.

Inside the madrasa one notes how deeply and richly carved the wall surfaces are, especially in the alternating white rows of the four centered arches of the liwans and in the spandrels of the main arches. The original blue painted background is still quite obvious. The bold black and white marble patterns on the floor are handsome, but you must ask to have the mats lifted in order to see them. The northwest liwan is curtained off for women and it contains a small loggia. Perhaps only the real enthusiast will want to trek back through the maze of streets on Qal'at al-Kabsh to find this mosque, but the reward is seeing a royal endowment that still serves the needs, albeit changed, of its neighborhood five centuries later.

Mosque of Ahmad ibn Tulun *** (No. 220) 876–79/263–65. Continue along Sharia Saliba from the Madrasa of Sarghatmish and take the first right. If one has time to see only one Islamic monument in Cairo, it should be this one. Its simplicity and grandeur of scale make it the most moving of all the great mosques.

Ahmad ibn Tulun was the son of a Turkish slave of the Abbasid khalif al-Ma'mun. He was sent to Egypt in 868 as governor of al-Fustat, but within two years he had been made governor of the whole country. Shortly thereafter, by refusing to send the annual tribute to the Abbasid court, he established himself as an independent ruler of the province. His family ruled in Egypt until 905. Ibn Tulun founded a new royal city around the Hill of Yashkur near the Muqattam range to the northeast of al-Fustat, razing the Christian and Jewish cemetery that was located on the hill to do so. This was a site to which many legends were attached: it was believed that Noah's Ark had landed here after the flood, that here God had spoken to Moses and Moses had confronted Pharaoh's magicians; nearby, on Qal'at al-Kabsh, Abraham had been ready to sacrifice his son to God. The city that Ahmad ibn Tulun built was called al-Qata'i', 'the wards,' descriptive of the allotments in which each group of his followers settled. In 905, when the Abbasids reestablished control, the city was destroyed and ploughed under. Of its magnificence and scale all that survives is the mosque that formed its center.

The mosque was built between 876 and 879 and is important for several reasons. It is the oldest intact, functioning mosque in Cairo. It also survives as a rare example of the art and architecture of the classical period of Islam, i.e. the ninth and tenth centuries, for it was built at a time when the influence of the Abbasid court in Iraq was dominant in the Islamic world. Its inspiration is thus almost exclusively Mesopotamian. Finally, this mosque provides one of the best examples of the classic congregational courtyard type of plan.

A bare limestone escarpment leads from the street to the outer wall. Between this wall and the inner wall is the *ziyada* or 'addition,' which separated, rather like a dry moat, the mosque itself from the bazaars and secular buildings that pressed upon it from all sides.

Early mosques in Islam had many entrances, located in each façade except the qibla façade, which usually had only a private connection with the ruler's residence. The crenellation above the walls is unique. It bears a resemblance to paper cut-outs of human figures with linked arms. Perhaps this show of solidarity was not intentional, but it provides a distinctive outline against the sky.

Inside the mosque one is immediately struck by its vast extent, which covers six and a half acres. This was the main congregational mosque of al-Qata'i', the mosque in which the whole community or congregation joined together for the Friday noon prayer. The original courtyard was not paved and filled with pebbles as it is today, for this space was intended for prayer. The arcades around the courtyard, which are deeper on the qibla or sanctuary side, are formed by arches on brick piers. Rosettes and windows form a continuous and simple decoration. The arches are pointed—two hundred years before similar arches made their appearance in Europe—and spring from oblong supports rounded at the corners by pilasters or engaged columns. The arches are outlined with an edge of carved stucco. Originally it would seem that all of the arcades had soffits of carved stucco similar to those that have been restored in the southern arcade. The use of red brick covered with stucco decoration is a feature imported from the court city of the Abbasids in Samarra, sixty miles north of Baghdad. This royal city existed from 836 to 886. Because it extended over a vast area and was quickly built, an efficient and rapid way had to be developed to decorate vast surfaces of brick. Wet plaster was stamped with carved and patterned wooden molds. It is this so-called Samarran decoration that one finds around and under the arches, on the capitals of the pilasters, and on the wooden panels over the entrances in the Mosque of Ibn Tulun. The ceiling is composed of palm logs boxed in by wooden panels.

The sanctuary hall is five aisles deep. In the middle of the qibla wall is the main mihrab, simple in form: a frame around a niche. Above the niche is an inscription in plain Kufic script of the shahada, the commitment that all Muslims make: 'There is no god but God. Muhammad is the Messenger of God.' This is followed by 'Greetings of God upon him and Peace.' To the right of the mihrab is the door through which Ahmad ibn Tulun would have entered the mosque from his palace, which adjoined it on that side. To the left of the main mihrab is a flat-paneled mihrab that was probably put there by the Amir 'Alam al-Din Sangar who was in charge of the mosque's restoration for Sultan Lagin (see below).

Over the years the mosque has been endowed with other mihrabs, which can be seen on the piers of the sanctuary. Two of them are on the piers that flank the dikka, or Quran-reading platform, and most probably date to the ninth century. The one on the right with a star hanging from a chain is most unusual. Two others are on the first arcade in from the courtyard; on the right is the one with which al-Afdal Shahansah, the son of Badr al-Gamali, the great Fatimid wazir, placed a Shi'i mark on the mosque in 1094/487; the one on the left pier is a copy of this mihrab by Sultan Lagin. These are the only mihrabs in Cairo that name the donors. On the pier just behind al-Afdal's mihrab is a panel of plain Kufic. This is the dedicatory inscription by Ahmad ibn Tulun. It begins with the Throne Verse (2:255).

The long band of inscription on sycamore wood that runs just below the ceiling and around the whole mosque contains verses from the Quran. The frieze is two kilometers in length and is calculated to comprise one fifteenth of the whole Book. There is

Arches and minaret of the Mosque of Ibn Tulun

a legend that some of the boards used for this inscription were left over from Noah's Ark. One hundred and twenty-eight windows light the interior. They are pointed in form and contain plaster grilles in various geometric combinations. Three are original: the fifth, sixth, and sixteenth from the left on the qibla wall. Six date from the 1296 restoration: the second on the southeast wall; the second and eleventh on the southwest wall; the ninth and twenty-fifth on the northwest wall; and the twenty-eighth on the northeast wall.

The Mosque of Ibn Tulun also shows that an interest in the restoration of important monuments in Cairo is not a modern one but goes back many centuries. The first such restoration was carried out by the Sultan Lagin in 1296. The Amir Husam al-Din Lagin was one of the accomplices in the murder of Sultan al-Ashraf Khalil ibn Qalawun (see Chapter 8), and during the period of unrest that followed, he successfully hid in the deserted mosque, much damaged by its use as a caravanserai for pilgrims from North Africa en route to the Holy Cities of the Hijaz in the twelfth century. In fulfillment of a vow that if he escaped he would restore the mosque, when he became sultan during al-Nasir Muhammad's first interregnum, he embellished several important areas. These include the marble lining and glass mosaic inscription in cursive script of the main mihrab, the dome over it, and the minbar, which is a splendid example of the wood carving and designs of the early Mamluk period. The domed building over the fountain in the middle of the courtyard belongs to Lagin's restoration. The Quranic verse inscribed here (5:6) describes the ablutions before prayer. The minaret was rebuilt—like other features of Ibn Tulun's mosque, the original minaret was probably inspired by that of the Great Mosque of Samarra, which in turn was inspired by the ziggurats of ancient Babylon. It was conceived as a spiral with its staircase on the outside. Lagin added the square base and the mabkhara finial that crowns it. During the eighteenth and nineteenth centuries the mosque was used first as a woolen factory and then as a hospice for the disabled. It was one of the first mosques restored by the Comité in 1890.

Cross the courtyard to the north side, where a door leads to the minaret. From the top there is a splendid view in all directions—of the mosque, of the Madrasa of the Amir

Sarghatmish next door, of Sharia Saliba, of the Citadel, and of Cairo extending west toward the Nile and the Pyramids.

Bayt al-Kritliya or the Gayer-Anderson Museum. ** The southeastern exit from the Mosque of Ibn Tulun leads to Bayt al-Kritliya, or 'House of the Cretan Woman,' so named either because it was acquired by a lady from Crete in the late eighteenth or early nineteenth century, or from Kretli, the name of a family who lived there previously. This is actually two medieval houses joined together, restored, and furnished by Major Gayer-Anderson, an Englishman who lived in them from 1935 to 1942, and which are now maintained as a museum by the Islamic section of the Egyptian Antiquities Organization. These are not the grandest of such houses in Cairo, but they are well preserved and furnished and give a good idea of the degree of comfort and luxury that could be attained by wealthy Cairenes three hundred years ago or earlier.

The narrow alley between the houses and the constriction of airspace by the overhanging windows above it hints at the beauty of medieval street patterns. The house on the right (No. 321, built in 1631/1041) has two grilled windows on its southwest corner, which mark a sabil, or free water dispensary, a rare feature in a private residence. This house belonged to 'Abd al-Qadar al-Haddad ('the smith'). When the two houses were joined, this house became the haramlik and the one on the left (No. 559, built in 1540/947), the house of Amna bint Salim al-Gazzar ('Amna, the daughter of Salim the butcher'), became the salamlik.

It is in the house on the right, the seventeenth-century haramlik house, that the tour begins. One enters through the courtyard, goes up to the maq'ad and the indoor reception room, through the harim qa'a and various small rooms, and up to the roof, which is enclosed by fine mashrabiya screens so that the ladies could use it to take the air. There one crosses over, to descend and exit through the house on the left, the sixteenth-century salamlik house. In the latter house the most interesting part is the large qa'a on the ground floor, which is perhaps the most magnificent sixteenth-century example of such a room in Cairo. With its marvellous polychrome central fountain, richly decorated ceiling beams, kilim covered pillows and alcoves, as well as the bank of mashrabiya windows in the upper gallery from which the ladies looked down on the entertainments below, it is the best qa'a in which to visualize the setting of life in pre-modern Cairo.

Each room of the museum has good identifying descriptions as well as interesting pieces of furniture. Although not belonging to the sixteenth and seventeenth centuries, they are nevertheless lovely. One complete room has been added: the Damascus room, which is from a seventeenth-century house in Damascus with walls and ceiling of intricate low-relief patterns of lacquer and gold.

These historic houses with their lovely architecture occupy a special place among the artistic and aesthetic monuments of Cairo. In addition to the local legends that surround the site itself, adjoining as it does the Mosque of Ibn Tulun, the Hill of Yashkur, and the Qal'at al-Kabsh, there are legends that belong specifically to the house of 'Abd al-Qadar al-Haddad. The domed tomb on the street side is said to be that of Sidi Harun, son of al-Husayn, a great-grandson of the Prophet and patron saint of the house. This saint has reputedly brought blessings, protection, and prosperity to the house. The house was built around a well, which can still be seen under an arch in the far right-hand side of the courtyard. It was supplied by waters left over from the Great Flood and was believed to possess magical and beneficial properties. This well was also the entrance to the vast subterranean palace of Sultan al-Watawit, the Sultan of the Bats and King of the Jinn, who lived amidst vast treasures guarded by his magic. It is here also that his seven daughters, each in a golden bed, lie asleep under a spell.

Mosque of Azbak al-Yusufi * (No. 211) 1494–95/900. Return to Sharia Saliba from Ibn Tulun, cross it and continue toward the tall, late Mamluk minaret before you. This is the complex of the Amir Azbak al-Yusufi. His career began in 1471. As one of the great 'Amirs of the Sword' he occupied several high posts and at the time of his death in 1498 was Counselor of State for the son of Sultan Qaytbay.

His mosque is a fine example of the late Mamluk style. It is situated on a corner and thus has two façades. The main or

northern façade contains the entrance. At its western end is a
drinking trough and the remains of other buildings, probably
including a maq'ad or reception hall; at the eastern end is the
sabil–kuttab. The Amir's blazon appears above the portal. It is
of the kind known as 'composite': in the upper field is a napkin
between a pair of horns pointing outward; in the middle field a
cup between another pair of horns; and in the lowest field a cup
between two napkins. The dispositions of the various devices
are difficult to understand, but it is thought that at this period
they are not so much representative of the duties of the amir as
they were a common badge used by a group of amirs of the same
sultan, since there are many blazons with similar arrangements.

Inside, the plan follows that of a mosque–madrasa, except
for the use of the southern liwan as a tomb area. Behind the very
lovely mashrabiya screen are buried Azbak, his wife the Princess Bunukh, and her son Farag by a previous marriage. In the
northwest liwan there is an inset loggia or dikka. The mihrab
is plain but the minbar is attractively inlaid. The interior is
richly decorated with marble floors, gilded ceilings, and wooden
frames around the doors. Each course of the four-centered arch
of the main liwans alternates between buff and red, and is
carved. As well as being an important architectural monument,
this mosque is also used by the inhabitants of the neighborhood
as a place of prayer and a place for Quranic study groups. It is
well taken care of by its custodians.

Mosque–Mausoleum of Hasan Pasha Tahir * (No. 210)
1809/1224. A short excursion beyond the mosque of Azbak leads
to this early nineteenth-century structure. Turn left on leaving
Azbak and turn right at the first corner, where there are the
remains of the *Sabil–Kuttab of Ahmad Effendi Salim* (No. 461,
1699/1111). Left again, and continue straight north until you
reach the façade on your right. This mosque was situated on the
banks of Birkat al-Fil ('Elephant Pond,' because of its long
extension that looked like a trunk), a landmark of medieval
Cairo that was drained in the early nineteenth century.

The mosque was built by Hasan Pasha Tahir and his brother
'Abdin Bey Tahir, two military functionaries in the days of
Muhammad 'Ali, when Ottoman influences were novel and

strong. Here, however, except that the tomb and the mosque are separated, Cairene influences prevail. The façade, ornately carved, contains the entrance, the minaret, and the sabil–kuttab. To the left stands the mausoleum, which is kept locked by the family. A short path leads to the mosque entrance. The interior is simple: a rectangle, with a marble-paved floor and a painted ceiling, divided into two arcades by six marble columns. There is a skylight in the center. The walls are plain and the decoration is confined to the pierced stucco windows filled with colored glass.

Near this group stands the *Mausoleum of Ahmad Pasha Tahir* (No. 565) 1817/1233. A nephew of Muhammad 'Ali, the builder was the Supervisor of Customs at Bulaq. This tomb, with a plan of a room of four liwans surmounted by a dome, was originally built behind the Mosque of Sayyida Zaynab, but was moved in 1951 to this new site.

Remains of Palace of Qansuh al-Ghuri (No. 322) 1501–16/906–22. Return to Sharia Saliba and continue east. A short distance up the street, on the corner of the first alley to the right, these remains are visible: the outline of a portal, console supports for an upper loggia, and roundel inscriptions of the late Mamluk period.

Mosque of Taghri Bardi * (No. 209) 1440/844. The Amir Taghri Bardi was a prominent amir in the reign of Sultan Barsbay. He led the army that invaded the Crusader kingdom of Cyprus. A man of somber character and violent language, he was murdered by his own Mamluks shortly after his appointment as grand dawadar or executive secretary to Sultan al-Zahir Gaqmaq. His madrasa, mosque, and sufi convent on the left-hand side of Sharia Saliba is a good example of how urban monuments in the late Mamluk period tended to be smaller and more compact because of the lack of large building sites.

The mosque has two façades. The main one on Sharia Saliba has a balance and unity that is pleasing. The entrance portal in the middle of the façade is elaborately decorated with ablaq and reversed trilobed forms in black and white marble with accents of colored stone characteristic of the late Mamluk period. To its left are the sabil–kuttab and the minaret, and to its right the façade of the tomb and the dome with interlocking ribs. The cut-out pattern of the kuttab eaves echoes the stalactite pattern of the tomb cornice; the pattern of the lintel over the door, that of the windows in the tomb façade. The second or eastern façade is on the side street. The round bull's eye window in the center panel is over the mihrab. From the street all seems extremely regular. Climb the minaret, however, and look down upon the complex to see how ingeniously the various parts have been tucked behind the façades and the various demands of the building have been met. These include a qibla orientation for the mosque, a position on the qibla wall and the main street for the mausoleum, symmetrically disposed windows and doors for the attached foundations, and as far as possible a symmetrical internal arrangement. The entrance corridor leads around the tomb and into the mosque–madrasa interior. One notices that the window to the right of the mihrab is much deeper than that on the left; that the way to the ablutions court is out through the northeast liwan; while in the southwest liwan, roped off for women, there is a peculiarly shaped closet or storage area. The small cubes of space in corners and angles that result from these adjustments and compromises are often used either as light and air shafts or are filled in as solid masses.

Sabil of Umm 'Abbas, 1867/1284. At the next intersection, on the left, is the fountain built by the mother of 'Abbas Pasha (see Chapter 7).

Mosque–Khanqah of the Amir Shaykhu ** (Nos. 147 and 152) 1349 and 1355/750 and 756. These two buildings face each other across Sharia Saliba with almost identical exterior aspects: two long and tall façades, two identical minarets mounted on similar portals. Yet they were not conceived and built at the same time, and the interiors serve completely different purposes. First Shaykhu built the mosque–madrasa on the north side of the street, in which twenty sufis were housed. Five years later he built the larger khanqah that included his mausoleum on the south side of the street.

The Amir Sayf al-Din Shaykhu al-Umari had a brilliant career. Purchased by Sultan al-Nasir Muhammad, Shaykhu rose through the ranks to become one of the leading amirs in the reign of al-Nasir's son al-Hasan. In 1351 al-Hasan was deposed by the Amir Taz, but Shaykhu restored him to power in 1354, at the same time becoming Commander-in-Chief and Amir Kabir or Great Lord, the first to be so called. His personal character alternated between cruel and mystical. In 1357, when he was more than fifty years old, he was assassinated by discontented Royal Mamluks. To endow his madrasa–mosque he purchased property from the merchants and householders living in the area. He established professorships in the four madhhabs or rites, in Prophetic traditions, and in Quranic readings. This was one of Cairo's largest pious foundations. The sufis were provided a stipend of bread, meat, oil, soap, and sweets. The institution retained great wealth until the famine of 1403–04/806, when Farag ibn Barquq confiscated some of its holdings, inaugurating a period of decline.

The entrance to the mosque leads into a vestibule. Embedded in three of the walls are pieces of polished black glass. Their purpose may have been decorative, but other possibilities are that they protected the establishment against jinns, or evil spirits, or that they were used as curing panels, which anybody seeking relief from an ailment could touch or lean against. To the right is a locked tomb, perhaps built by the founder for his own use, but abandoned by him when the tomb in the khanqah was built. It is locked and the man with the key cannot always be located.

The interior plan of the building is that of a small congregational mosque. Immediately to the left as one enters the courtyard is a small mashrabiya enclosure that extends from the wall. This was made to contain water jars, and probably dates to the mid-eighteenth century. An interesting feature of the sanctuary is the way the qibla is bent in a diagonal away from the street. Another is the stone minbar. The carved geometric decoration of the sides has been eroded away but its nature is suggested by what remains along the balustrade. The tight geometric patterns of the railing, however, suggest that this minbar was a later (late fifteenth- or early sixteenth-century) gift to the mosque. The carved stone dikka is handsome. An inscription dates it to 1555/963. The mihrab with its radiating courses of red, white, and blue stone and its marble paneling belong to the type favored in the mid-fourteenth century;

however, the glazed tiles of the lowest register seem to have been imported from North Africa or Spain, and embedded at a later date.

The khanqah, on the opposite side of the street, is a much larger building, and was built when Shaykhu was at his most powerful. One enters beneath a pharaonic cornice, deliberately placed—in contrast to the usually somewhat haphazard use of such materials by Islamic builders—and through the twisted entrance corridor to the courtyard. The khanqah originally accommodated seven hundred sufi dervishes or mystics who lived in a warren of passageways and cells surrounding the courtyard on the south and west sides. These upper corridors are easy to get to and very interesting to walk along.

The sanctuary liwan is a large and spacious hall divided by the columns of two arcades attached by tie-beams. There are two domes in the ceiling, one over the middle of the second aisle and the other over the mihrab. The eighteenth-century decoration of the ceiling is very handsome and the blue and white colors impart a peaceful and restful quality to the place. The inscription under the beamed ceiling is Quranic and alludes to the giving of alms to the poor. It is from the chapter called "Man," (76:5–9):

> Surely the righteous shall drink of a cup flavored with camphor, of a spring from which drink the servants of God, causing it to gush abundantly. They fulfil their vow, and fear the Day whose evil shall spread widely; they give food to the needy for love of Him, and to the orphan, the captive: 'We feed you only for the Face of God, desiring neither reward nor gratitude.'

The mihrab is unusual for this period: the hood design is made up of radiating red and white courses of stone extending into a carved spandrel. The rounded mashrabiya front of the minbar is also unusual and dates to the late seventeenth century.

The tomb chamber is in the northeast corner of the sanctuary, in an area screened off with a mashrabiya railing and projecting outward into the street. The two cenotaphs that were there in 1983 have disappeared. The smaller one belonged to Shaykhu, the other to the Hanafi Shaykh Akmal al-Din Muhammad, who was appointed by Shaykhu as the first

superior of the khanqah and who died in 1378/780. The plaque
on the street wall states that the tomb chamber was restored in
1684/1095 by Bilal Agha. It is from this restoration that the
painted representations of the mosques of Madina and Mecca
on the walls date. The mashrabiya windows between the
sanctuary and the courtyard, and the dikka nearby, are also
most likely from this date. The two domes in the sanctuary may
also be from this time.

On the south side of the prayer hall a door in the wall leads
into a large room with two arched openings across a roofed
courtyard. There is no mihrab in the hall. This may have been
an assembly hall for the sufis to gather in for the daily hudur
service at which the dhikr was perfomed. The mashrabiya
maqsura dates presumably to the seventeenth century.

Outside, on Sharia Saliba, a projecting mashrabiya window
at the end of the complex is all that remains of the *Hod of
Shaykhu* (No. 323, 17th/11th century), presumably part of Bilal
Agha's restoration.

On the corner are the remains of the *House and Sabil of the
Amir 'Abdallah* (No. 452, built in 1719/1132).

Mosque of Qanibay al-Muhammadi (No. 151) 1413/816.
Sixty meters up the street from the hyphenated complex of
Shaykhu is this mosque on the right. It is small and compact.
The tomb chamber, under its chevron-covered dome, projects
into the street. The minaret stands next to it over the entrance.
Inside, the plan is that of a large oblong room bisected twice by
four-centered arches. It is plainly decorated. At the sanctuary
end, a coat of paint now covers the beamed ceiling with its
support of niches that once must have been ornately decorated.
There is a malqaf (wind-catcher) over the sanctuary sahn. To
either side of the mihrab in the tomb are two white marble
panels carved with a central medallion and quarter medallions
in the corners. This tomb has no historic inscription, but
literary evidence suggests it was built by Qanibay, who rose to
be Viceroy of Damascus. He rebelled against Sultan Muayyad
Shaykh and was executed in 1415.

Sabil–Kuttab of the Sultan Qaytbay ** (No. 324) 1479/884.
This building lies on a small wedge another sixty meters up the

street on the right. It is the first example in Cairo of a free-standing sabil–kuttab, one which is not attached to a larger complex. The building offers a good example of the trend in the later Mamluk period to apply a variety of rich decoration to the exterior of buildings. This is particularly evident in the entrance portal, which with its ablaq courses of red, white, and black is very handsome, and in the areas between the windows of the sabil and the base of the kuttab, on the west and north façades. These are focal points of the building's exterior decoration. Take an extra minute or two to look carefully at the roundels, lintels, joggles, and corner columns of these areas, since the marble veneer and carving are exceptionally fine.

In Ottoman times these free-standing water-and-Quran dispensaries became favourite structures because they dispensed economically and efficiently the 'two mercies' most commended by the Prophet: water to the thirsty and instruction to the ignorant. The building today is still in use as a center of instruction, for it houses women's sewing classes, a weaving center on the ground floor, and a child–care nursery school. The sabil is being used as the director's office. Its interior decoration and the carved marble panel over which the water flowed, for both cooling and aesthetic purposes, are still visible. The entrance is no longer through the main portal, but through a plain door in the back of the building.

5 ◊ The Madrasa of Sultan Hasan and Bab al-Wazir

Madrasa of Sultan Hasan ∗∗∗
Rifa'i Mosque ∗∗
Gate of Mangak al-Silahdar
Mosque of Gawhar al-Lala ∗∗
Mosque of Amir Akhur ∗
Mosque of Mahmud Pasha ∗∗
Bab al-'Azab
Palace of Qawsun or Yashbak min Mahdi ∗
Maristan of Sultan al-Muayyad ∗
Mosque of Mangak al-Yusufi ∗
Mausoleum of Yunus al-Dawadar ∗

See maps 2, 3 and 4

The monuments in this chapter are primarily those that ring the great square below the Citadel known as the Maydan al-Qal'a (Citadel Square) or Maydan Muhammad 'Ali. The square, which today seems no more than a busy vehicular intersection, was once the setting for elaborate court ceremonies, equestrian games, military exercises, and religious processions. It was a defined and very prestigious area of urban space, and it is to emphasize this fact that the Egyptian Antiquities Organization included these buildings in a major restoration program of the Citadel it completed in 1988. The Madrasa of Sultan Hasan and the mosques of Gawhar al-Lala, the Amir Akhur, and Mahmud Pasha all received structural repairs, cleanings, information blurbs, plans on plaques, and new furnishings.

Sharia Muhammad 'Ali, or Sharia al-Qal'a, now stops at the triple-arched portal that is the entrance to a newly created Sultan Hasan–Rifa'i compound. The canyon-like street that once ran between these monuments has been converted into a breezy, marble walkway, whose broad lateral railings provide a sort of continuous, convenient bench upon which to sit and observe the flowing crowd. Refreshments are available in the

65

open garden restaurant between the portal entrance and the elevated entrance of Sultan Hasan. In medieval times this site was a large commercial annex that financed the upkeep of Sultan Hasan's complex.

Madrasa of Sultan Hasan *** (No. 133) 1356–63/757–64. (Refer to map 4.) This is unquestionably one of the masterpieces of Mamluk architecture in Cairo. It is an excellent example both of the massive monumental style of the Bahri period (1260–1382) and of the cruciform madrasa plan.

Sultan Hasan was one of the sons of Sultan al-Nasir Muhammad, the son of Sultan Qalawun whose descendants dominated the Bahri period. He came to the throne at thirteen, and reigned for fifteen years, from 1347 to 1351 and from 1354 to 1361. The mosque was begun in 1356 and took seven years to complete. But Sultan Hasan was assassinated in 1361 and did not live to see its completion. He was not a glorious and impressive sultan, but rather a puppet in the hands of powerful and manipulative amirs, such as the Amirs Taz, Shaykhu, and Sarghatmish. He was able to build such an imposing monument because the estates of victims of the Black Death, i.e. the plague of 1348, had swelled the coffers of the treasury with money to be used for royal endowments.

The Madrasa of Sultan Hasan is best seen in the morning when the sun lights up the mausoleum and the western liwan. To get there, take Sharia al-Qal'a from the southern side of Maydan al-'Ataba, just behind Opera Square, and follow it for just under two kilometers, at which point one arrives at the new entrance portal at the end of Sharia Muhammad 'Ali. Alternatively, take Sharia Salah Salim along the aqueduct as though going to Heliopolis or the airport. Nearing the Citadel, do not mount the overpass but stay to the right. Turn left at the first opportunity where the road crosses the tram tracks. The street leads to Maydan Muhammad 'Ali between the madrasa and the Citadel.

The entrance is on Sharia al-Qal'a and the porch is a convenient place to pause and notice several points about Mamluk architecture in general and about this building in particular. The view, looking back at the length of the façade as it stretches toward the Citadel, is an excellent example of how

Bahri Mamluk architecture was intended to dominate the urban setting. The dimensions of the building are colossal: the façade from the entrance is seventy-six meters long, and thirty-six meters high. The horizontal mass of the façade is given extra emphasis by its division into thin vertical bays that end in the bold honeycomb cornice running along the top of its walls. Originally there was a fleur-de-lys cresting above. It remains today only around the tomb chamber.

The portal is offset, i.e. not in the middle of the façade, and it inclines from the rest of the façade by a thirty degree angle. Originally, additional drama was intended by surmounting it with two minarets, one on each side, a feature characterstic of the thirteenth-century madrasa in Anatolia and of mosques in fourteenth-century Mongol Persia, but in February 1360 one of them toppled. Three hundred people were killed in its fall and the construction of the other was abandoned. The tremendous height of the portal is emphasized by the spiral-cut pilasters, as well as by the vertical panels on each side of the porch. These panels are uncarved and therefore unfinished. Further evidence that the madrasa was unfinished in 1363 lies in the oval medallions just over the mastabas. The first one, on the left has been finished, but on the others the design has been sketched in but not carved out. Presumably a master craftsman pointed the way for completion by apprentices. The black basalt stone embedded in the façade appears in other buildings of the period and perhaps symbolizes the black stone at the Ka'ba in Mecca. Just before stepping over the threshold, look up and note the effect produced by the stalactites over the entrance. It is like entering a magical cave, passing through to an otherworldly experience.

From the richly decorated vestibule, with its stalactite-covered dome, one passes through a long, double-bending passageway, which empties into a magnificent marble-paved courtyard surrounded by four enormous vaulted liwans. The sense of transition, from entrance to courtyard and from darkness to light, in which one leaves behind the urban secular scene for the peaceful grandeur of the interior, is dramatic and impressive.

Although the exterior of the building is of stone, the interior is of brick covered with stucco except for stonework finishing details. There are some fine details to be noted, aside from the magnificent manipulation of voids and solids that gave the courtyard its soaring thrust toward the sky. The little gazebo in the middle of the court was originally designed as a decorative fountain and not for ablutions, its present function. Much altered and repaired, in its present shape it dates from the Ottoman period. On great occasions the fountain dispensed sherbet. The hundreds of chains hanging down from the great arches once held enameled glass oil lamps, some beautiful examples of which can be seen in the Islamic Museum. When lit at night they must have made a splendid spectacle. The inlaid marble paving of the courtyard dates back to the Comité restoration of 1912. The intricate designs of the scattered panels provide an attractive and cool substitute for woven rugs.

This was a functioning mosque with four madrasas, or colleges. Each of the vaulted recesses was for teaching one of the legal rites of Sunni Islam: the Shafi'i, Hanafi, Hanbali, and Maliki rites. The shaykh or teacher sat on a stool or a platform while his students sat crosslegged around him. The four doors that lead off from the courtyard belong to the internal areas of each madrasa. Here in the corners of the building, between the arms of the liwans, were lodgings for students and teachers. Each madrasa had its own courtyard and four or five stories of rooms. The Hanafi madrasa is the largest and is particularly worth visiting. As one faces the qibla, the entrance is in the south corner. (The entrance of the Hanbali madrasa, the smallest, is in the west corner. These are both on the right side of the courtyard. The Shafi'i madrasa and the Maliki madrasa are on the left side of the court, in the north and east corners respectively.)

Enter and look with care at the decoration of the door. The ablaq courses of black and white marble, the colored mosaic decoration, the joggled voussoirs on arches and lintels, and the dripping stalactites on the cornice are standard elements of doorway decoration in this period. The skill of inlay is very high: here the voussoirs interlock from both the sides and the bottom forming a three-dimensional puzzle.

The eastern liwan was also the mosque sanctuary. The use of marble paneling is one of the most characteristic features of Mamluk decoration and here the mixture of soft colors in flat rectangles contrasts strikingly both with the dusty plastering of the walls and with the deep relief carving of the Quranic inscription. Circumscribing the liwan are the first six verses of Sura 48, which begins:

> In the Name of God, the Merciful, the Compassionate. Surely We have given you a resplendent victory, that God may forgive you of all your blame past and to come, and may perfect His favor upon you, and guide you on a straight path; that God may help you with a mighty help.

This inscription is in monumental Kufic. Here the combination of the forward motion of the plain letters against the circular paterns of the arabesque background scrolls is both complementary and dramatic. The decorator, 'Abdallah Muhammad 'Ali, has left his name. The stone minbar was originally decorated with an inlaid pattern like the one in the Blue Mosque, but today it is plain. The platform or dikka in front of the mihrab was for readers or chanters of the Quran to sit upon so that their voices could project out into the courtyard.

On either side of the mihrab, doors lead into the mausoleum. The door on the right, of bronze inlaid with silver and gold is original and of exceptional workmanship. When cleaned it is dazzling. The design of the door combines central star shapes with small polygonal satellites, a design also popular in wood-work. The inscription in silver at the base is in Thuluth script, much favored in the Mamluk period. Thuluth means 'third,' and in this script the letters are three times as high as they are wide.

Inside the mausoleum the chamber is lofty and somber. One corner of it has been restored to give some idea of its original richness. Above the marble paneling the chamber is circum-scribed by a carved and painted inscription in Thuluth from the "Throne Verse" of the Quran (2:255):

> God—there is no God but He, the Living, the Self-subsisting. Slumber seizes Him not, neither sleep; His is all that is in the heavens and on earth. Who is there that shall intercede with Him, except by His leave? He knows what lies before them and behind them, and they compre-hend nothing of His knowledge, except as He wills. His throne comprises the heavens and the earth; the preser-vation of them wearies Him not; He is the Sublime, the Almighty.

Mosque lamps pendant from the octagonal support supplied the lighting. In the corners stalactite pendentives with niches of lavishly gilded and painted decoration support the dome. The Quran kursi, or lectern, has recently been cleaned: the royal Qurans were so large they required special stands. The front and back of the book rested on inclined planes, while the reciter sat crosslegged in front of it on the dais. The straight multicolored marble paneling combines and contrasts well with the rich polychrome surface of the wooden stand. The geometric star pattern exactly encloses its four sides, and is outlined and given emphasis by the use of ivory. The overall effect, both of pattern and technique, is similar to that of the bronze door.

Sultan Hasan's mausoleum has been given great prominence. The engineer builder or master planner has ingeniously solved the problem of maximum urban visibility with maximum religious blessing or baraka. The tomb's external site is on the maydan under the Citadel, overlooking the parades and feasts that took place there and had done since the time of his father al-Nasir Muhammad. Its internal location is behind the qibla wall toward which all Muslims face when saying their prayers. Sultan Hasan, however, is not buried here. After his assassination his body was not recovered, and behind the wooden lattice screen lie two young sons.

The architectural conception of the mausoleum is also very dramatic. The chamber, flanked by two minarets, was conceived as projecting in full mass onto the maydan. In 1616 the dome was described by an Italian traveler as unique, "in that it commences narrow, then swells out, and then contracts to a point like the egg of a hen." In 1660 it was described as full of holes made by cannonballs fired at the building from the Citadel. Twice the madrasa of Sultan Hasan was used as a fortress. During the reign of Sultan Barquq (1391) dissident amirs mounted on the terrace and hurled projectiles at the Citadel until the sultan ordered the steps and platform of the entrance destroyed and the entrance boarded up. Again in 1517 the madrasa was bombarded by cannonballs when it served as a refuge for the fugitive Tumanbay, the last Mamluk sultan. The northeast minaret fell in 1659, and both that minaret and the present dome date to restorations of 1671–72.

Rifa'i Mosque ** 1869–1912 (see map 4). This enormous
structure lies opposite the Madrasa of Sultan Hasan, upon the
site of a former Rifa'i zawiya, acquired and demolished by the
Princess Khushyar, consort of Ibrahim Pasha and the mother
of the Khedive Isma'il (ruled 1863–79). The architect Husayn
Pasha Fahmy was empowered to build a mosque with tombs for
Shaykh 'Ali al-Rifa'i, a saint formerly buried in the zawiya, and
Shaykh 'Abdallah al-Ansari, a companion of the Prophet, as
well as mausolea for the founder and her descendants. The
mosque was begun in 1869, but a series of vicissitudes, structural and financial, followed by the deaths of both the architect
and his patroness, led to the suspension of work in about 1880.
It was not until 1905 that work was begun again and the
mosque was finished more or less as originally planned by
Husayn Pasha. The decorations, for which the architect had left
no plans, were executed by Max Herz Bey, chief architect for the
Comité, from models taken from the best Cairene mosques.

The main or royal entrance, at the western end of the
building, is now closed. One enters from the south side, across
from Sultan Hasan. Immediately in front is the tomb of Shaykh
'Ali al-Rifa'i, the head of the Rifa'i tariqa or order of dervishes.
He was considered a saint in his lifetime and people still walk
around his tomb, touching their hands to the sandalwood
screen, while seeking his blessed intercession in their lives. To
the left of this tomb, behind the mashrabiya screen, in other
chambers lie the cenotaphs of King Fuad (ruled 1917–36) and
his mother, and Muhammad Pahlevi, the last Shah of Iran,
buried here in 1980.

To the right of Shaykh 'Ali's tomb is the sanctuary of the
mosque. It is an impressive place, both in its monumental size
and in the massing and variety of its ornamentation. A late and
dazzling compendium of Cairene ornamentation, it is not possible to take it all in at a glance. Plan to stay a while and let the
eye wander over its cool surfaces.

Its statistics are also impressive. Nineteen different kinds of
marble from seven different countries are used; the forty-four
grand columns, and the eighteen intricately worked window
grilles, each cost LE 1,000. Gold for gilding the ceiling was
imported from Turkey for LE 25,000 between 1906 and 1912,
when such a sum was large.

The patroness and her family are buried in funerary chambers along the north walls. To get to these tombs exit from the sanctuary by a door to the left of the qibla wall. Herein lie Isma'il, his mother, two daughters, two sons, and three wives, one of whom was French, as indicated by the crosses on her cenotaph. Sultan Husayn Kamil, who reigned from 1914 to 1917, and his wife are also buried here.

Gate of Mangak al-Silahdar (No. 247) 1346–47/747–48. Leaving Rifa'i, go back to the triple-arched entrance portal, turn right, and walk a few yards to the first street on the left, Suq al-Silah. At the corner is a ruined domed structure. This is the gate to the palace of Mangak al-Yusufi al-Silahdar (the swordbearer or armorer)—the same Mangak whose funerary complex is in the Bab al-Wazir cemetery. The gate was built at the beginning of his career, and his blazon with the sword of office is a prominent decoration. The shallow dome is also interesting, being an example of a pure pendentive system. The collar of red stones in a zig-zag pattern below the interior dome is striking. This gate was at the edge of the Suq al-Silah, or 'bazaar of the armorers,' whose location near the Citadel was a logical consequence of its strategic importance and of the number of Mamluks quartered there. The trade of metal working is still practiced in this area.

Other monuments along this street, which leads to Bab Zuwayla, are described in Chapter 6.

Mosque of Gawhar al-Lala ** (No. 134) 1430/833. Gawhar was a free slave, first in the service of Sultan Barsbay (d. 1438), for whom he served as chief eunuch, and then of Barsbay's son, who succeeded Barsbay briefly for three months and for whom Gawhar was chief tutor (*lala*). Under Sultan Gaqmaq he fell from grace and was thrown into prison, where he died of an epileptic attack. His mosque–madrasa–mausoleum–sabil-kuttab is to be found behind and east of the Mosque of Rifa'i. Climb a flight of stairs. The attenuated dome and squat minaret, which seem off scale, will identify it.

After Rifa'i the inside will seem to be on an almost miniature scale, but it is charming and incorporates all that is best decoratively of the mid-Mamluk period: attractive marble panels on floors, a handsome though faded lantern covering the sahn, a qibla wall paneled in slabs of cool marble, and soft colors. If the minbar seems different it is because all of the inlaid polygonal inserts were missing and have been replaced with plain forms. There is a gallery in the northwest liwan which has been draped so that women may pray there. Notice the way the windows in the qibla wall are angled to adjust between the difference in the line of the street façade and the line of the qibla, that is, between two conflicting orientations, between the ostentatious desire to have the façade, its dome, and minaret clearly visible from the maydan, and the religious need to have the inside correctly oriented toward Mecca. The Comité restored the mosque in 1896.

Mosque of Amir Akhur * (No. 136) 1503–04/909. This mosque complex belongs to Qanibay al-Sayfi, also known as al-Rammah ('the lancer'), who was Amir Akhur Kabir, or grand master of the horse, during the reign of Sultan al-Ghuri. The site is appropriate, since the horse market and stables of the Citadel were originally located below the Citadel, just off the maydan.

The features that immediately identify this building as one built in the very late Mamluk period are the double finials of the minaret, the forked lower leaves of the fleur-de-lys cresting, and the handsomely carved arabesque surface of the stone dome, with its triangular corner supports. The master builder has ingeniously dealt with the problem of the ascending ground level. The sabil–kuttab on the left is at a lower level. The mosque unit, above storage rooms, is up another flight of stairs.

The plan of the interior is that of the late Mamluk madrasa-mosque style. The original roofing of the sahn is now missing. The shallow dome on pendentives in the qibla liwan is unusual but the lavishly carved surfaces are not. The mausoleum to the right of the qibla is preceded by a small vestibule where the Quran was read. There is a good view of the city from the minaret. The complex was first restored in 1895. Qanibay al-Rammah built another mosque in the vicinity of the mosque of Sayyida Zaynab, which in 1989 suffered much damage when its minaret collapsed.

Manzil of 'Ali Effendi Habib (No. 497) 18th century. Turn left around the outer wall of the tomb chamber of the Amir Akhur.

*Dome and minaret of Amir Akhur and
House of 'Ali Effendi Habib*

This is the Darb al-Labbana. On the left is an attractive house with a façade of mashrabiya windows. It is notable as the home of Hasan Fathy, the famous modern architect who died in 1988.

Porch of Takiyat Taqiy al-Din al-Bistami (No. 326) 1443/847. At the end of the Darb al-Labbana, the entrance, with a mere trace of turquoise decoration, is all that is left of this monument.

Mosque of Mahmud Pasha ** (No. 135) 1568/975. To the south of the Mosque of Amir Akhur, southeast of the Madrasa of Sultan Hasan, is this mosque built by Mahmud Pasha, Governor of Cairo from 1565. Rapacious and sanguinary, he never went out except with his executioner, to whom he would indicate with a gesture of his hand those destined for death. In 1567 he met his end by an assassin's bullet through his cheek.

The exterior form and arrangements of the building are typical Mamluk: façade divided into bays with stalactite cornice, double-leafed merlons, and windows of one light over two. In back, the projecting tomb chamber in fact imitates that of Sultan Hasan. The only real Ottoman element of the building is the minaret, a slim, cylindrical shaft with a conical cap. The interior is surprisingly pleasant. A lowered aisle leads straight across the rectangular sanctuary from the entrance to the ablutions fountain. In the center four massive granite columns support a lantern covering that is similar to late Mamluk prototypes. The walls at one time were striped red and white; fortunately, the paint has almost faded away so that the stripes do not detract from the glowing colors of the windows or from the remaining patterns of the ceiling. This is a pleasant and restful place in which to contemplate the present and the past.

Bab al-'Azab (No. 555) 1754/1168. This gate that projects out into the Maydan was added to the Citadel by Radwan Katkhuda. It was used by the 'Azaban, 'the young men levies,' the infantry corps that occupied the lower levels of the Citadel as distinct from the older Janissary corps, which occupied the northern enclosure. It was here in 1811 that, on orders from Muhammad 'Ali Pasha, the Mamluks—and an institution that had endured more than 550 years—finally met their end (see Chapter 12).

Canopy portal of the Palace of Qawsun

Palace of Qawsun or Yashbak min Mahdi * (No. 266) 1337/
738 (see map 2). Circle around the tomb of the Madrasa of
Sultan Hasan and continue west. Take the first turning to the
left after the blocks of lower-income flats, into Sharia Manakh
al-Waqf. The remains of the palace are visible from the street.
About twenty meters on the right is a bright blue door. Knock
and the custodian will escort you to what is left of the palace.

Although many splendid examples of religious architecture
remain in Cairo from the Mamluk period, there are few surviving secular buildings. This palace, which originally included an
enormous stable and lodge, was built between 1330 and 1337 by
the Amir Qawsun, cupbearer and son-in-law of Sultan al-Nasir
Muhammad ibn Qalawun. His successors added to it, most
notably Yashbak min Mahdi, an important amir under Sultan
Qaytbay. It is a rare survivor from a royal quarter that once
spread down from the Citadel toward the Nile. The entrance is
set in a bay, with a superb canopy of dripping stalactites in a
star-shaped pattern. The portal is similar in its main components to those of mosques and madrasas. The palace, although
two thirds destroyed and otherwise inaccessible, still gives an
idea of Mamluk grandeur and scale under the sons of Qalawun.

Maristan of Sultan al-Muayyad * (No. 257) 1418–20/821–23
(see map 3). In the same quarter is the great hospital built by
the Mamluks to serve the Citadel area. It is their second
important hospital, the first being that of Qalawun (Chapter
11). Facing Bab al-'Azab at the foot of the Citadel, go left up the
hill two-thirds of the way to Sharia al-Mahgar. Turn left into it
and proceed thirty yards until the first turning on the left,
Sikkat al-Komi. Another thirty meters down Sikkat al-Komi
one comes quite suddenly upon the façade of the Maristan.

Its unexpected appearance amid mean surroundings, its
natural elevation, as well as the grandeur of the monument
itself, make it one of the most impressive sights of Islamic
Cairo. After Muayyad's death the building was used as a
residence for foreigners coming to Egypt. Today it is in ruins
and only the main façade remains. The raised portal, similar to
that of al-Muayyad's mosque, shows Persian influence; the
prominent use of the Fatimid keel arch is local. The large
medallions flanking the portal were once inlaid with contrast-

ing tile or stone such as one sees on other Mamluk monuments. The tall engaged column to the left of the entrance is a beautiful example of intricate stone carving.

Mausoleum of Qansuh Abu Sa'id (No. 360) 1499/904. This tiny tomb is on the left just before Sharia al-Mahgar. When Qansuh became sultan he built another, much grander tomb in the Northern Cemetery.

Zawiyat Hasan al-Rumi (No. 258) 1522/929. Opposite is this small and undistinguished structure, mentioned to give it a name and a date for those who wonder.

Mausoleum of Ragab al-Shiraz (No. 476) 1379/781. Continuing north one passes this curiously outlined tomb next to a mosque of recent construction. Perched on a hill, it is an octagonal structure with a saw-tooth crown around a plain dome.

Mosque of Mangak al-Yusufi * (No. 138) 1349/750. To the northeast along the same street a stone newel post marks the left turn-off into Sharia Qarafa Bab al-Wazir. This downhill street leads to a cluster of monuments nestled in a hollow behind the site of the former Bab al-Wazir, one of the medieval gates of the city. Many high-ranking amirs were buried in this cemetery which was within the city walls because in the main cemeteries outside tombs were subject to looting and bodies to desecration. One sultan sent six hundred men to protect his mother's grave.

Mangak al-Yusufi started his career as a mamluk of al-Nasir Muhammad ibn Qalawun, and he rose successively to the highest offices until he became viceroy of Egypt and com-mander-in-chief of the army. He died in 1375. His mosque complex, which included a khanqah and his mausoleum, was built when he was wazir and majordomo. Approximately one block down Sharia Qarafa Bab al-Wazir, on the left, the upper windows of the mosque are visible behind shop fronts. Turn left into Darb al-Manashka, proceed through an arched entrance and turn left. The minaret, with its unusual puffed or cushion mouldings under the balconies, is free-standing before the monument. The plan of the complex is curious, for it is on two levels. The main entrance leads into the mosque, which is of the congregational type but the sahn is smaller and roofed over. The present fountain area near the sahn is a later addition. The mosque is in need of refurbishing, but the minbar can be admired. The khanqah is reached by a flight of stairs in the north wall. It is a large room, with a mihrab, in which the amir and his wife are buried. In the back wall there is a tunnel, which reportedly leads to the Citadel. A strong flashlight is required to explore this hypothesis.

Sabil and Hod of 'Abd al-Rahman Katkhuda (No. 260) 18th century. All that remains of this fountain and watering trough is part of the façade opposite Mangak's complex. Originally, the façade on the street was open, i.e. it had a two-arched, one-column front. The other three sides were closed.

Mausoleum of Yunus al-Dawadar * (No. 139) 1382/783. The elongated, melon-shaped, ribbed dome with a return curve on the left marks this earliest monument of the Circassian Mamluk period, a complex much ruined except for the tomb chamber. This is the tomb of Yunus al-Dawadar ('Jonah the inkstand-holder'), the executive secretary or royal messenger who supervised the execution of the sultan's orders: in his case, they were Sultan Barquq's. Like the earlier dome of the Sultaniya (Chapter 8), this one prefigures the Central Asian style associated with the period of Timur or Tamerlane. The base of the dome is decorated by alternating windows and panels. The emblem incised on these panels, however, is that of a cup, not a penbox. The sultan chose his cupbearers from the most engaging and fetching boys at court. The cup in this instance is from an earlier office and may have been used from an old man's desire to be remembered for his beauty rather than his brains. The shallow relief carving of arabesques around the windows in the transition is very attractive.

  Yunus al-Dawadar is not buried here: he was killed in battle in Syria and his grave is unknown. Anas, the father of Barquq, was buried here but moved after the construction of Barquq's khanqah in the Northern Cemetery (Chapter 13).

Hod of Shaykhu (No. 144) 1354/755. Across from Yunus's tomb is the watering trough of Shaykhu, a decorated, five-arched

Mausoleum of Yunus al-Dawadar

niche let into the side of the hill. It was built when he was cupbearer, as the blazons indicate. Bab al-Wazir was the entrance to the city for travelers coming overland from Syria and here was the first municipal service for the weary and thirsty.

Mosque and Khanqah of Nizam al-Din (No. 140) 1356/757. On the hill above the hod is a large but ruined tomb complex. It was built by a man from Isfahan whom Sultan al-Nasir Muhammad placed in charge of his famous khanqah at Siryaqus, twenty kilometers north of Cairo. Nizam al-Din spent a large fortune building this complex.

This cemetery area can also be approached by the road passing under Salah Salim from the Northern Cemetery.

6 ◇ From Sultan Hasan to Bab Zuwayla

A. *Sharia Bab al-Wazir:*
Mosque of Aytmish al-Bagasi
Gate–Sabil–Kuttab–Mausoleum of Tarabay al-Sharifi *
Palace of Alin Aq *
Mosque–Mausoleum of the Amir Khayrbak **
Mosque of Aqsunqur (The Blue Mosque) **
Madrasa of Umm al-Sultan Sha'ban **
Bayt Ahmad Katkhuda al-Razzaz **
Minaret of Zawiyat al-Hunud *

B. *Sharia Suq al-Silah:*
Madrasa of Ilgay al-Yusufi **
Sabil–Kuttab of Ruqayya Dudu **
Hammam of the Amir Bashtak
Mosque of Alti Barmaq *

C. *Darb al-Ahmar:*
Mosque of Altinbugha al-Maridani ***
Mosque of Ahmad al-Mihmandar *
Sabil–Kuttab of Muhammad Katkhuda Mustahfizan
Mosque of Qajmas al-Ishaqi ***
Mosque of Aslam al-Silahdar *

See map 4

The street that connects Bab Zuwayla with the Citadel is another of Cairo's streets that has several names: Darb al-Ahmar, al-Tabbana, Bab al-Wazir, Sharia al-Mahgar. It also forks in the middle, so there are three parts to this walk. This quarter, outside the southern wall of the Fatimid city, was originally the site of Fatimid and Ayyubid cemeteries. It was not until Sultan al-Nasir Muhammad developed the Citadel as the seat of political, military and administrative power that,

with the sultan's active encouragement, it became a fashionable place in which to build. Most of its present monuments date
therefore from the fourteenth century. In the nineteenth century the area received another developmental impetus from
those who wished to be near the Citadel expansion and development of Muhammad 'Ali. As one walks down the street there
are some fine remnants of projecting and carved wooden windows, and glimpses of twisting, narrow alleys.

If one has a car it is easier to park it near Sultan Hasan than
Bab Zuwayla, and for this reason the walk begins at the Citadel
end of the street.

A. Sharia Bab al-Wazir

Mosque of Aytmish al-Bagasi (No. 250) 1383/785. From Bab
al-'Azab proceed past the Mosque of Mahmud Pasha as though
going to the Maristan of al-Muayyad (Chapter 5). After two
hundred meters a street branches to the left. This is Sharia al-
Mahgar, the beginning of Sharia Bab al-Wazir. The Mosque of
Aytmish is some 250 meters ahead to the right. It was built by
a Burgi Amir who for a few months in 1399 was regent for Farag
ibn Barquq. The façade has its sabil–kuttab on the northwest
corner, a decoration of inverse heart-shaped leaf patterns over
the main entrance, and a dome with slanting ribs. The slanting
angle of the ribs is an example of the experimentation with
ribbing that was in vogue from 1360 to 1400. The interior is
extremely plain both in shape and in decoration. A drinking
trough (No. 251) is located behind this mosque. One can reach
it via Sharia Bab al-Turba ('Gate of the Tomb') on the mosque's
north side, the site of a former city gate.

Gate–Sabil–Kuttab–Mausoleum of Tarabay al-Sharifi*
(No. 255) 1503–04/909. Just north of the Mosque of Aytmish,
this large complex really belongs to the group of monuments
described in the Bab al-Wazir cemetery (Chapter 5), but it is
easier to get to it from Sharia Bab al-Turba. The building was
restored by the Comité in 1905/1323. The tomb, a large domed
cube typical of late Burgi buildings, is set within an enclosure
into which one enters through the gate opposite Aytmish's
drinking trough. The tomb, all that remains of a much larger
complex, is a magnificent example of late Mamluk workman-

ship: double-leaf cresting, windows in the form of three oculi over three arched panels, roundel inscriptions with the Amir's name, double bands of molding, and decorated shoulder cascades in the transition zone. Amir Tarabay was chief of the Mamluks in Egypt (but not of those in Syria) under Sultan al-Ghuri.

Palace of Alin Aq * (No. 249) 1293/693. Return to Sharia Bab al-Wazir and continue northward. Just before reaching the complex of Khayrbak (below) you will pass on the right the remnants of what once must have been a very impressive early Bahri residence. Alin Aq was an amir and cupbearer to Sultan al-Ashraf Khalil ibn Qalawun. The portal lies to the right in an open area behind an iron railing just off the street. The canopy hood has a pattern of stalactites that hang from an eight-petaled rosette.

Mosque–Mausoleum of Khayrbak ** (No. 248) 1502–20/ 908–26. The Amir Khayrbak was one of the chief amirs of the Mamluk empire. Although he was viceroy of Aleppo, his ambition led him to intrigue with the Ottomans and to betray his master, Sultan al-Ghuri, at the battle of Marj Dabiq near Aleppo in 1516. There the Ottomans routed the Mamluk army and opened the door to the conquest of Egypt. As a reward, Khayrbak was made the first Ottoman viceroy of Egypt. He was rapacious and cruel.

His mausoleum was built in 1502, but the mosque and sabil attached to it date from 1520. This monument thus straddles the transition from the Mamluk period to the Ottoman, but architecturally it is in the Mamluk tradition and does not incorporate new and foreign architectural features.

The best view of the complex is from the direction of the Citadel. Khayrbak annexed the former palace of Alin Aq in the foreground and heavily restored it as his residence. Behind stand the dome, with its triangular shoulders and richly carved tapestry of interlacing leaves and hearts, and the minaret, unfortunately missing its upper story. The sabil–kuttab next to the entrance protrudes slightly and balances the protrusion under the minaret at the other end of the façade. One enters the complex through a corridor, on the left of which is a door to the

Mosque of Khayrbak

sabil; on the right steps lead up to the mosque. This is an unusual aproach. The portal with its stone benches on either side cannot be seen from the street. One steps over a threshold made from a block of pharaonic stone. The custodian claims that these hieroglyphic inscriptions, which include a figure of the mummified Osiris, have kept all flies and insects from the mosque.

The interior is covered with three cross vaults: the central one with a small lantern in the roof. The mosque, however, appears to have been finished in a hurry and according to an abbreviated plan, for the arches cut straight across the windows of the qibla wall. Beyond the minbar is the entrance to the tomb chamber. The mausoleum is not lavishly decorated but one is surprised by its extraordinary height. The depth of the windows increase so that both the façade alignment with the street and the internal regularity of the mosque is maintained. A door in the qibla wall to the left of the mihrab hides the stairs that communicate directly with Alin Aq's palace; on the opposite wall is a closet. From the mausoleum one gets a good view of both the palace and the city walls built by Salah al-Din, which abut the courtyard from behind and to the east. The cemetery of Bab al-Wazir is just beyond.

House–Waqf of Ibrahim Agha Mustahfizan (No. 619) 1652/ 1062. This lies between the Mosque of Khayrbak and the Mosque of Aqsunqur, with the ruins of the *Rab' of Ibrahim Agha Mustahfizan* (No. 595) opposite. These monuments, of which little survive except the parameters, were built by a commander of the Citadel guards, who intended perhaps to make them the center of a general restoration for this quarter.

Mosque of Aqsunqur ** (No. 123) 1346–47/747–48. (Also known as the *Mosque of Ibrahim Agha Mustahfizan* 1652/1062, and the *Blue Mosque*.) This mosque is located on the right-hand side of the street, just next to the previous two monuments. Beloved of tour guides, it is on all their itineraries. The minaret projects from the southwest corner of the mosque and dominates the street. Its simplicity and good proportions make it noteworthy, as does its uncommon circular shaft. The entrance is distinguished by the lovely weathered panels of blue-gray marble on its façade.

Shams al-Din Aqsunqur ('Sun of Religion, White Falcon') an amir of one hundred and a commander of one thousand, was al-Nasir Muhammad's Master of the Hunt, and his son-in-law. He was one of the most important amirs at court, especially under the ephemeral successors of Sultan al-Nasir. In 1346 he organized a successful plot against Sultan al-Kamil Sha'ban on behalf of his half brother al-Muzaffar Hajji, who rewarded the amir by having him strangled in 1347.

The main entrance to the mosque on Sharia Bab al-Wazir is in a recess covered with an arch supported on two beautiful fan-shaped brackets. To the left is a salient formed by the mausoleum and a circular window of fine pierced stucco. Below this is the foundation slab bearing the name of 'Ala al-Din and the date 746 (1345). 'Ala al-Din, the Sultan al-Ashraf Kuchuk ('Little One'), was one of the nine sons of Sultan al-Nasir Muhammad. Kuchuk ruled for five months at the age of six but was deposed and imprisoned at the Citadel, where he was strangled three years later on the orders of his brother Sultan al-Kamil Sha'ban. He is buried in this tomb chamber just inside the mosque on the left, presumably because he was Aqsunqur's puppet as well as his brother-in-law. Aqsunqur himself is buried in the plain, unadorned tomb on the right wall of the mosque just before the sanctuary.

The plan of the mosque is that of an open sahn surrounded by four riwaqs. The qibla riwaq was originally covered with crossvaults, the arches of which rested on octagonal piers. There is a small dome over the mihrab. A dikka faces out into the courtyard. The fountain in the middle of the courtyard was added by Amir Tughan in 1412/815. The mosque was constructed in 1347 but the blue tiles for which it is famous were installed between 1652 and 1654/1062 and 1064 by Ibrahim Agha, who usurped and redecorated the mosque. With the Ottoman conquest the chronological development of the cemeteries came to an end. Most Ottomans were buried in the courtyards of mausolea already in existence—here we have a vivid example. Ibrahim is buried in the tomb chamber he built for himself next to the minaret entrance on the right side of the courtyard. The combination of Mamluk-style marble dadoes, Ottoman tiles, and painted ceilings with which the tomb is decorated is very rich.

The tiles were imported either from Istanbul or from Damascus. They are typical of the tiles called Iznik, made in that city, although later imitated in other places. During the sixteenth and seventeenth centuries they were an important feature of interior decoration of Ottoman mosques. The beautiful combination of light indigo and turquoise is the characteristic color scheme, while the designs show growing plants or cut flowers: cypress trees, carnations, tulips, bluebells, peach blossoms, and the long, serrated leaves known as saz. Ottoman tiles are used sparingly in Cairo, and in view of the Ottoman fondness for them and the nearness of Damascus where Iznik tiles were imitated until 1759, that is surprising. The tile wall decorations in the tomb chamber and on the qibla wall in this mosque exhibit the most lavish use of them locally.

The mihrab is a handsome example of Mamluk inlaid mihrabs, with its geometirc interlace design in the spandrels, joggled lintel panels, painted relief carving of the hood, and registers of carved marble, marble and mosaic inlay, and marble panels. The minbar, the oldest of the few remaining marble minbars, is especially attractive with its bold, rounded, white separation lines and its combination of salmon, plum, light gray, and green stone insets. The handrail, with its sweeping, undulating leaf and grape cluster design, is also well carved.

When Ibrahim usurped the mosque he did not really alter its main features, and with the trees growing in the courtyard and the birds twittering and singing in the branches it is another of those pleasant places in which to sit for a while to rest and to contemplate. The Comité restored the mosque in 1908.

Sabil and Tomb of 'Umar Agha (No. 240) 1652/1062. This small domed tomb with a sabil on the corner stands directly opposite the mosque of Aqsunqur and next to the Rab' of Ibrahim Agha Mustahfizan.

Madrasa Umm al-Sultan Sha'ban ∗∗ (No. 125) 1368–69/770. The street now becomes Sharia al-Tabbana. Seventy meters further down on the left, this monument is distinguishable by its handsome façade and double domes. This is the only royal foundation on this main artery leading from the Citadel toward

Bab Zuwayla. It was begun in 1368–69 by Sultan al-Ashraf Sha'ban for his mother Khwand Baraka (Lady Blessing) while she was making the pilgrimage to Mecca and Madina. When she returned in 1369–70 she endowed the mosque. She was the concubine of Husayn, a son of al-Nasir Muhammad, and rose to fame when her son came to the throne at the age of ten. After her first husband died in 1362, Khwand Baraka married Ilgay al-Yusufi, whose monument is in the Suq al-Silah. Sultan Sha'ban himself began building a khanqah–madrasa–mosque at the foot of the Citadel, but when he was murdered in 1376 his complex was left unfinished and he was buried in his mother's madrasa.

To the right of the entrance is a drinking trough with inscriptions above; to the left a sabil, the opening of which is covered with a screen of mashrabiya work in beautiful geometric designs. The main feature of the façade is the beautiful entrance, which stands in a recess covered by a nine-row muqarnas tier. The frame around it is decorated in flat relief carving. Both tier and frame were painted originally in gold, red, and blue. Around the entrance itself extensive use is made of ablaq or striped masonry. The main façade of the complex is unusual. The portal, the sabil, and the minaret are aligned with Sharia al-Tabbana. Then the façade makes a 45° turn to the back. The monument is now being used as an elementary school, and if the main entrance is closed, walk round the exterior until you reach the entrance in the back.

The internal plan is that of a cruciform madrasa, although it was built to teach only two madhhabs, the Shafi'i and the Hanafi. The qibla liwan is flanked by two lofty-domed tomb chambers. They are both rather unusual in that the domes rest on simple squinches rather than on tiers of stalactites; the walls are plain, not marble-covered. Each tomb chamber has a window opening onto the qibla sanctuary. The wooden shutters are quite fine, with large polygons of bone in carved leaf forms alternating with small ones of mosaic inlay. The large tomb chamber on the left is that in which Khwand Baraka and a daughter Khwand Zahra are buried. In front of it is an irregularly shaped room that was probably for storing large Qurans or for special Quran recitations. The smaller tomb on the right, with no decoration and no mihrab, is the final resting place of

Sultan al-Ashraf Sha'ban and his son al-Mansur Hajji (ruled
1377–81). There is no Quranic law requiring the separate
burial of men and women, but by the end of the fourteenth
century the custom had become established.

Bayt Ahmad Katkhuda al-Razzaz ** (No. 235) 15th/9th
century and 1776/1192. Immediately next to the Mosque of
Sha'ban, and identifiable by its second-story mashrabiya windows, is Bayt al-Razzaz, a palace built by Sultan Qaytbay in the
fifteenth century. It has been so extensively added to by subsequent occupants that it contains some eighty-odd rooms and
stretches from Sharia al-Tabbana to Sharia Suq al-Silah,
where there is a second entrance, now blocked up. A left turn
down the passageway from the Sharia al-Tabbana entrance
and then a right turn will bring you into the first or north court,
which occupies more than four hundred square meters; immediately to your left as you enter this court is the original
entrance of Qaytbay. Stairs lead to the qa'a behind the beautiful
mashrabiya that overlooks the courtyard. The projecting alcoves, where porous earthenware jugs were placed to cool by
evaporation, are what give these lattice windows their name:
literally, 'drinking-place thing.' To your right as you enter the
courtyard another stairway goes to the qa'a and mashrabiya
windows that overlook the street. As in most double houses, this
area was the preserve of the ladies. The women used the
upstairs apartments of both houses, connected by passageways, while the men used the downstairs rooms. At the southwestern corner of the first court is a passage leading to the
second court, which was for the men. There is a large maq'ad
overlooking this court. Just to the left is a door that opens into
a passage leading to an eighteenth-century qa'a in ruinous
condition but with magnificent vestiges. At a height of about
four meters a carved cornice projects into the room, perhaps to
give human scale to the grand elevation of the ceiling. In the
middle of the room was a fountain with a high-domed opening
above it. The ceilings, whether beamed (as over the southern
end) or with a central rosette (as over the northern end), are
painted in reds and blues. There are mashrabiya galleries over
the side liwans from which the ladies of the harim looked down.
Upstairs was also a qa'a and a private bath area in the back.

House–Waqf (No. 595) 1652/1062 *and Sabil* (No. 238) 1639–40/ 1049–50 *of Ibrahim Agha Mustahfizan*. This façade ending in a sabil of Ibrahim Agha lies opposite the Madrasa of Umm Sha'ban. If one looks down the alley or enters the children's school at 49 Sharia al-Tabbana, one sees next to a palm tree a minaret.

Minaret of Zawiyat al-Hunud * (No. 237) 1260/660. This is the oldest surviving minaret of the Bahri Mamluk period and is interesting as being a direct descendant of the Fatimid– Ayyubid minaret with its ribbed keel-arched mabkhara finial, and its inverse S-curve windows.

Another 140 meters down this street is an intersection where Sharia Suq al-Silah comes in from the left. If one is tired or sated this is a good place to turn back along Sharia Suq al-Silah for Sultan Hasan.

B. Sharia Suq al-Silah

Gate of Mangak al-Silahdar (No. 246) 1346–47/747–48. To the north of the Madrasa of Sultan Hasan is a small park. At its western end, off Sharia Muhammad 'Ali on the right, Sharia Suq al-Silah enters what was in the medieval period the Armorer's Bazaar. On the left is what remains of the domed palace gate that is described in Chapter 5.

Madrasa of Ilgay al-Yusufi ** (No. 131) 1373/774. Visible from the top of the street is this handsome late Bahri complex, with its three-storied minaret and its unusual dome of twisted ribs. Between the stepped shoulders of the transition zone there is a new window form. From now on the standard fenestration for domes becomes three round windows, one over two, above three arched windows. The main façade is beautiful with regard to its fine proportions and its masses. It is divided into four bays: two wide ones topped with stalactite cornices, and two narrow ones with fluted keel arches. Inside these recesses are an arrangement of thirty-six windows in three registers.

Also, by the end of the Bahri period the style of Mamluk architecture had been set. The main dramatic and visual interest of a Mamluk façade lies in the careful positioning of

Madrasa of Ilgay al-Yusufi

contrasting shapes and masses such as the vertical thrust of the minaret, the hemispherical counterbalance of the dome, the horizontal mass of the façade, and the rectangular outline of the portal. The difference in each building lies not so much in new shapes and forms for individual features of the structure, but in their placement, in their relationships with each other, and in the effect of the building as a whole on its site.

Also, by the end of the Bahri period sabils has acquired a place at the northwest corner of the complex. Originally the sabil was open to the street on two sides, which were screened off by mashrabiya grills. In this complex the space above the sabil was used for the kuttab or Quranic school, the first instance of what was to become a standard Cairene practice.

The Amir Sayf al-Din Ilgay, an amir of the sword, rose through the ranks. His monument was built shortly after his appointment as Commander-in-Chief of the Armies and his marriage to Khwand Baraka, the mother of Sultan Sha'ban (1363–77). For a few months Ilgay was the real head of the government; however, when Princess Baraka died, a quarrel with the sultan over her property obliged Ilgay to flee. He drowned crossing the Nile on horseback. His body was recovered by divers and brought back for burial in his madrasa. The blazon of the saqi, or 'cupbearer,' a cup in the middle field of a three-register shield, appears in the dating inscription over the entrance. Here again, as in the case of Yunus al-Dawadar, by picking the cup from the various court ranks he had held, he is reminding the world forever that he had once been 'surpassing fair.'

The interior plan is that of a cruciform madrasa with a large open sahn surrounded by four liwans, each with a frontal arch. Remains of the gilded decoration on the ceilings of the lateral liwans show the beauty and richness with which all four ceilings must once have been decorated. The qibla liwan has no marble dado. The minbar, although it has lost its top, has fine carving and inlay.

Sabil of Mustafa Sinan (No. 246) 1630/1040. This stands opposite the northwest corner of Ilgay's monument, and is all that is left of a structure that once also included a kuttab. The use of tiles in the rosettes on either side of the foundation incription is very attractive.

Sabil–Kuttab of Ruqayya Dudu ** (No. 337) 1761/1174.
Another hundred meters up the Suq al-Silah, on the right, is
one of the most remarkable sabil–kuttabs in Cairo, that of
Ruqayya Dudu. She was the daughter of Ridwan Kahya al-
Julfi, a regimental Mamluk officer and leader of the Julfiya
group, one of the Mamluk parties into which local lords were
divided in the Cairo of the eighteenth century. Ridwan supported Ibrahim Bey al-Kabir, who from 1748 to 1754 held
effective political power in Cairo. Ridwan, however, had no
interest in affairs of state but occupied himself with building
magnificent residences, with luxurious living, and with patronage of poets. Ruqayya died in 1758, four years after her father,
and it was her mother the Lady Badawiya Shahin who built this
monument for her.

The sabil is a fine piece of gingerbread. The eye is first
caught perhaps by the undulating eaves of the kuttab, the
fringes of scalloped woodwork around the projecting roofs, and
the magnificent iron grillwork of the windows of the sabil. Then
it is the collection of tiles in the spandrels, or the rich patterns
and floral forms, or the elaborately carved frames, columns,
and recesses that draw the eye. The recessed, rectangular
panels to either side of the rounded front serve to frame the
monument. The kuttab at the top must have been an especially
good place from which pupils could peer out at the traffic in the
street. The edifice is now in disrepair; a great shame for what
is truly a noble building in the Cairo–Ottoman baroque style.

Hammam of the Amir Bashtak (No. 244) 1341/742. The
striking portal on the next monument on the left belongs to the
bath of the Amir Bashtak. The red rhomboid in the center of the
ribbed keel arch is the blazon of the jamdar, the master of the
robes, an office that is represented by a napkin. The strapwork in
white and black around it makes a fine effect. The inscription
over the door reads: "Ordered to build this blessed bath, His Most
Noble and High Excellency, our Lord, the Great Amir, Sayf al-Din
Bashtak, (officer) of al-Malik al-Nasir, may his glory last for ever."
Although still in use as a bath, it is only the portal that survives
from the fourteenth century. Today, as in the medieval period, it
provides bathing facilities for women of the lower and middle
classes who live in the surrounding rooms or rab's.

Sabil–Kuttab of Ruqayya Dudu

Mosque of Sudun Min Zada (No. 127) 1401/804. This building once occupied the whole left-hand corner of Sharia al-Ghandur, which goes off Suq al-Silah to the right, opposite the Hammam. All that remains today, if you look closely, are the qibla wall and remnants of a few arches.

Mosque of Alti Barmaq * (No. 126) 1711/1123. This mosque, fifty meters farther up Sharia al-Ghandur on the right, was built by a Turk of whom little is known. From the outside it is a recognizably Ottoman structure with a subdued mamluk façade and an Ottoman minaret. At ground level there are shops, whose rent contributed to its upkeep. One ascends to the mosque by a flight of stairs. Inside, the plan is exceptional: three pairs of polyfaceted piers give the rectangular sanctuary a basilican feeling. The main aisle is flat-roofed; the side aisles are covered by groined vaults. The vividness of the ablaq masonry is not natural, but is due to paint. Opposite the mihrab is an open, suspended loggia, either for Quran readers or for women.

The mihrab is decorated with a fine set of Iznik tiles manufactured between 1555 and 1700 and called 'Rhodian' because it was once imagined they were made on the island of Rhodes. They are distinguished by their rich 'sealing-wax' red, a slip of highly ferruginous clay, which was so thickly applied as to stand up in perceptible relief. The lotus, tulip, and carnation forms are recognizable as well as the long, serrated saz leaves. The tiles were probably made earlier than the building. Unfortunately many of them have been broken or removed, but altogether they constitute a fine, tiled mihrab.

Sabil–Kuttab of Hasan Agha Koklian (No. 243) 1694/1106. Return to Suq al-Silah and continue north. This little monument with its nice lunette of blue and white tiles is at the next corner on the right.

Madrasa of Qatlubugha al-Dhahabi (No. 242) 1347/748. The façade is on the left as one continues up the street. This amir was one of the supporters of Sultan al-Muzaffar Hajji (ruled 1346–47) and took part in the first deposition of Sultan Hasan. Next on the right is an Omar Effendi department store and then a tile and marble factory. The street opens up here into a little square.

Zawiya Arif Pasha 1866/1282. This is the plain Ottoman structure on the left at the corner where Suq al-Silah joins Sharia al-Tabbana. At this point if time is limited one can turn right at Sharia al-Tabbana and return to Sultan Hasan. If not, by turning left to the north one can visit the monuments on the Darb al-Ahmar and end up at Bab Zuwayla.

C. Darb al-Ahmar

Mausoleum of Abu al-Yusufayn (No. 234) 1329–30/730. Thirty meters north of the intersection of Sharia Suq al-Silah and Sharia al-Tabbana, on the right, stands this little monument. It is locked. Nearby is a bakery that produces very good baladi or dark bread.

Mosque of Altinbugha al-Maridani *** (No. 120) 1339–40/ 739–40. A little further up the street on the left is this mosque, one of the finest monuments of the fourteenth century. The Amir Altinbugha ('Golden Bull') al-Maridani was one of Sultan al-Nasir Muhammad's sons-in-law, like Aqsunqur down the street. He was his father-in-law's cupbearer (saqi) and finally governor of Aleppo, where he died in 1341 at the age of 25. Judging by his name, his original owner came from Mardin in Turkey.

Since the façade follows the curve of the street, the discrepancy between the orientation toward Mecca and the street alignment is taken care of by the stair-step arrangement of the exterior. The façade is divided into shallow panels with stalactite hoods, with two windows in each panel. A Quranic inscription (36:1–18) runs along the top.

The minaret, next to the main entrance, shows new elements that set the style to which future minarets will add little but refinement. The square shaft of the first stage has become almost entirely reduced or omitted, and is now no more than a transitional area between mosque and minaret. The mabkhara finial is eliminated, and a little dome supported on slender columns serves as a final stage: it is the first instance of this type of minaret finial, which is to become the distinguishing mark of Mamluk minarets.

There are three entrances to the mosque, the principal one being in the north façade. The entrance in the south façade is the one to which one should go if the main entrance is closed. The northern entrance is set in a plain vaulted recess and is strikingly enhanced by its stalactite frieze, inlaid black and white marble panel, joggled voussoirs, and the complex pattern of the lintel made up of alternating and reverse ablaq forms.

Unlike the cruciform madrasas, this is a mosque with an open courtyard surrounded by four riwaqs. The elements of the courtyard are familiar from previous structures and exhibit the conservative use of ornamental units: stair-step crenellation with arabesque designs like the crenellation of the Bayn al-Qasrayn complex of Sultan Qalawun, keel-arched ribbed blind arches with lozenges and medallions as in the Mosque of al-Azhar, and corner posts with finials like those of the Mosque of Ibn Tulun, originally sheathed with green faience. Recently several poinciana or flamboyant trees have flourished in the courtyard. Although they are not an authentic part of the mosque they provide color and shade.

The qibla riwaq is separated from the rest of the mosque by a superb mashrabiya screen. In Cairo, because good wood was scarce and therefore prized, it was used primarily for decoration. This screen belongs to the earliest period of mashrabiya work. Mashrabiya work is an Islamic craft that was stimulated in Egypt by the shortage of fine wood for paneling. The basic principle is straightforward: a lattice is constructed of turned oval shapes joined together by short turned and ribbed links. Although this screen has been restored, its basic fabric is original, which gives some idea of the durability of wood in the dry, open air of Cairo. It is finely carved on both faces and from either side; whether from the courtyard or in silhouette from the sanctuary, it adds a fine extra element to this mosque.

In front of the mihrab there is a three-bay by three-bay domed area, whose arches are supported by eight red granite pharaonic columns. The lateral aisles are supported by reused church columns with a variety of capitals (although in the main Corinthian) and by Mamluk columns with polyfaceted edges and hourglass-shaped capitals. This plan resembles that of the mosque built by Sultan al-Nasir Muhammad on the Citadel. Ample documentation attests to al-Nasir Muhammad's great interest in building, not only in his own foundations, but also in his frequent encouragement of his amirs to build for themselves. He sent them official contributions of various kinds: marble, wood, workmen, builders, or architects. This is particularly true of this mosque, for not only were marble and wood provided out of the privy purse, but as a special mark of favor the chief architect of the court, Mu'allim ibn al-Suyufi, was sent to lay out the mosque.

The mihrab, with its mosaic and mother-of-pearl inlay, its turquoise colonettes, it joggled voussoirs in ablaq, and carved marble frames, although especially fine, is typical of the decorative fashion in mihrabs introduced by the mihrab of Sultan Qalawun's mausoleum. The minbar, like other Mamluk minbars, is of a woodworking techinque that makes use of small panels joined together to make larger items. In this way there is no waste of wood, and the distortion caused by warping and shrinking in a dry, hot climate is minimized by being evenly distributed over smaller units. The raised platform (the dikka) is for the recting and chanting of the Quran.

On the wall just above the minbar and below the dome there is an unusual kind of stucco ornament. It shows tree forms, which might allude to the Quranic verse, "A goodly saying, as a goodly tree—its roots firm, and its branches in heaven." (14:24). Other aspects of the interior decoration that are noteworthy are the panels of square Kufic, the marble inlaid panels with mother-of-pearl with arrow designs, and the strapwork interlace designs that appear often in the Bahri period. The roofing is of simple beams richly ornamented with patterns of gilt and paint. One corner of the domed area has been restored, which imparts a sense of the original richness of color. This mosque was extensively restored by the Comité in 1895–1903/1313–21 but is again in need of work.

Mosque of Ahmad al-Mihmandar * (No. 115) 1324–25/725. This Amir was one of the great civilian dignitaries in the reign of Sultan al-Nasir Muhammad. As mihmandar he was chief of protocol, the offical meeter and greeter. He later became the Amir al-Hajj, in charge of the annual pilgrimage to Mecca. He died in 1332. His mosque, a charming little structure, lies further down the Darb al-Ahmar, on the left. It is one of the oldest buildings of the quarter. The façade is very handsome and is a good example of the Mamluk style, which was established early and has endured for religious monuments even to the present day. The façade contains shallow recesses topped by stalactite hoods that run right up to the cornice crowned with trilobed merlons. In a country where there is little rain and flat roofs are general, some sort of crenellation is useful to relieve the monotonous horizontal lines of the roof. The upper windows framed with black and white ablaq and the keel-arched hood to mark the mihrab are especially ornate touches, but they harmonize with the richly emphasized entrance. The whole façade is divided horizontally by a great tiraz or historic inscription band. It starts with Quran 2:255, the "Throne Verse," and continues:

> The erection of this mausoleum and of the blessed mosque has been ordered of his own pure wealth from that which God has given him, and been endowed for all Muslims, in his desire for God's satisfaction and for the palace of the Hereafter, and in the desire to build houses for God and the accomplishing of what is due Him and for the recitation of His Book and making permanent mention of Him, by the slave needy of God—exalted be He—Ahmad the Mihmandar, Chief Syndic (*Naqib*) of the victorious armies of al-Malik al-Nasir.

The interior plan is that of a small courtyard mosque. Two columns form an arcade on the qibla side, while one column supports the ceiling on each side. The north liwan is arched. All the walls and the mihrab are plain. The mosque was restored in the name of the Turkish Sultan Ahmed III in 1722–23/1135. To this date belong the stained glass windows, the minbar, and the wooden dikka across the north liwan, and possibly the roof over the courtyard.

Sabil–Kuttab of Muhammad Katkhuda Mustahfizan (No. 230) 1677/1088. Just next to Ahmad's mosque stands this monument, with two façades that make a shallow angle on the corner. The left face has a lunette of tiles; the right face has an historic–poetic inscription set between panels of blue and while tiles. The window grills have cut-out inserts with the name of

Allah. Some of those on the right-hand grill are missing, which gives the placing of the remaining ones a random look. If the sabil is locked one can still get an idea of the interior by looking through the window. The rooms is lined with blue and white tiles. Opposite the windows, under a wooden stalactite hood, is the salsabil, the carved marble panel over which the water sparkled and cooled as it ran.

The Mosque of Qajmas al-Ishaqi *** (No. 114) 1480–81/ 885–86. Further up the street on the right stands this jewel-like structure from the Circassian Mamluk period. The complex is not far from Bab Zuwayla, and it is coming from that direction and proceeding toward the Citadel that the complex is best viewed. In fact, it is only from that direction that the real beauty and drama of the façade is truly apparent. The monument is situated on a triangular piece of land at the intersection of two streets, and provides an excellent example of the ingenious way in which architects of the late Mamluk period adjusted the parts of the building to the available site. A maximum use is made of both street façades, whose various sections are unified by the decoration. The sabil–kuttab, which in this period had become an integral part of the planning of all monuments, was built as a separate structure across the street. It is connected to the mosque by a raised passage over the street. The mashrabiya windows above the passage indicate that this area was intended as a residential unit for dependents and heirs. The plain dome and plain central section of the minaret are unusual for this period, and difficult to explain.

The mosque is built over shops, which are continuous on all of its exterior faces. Near the entrance behind the grilled windows is a sabil. It is marked by handsome marble inlay lintels over the windows. If you look closely at the knots of the grills you will see the blazon of Qajmas. It is of the composite kind and shows the following: a napkin in the upper field; a cup charged with a penbox placed between 'horns of plenty' in the middle, and a cup in the bottom field. Notice also the rich carving of the engaged corner column.

Above the entrance is a magnificent panel of ablaq marble, a swirl of six leaf forms in red, black, and white with turquoise touches. It is to this focal point that the marble mosaic lintels

Mosque of Qajmas al-Ishaqi

above the various windows seem to be leading. On the door, a central medallion pattern in bronze has replaced the solid bronze facings of the early Mamluk period. This was partly due perhaps to the general problem at this date of obtaining raw material, but it was also due to a change in taste, from the massive solidity and stability of the earlier monumental architectural forms to the lighter and airier elegance of rounded and curving forms. The entrance leads into a square vestibule with a richly gilded ceiling. Turn left, noticing as you pass into the open corridor that is part light source and part ventilator, that you are entering through a sliding door with two halves, similar to modern ones.

The mosque was restored in 1894/1312 and again in 1982. The interior is a perfect example of the typically Cairene evolution of the cruciform madrasa, the qa'a plan, in which the whole scale has been compressed, the sahn covered, and the lateral liwans reduced. This is one of the most important mosques of the Qaytbay period because of the high standard of skill shown in the various crafts employed in its decoration, such as the color harmonies of the marble paneling, the fine stone carving of the walls, and the splendid wood ceilings beautifully decorated and gilded.

The mihrab in this mosque is richly decorated. Here a new technique is used: black bitumen and/or red paste fill grooved designs in white marble, possibly because by the mid-fifteenth century supplies of antique marble were being depleted, but also because it was possible to achieve a more sinuous and compact effect this way. In the center of the mihrab, in a mirror-image cartouche, the craftsman in charge of the mosque's decoration has signed his work: "Made by 'Abd al-Qadir the Designer" (or 'Engraver,' *al-Naqqash*). The main pattern of the minbar, a central star with raised boss, is geometric.

The stained glass windows glow with color, but the presence of the cypress tree suggests that they are restorations from the Ottoman period. The floors have handsomely paved marble panels, but one has to ask the custodian to lift the mats. The paving in the qibla liwan is particularly fine.

A good view of the Bab Zuwayla and the surrounding quarter is obtained from the minaret. The kuttab is in use today as an elementary school.

The Amir Sayf al-Din Qajmas occupied several important posts during the reign of Sultan Qaytbay. He was master of the horse and officer in charge of the yearly pilgrimage to Mecca. He was also governor of Alexandria, Grand Marshal, and ended his career as viceroy of Syria, where he died peacefully in 1487. Described as pious, benevolent, and highly respected, Qajmas is buried in Damascus.

His tomb chamber, entered through the qibla liwan and located on the corner of two streets, has been occupied since 1852 by a holy man, Abu Hurayba, from whom the mosque takes its popular name. The chamber is plain and dignified, with a feeling of loftiness imparted by the dome.

Mosque of Aslam al-Silahdar * (No. 112) 1344–45/745–46. Take the street that runs between the Mosque of Qajmas and its kuttab. At a small vividly painted shrine the street forks. Either fork is all right. About three hundred meters to the east, you will come into an open square by this mosque.

Baha al-Din Aslam was a Qipchak Mamluk who became the swordbearer of Sultan al-Nasir Muhammad, who appointed him an amir of one hundred and commander of a thousand. As a victim of vicious slander he was imprisoned for six and a half years and it was not until the end of al-Nasir's reign that his rank was reinstated. The historian al-Maqrizi describes him as a kind man, known for his good deeds, and a pious man who sat at the head of halqas or circle of students, i.e. he was also a teaching shaykh.

This area outside the Bab Zuwayla was until the thirteenth century a Fatimid–Ayyubid cemetery, and it is likely from the arrangement of his building that Aslam built his mausoleum first and subsequently added to it the mosque.

There are two façades. The most attractive feature of the main one is the large rectangular marble panel with its red, black, and white interlace of trilobed forms. The brick dome of the mausoleum has stucco ribs and a band of faience mosaic around the base, which is best viewed from the east because so much of it has disappeared. The inscription is the "Throne Verse," Quran 2:255.

The interior plan is a variation of the cruciform madrasa and presents several surprises. The first is that the entrance leads

directly into the mosque. The north and osuth liwans have
arcades of two columns each; the east and west liwans are
arched. The east liwan, which contains the qibla, has a rather
garish mihrab and a small minbar. The side walls have arched
recesses with large stucco carved roundels. The roundel over
the mihrab has red and blue glass hearts hidden in the arabesque leaf pattern. The second surprise is that the liwans are
of different heights. Over the north and south liwans with their
flat ceilings are rooms for the inhabitants of the establishment.
They are set behind the courtyard façade, which is made up of
a triple register of windows with carved screens, carved stucco
lozenges and medallions, and cusped keel-arched panels. Over
the east liwan, because the arched opening is higher than the
north and south arcades, there is only one row of medallion–
lozenge–panel decoration. Over the west liwan there is no
courtyard ornament. This liwan is another surprise. Above the
arched recess there is an open balcony. This was probably used
by students, shaykhs, or sufis, since there is no separate access
to it for women other than by the staircase leading through the
living units. A second balcony, no more than a bridge, spans the
opening at the base of the liwan. This was probably the dikka.
The present roofing of the sahn was put up in 1900 to protect the
interior.

The tomb chamber on the southeast corner is now being used
as a storeroom. The walls are pocked and pitted, which is
generally an indication that some sort of previous surface
decoration (usually stucco) is now missing. There is a mihrab,
of carved stucco, which is unusual for this date, when marble
panels were the vogue. The room is enormously high. Between
the square room and the transition zone with its stalactite
squinches there is a level in which stained glass windows are
set.

Upon leaving the mosque, it is best perhaps to retrace one's
steps. However, the street that leads from the southwest corner
of the square, Sharia Nabawiya, leads into Sharia al-Tabbana
at the point of the wedge-shaped open space with the Madrasa
of Umm al-Sultan Sha'ban to the south or left and the Mosque
of Maridani to the north or right.

7 ◇ Bab Zuwayla to Sharia Saliba

A. Bab Zuwayla to Sharia Muhammad 'Ali:
Mosque of Salih Tala'i' **
Zawiya–Sabil of Farag ibn Barquq
Qasaba of Ridwan Bey **
Maq'ad of Ridwan Bey
Mosque of Mahmud al-Kurdi *
Madrasa of Inal al-Yusufi *
Zawiya of 'Abd al-Rahman Katkhuda *
Madrasa of Amir Gani Bak *
Mosque–Mausoleum of Ganim al-Bahlawan **
Takiya of Sulayman *

B. Sharia Muhammad 'Ali to Sharia Saliba:
Mosque–Mausoleum of Amir Ilmas *
Tomb of Amir al-Muzaffar 'Alam al-Din Sangar *
Mausoleum–Madrasa of Amir Sunqur Sa'di *
Khanqah al-Bunduqdariya *
Sabil–Kuttab of 'Ali Agha Dar al-Sa'ada
Sabil of Umm 'Abbas *

See map 4

A. Bab Zuwayla to Sharia Muhammad 'Ali.

Bab Zuwayla is the starting point for several interesting walks. This one can be done in two easy stages or in one fairly long excursion, depending on how many monuments one examines carefully along the way. The Street of the Tentmakers is the continuation of the Qasaba and leads from the southern gate of the Fatimid enclosure, i.e. Bab Zuwayla, to the Qarafa, or City of the Dead. Dotted with monuments throughout its length, this was the longest street of the medieval city.

Mosque of Salih Tala'i' ** (No. 116) 1160/555. Facing Bab Zuwayla, on the right is the Mosque of Salih Tala'i', named for the Fatimid wazir who built it. The last of the Fatimid mosques in Cairo, its simplicity gives it a charm that restoration has done much to preserve. When it was built, the street level was that of the row of shops behind the iron railing. The shops were part of the endowment or waqf, and their rents helped pay for the upkeep of the mosque and the employment of its personnel. There are seven shops in the front, with twelve each on either side, but none on the qibla wall. This mosque is the first of the 'suspended' or hanging mosques.

The porch or narthex above the shops, in which the entrance is set, is unique in Cairo. The style of the five keel arches, ribbed and cusped and on classical pillars, dates to the mosque of al-Aqmar (Chapter 11). The mashrabiya screens of the porch were added to the mosque when it was restored after being damaged in the terrible earthquake of 1303. The bronze facings on the exterior of the main door are also from 1303, but the carving on the inner side is a copy of the original door, which is in the Islamic Museum.

The interior plan is that of a congregational mosque: a large central courtyard with colonnades on four sides. Vestiges of the original decoration can be seen in the carving of the tie beams and in the Quranic inscriptions that outline the arches. This type of script, common in the Fatimid period, Kufic letters on an arabesque background, is known as floriated Kufic. The sanctuary has three rows of columns held together by tie beams, which are both decorative and functional as they give additional support to the arches. No two captials of the columns are the same: all are reused from pre-Islamic Christian buildings.

The minbar dates to 1300. It was the gift of the Mamluk Amir Baktimur al-Jugandar, or the Polo Master. It is a very fine example of Mamluk wood carving. The decoration is a geometric repeat pattern based on star shapes with polychrome accents. Above the minbar is the opening for the malqaf, a windscoop facing north, through which cool breezes were channeled into the sanctuary. Seven arched windows in the qibla wall illuminate the sanctuary. The carved frames, decorated with Kufic and palmettes, are original. The mosque was badly damaged in the earthquake of 1303. It lost its minaret, which would have been over the porch. If one climbs up one of the minarets on the Bab Zuwayla, one gets a good overall view of the mosque.

Zawiya–Sabil of Farag ibn Barquq (No. 203) 1408/811. This small sufi establishment opposite Salih Tala'i' is noteworthy primarily for the lovely panels of inlaid polychrome stone on the exterior. Bang on the door and the shaykh will let you in. The little room on the left has a very handsome wooden ceiling.

Qasaba of Ridwan Bey ∗∗ (Nos. 408, 409) ca.1650/1060. Just outside and opposite the Bab Zuwayla is this bazaar, which is one of the best preserved examples of a covered market in Cairo. The area is popularly known as the *Khiyamiya* or Tentmakers' Bazaar. Here articles and trappings for caravans were sold, an economic activity that is continued today in the sewn canvas goods and appliqué work carried on in the small stalls bordering the street. The market was built by Ridwan, a Mamluk bey and the leader of a faction known as the Faqariya, who dominated political life in Cairo from 1630 to 1656. For twenty-five years Ridwan Bey held the post of Amir al-Hajj, commander in charge of the annual pilgrimage to Mecca. From Mamluk times until 1962, the *kiswa*, the black velvet drapery used to cover the Ka'ba, the holy sanctuary in Mecca, was woven in Egypt. It was sent with the annual pilgrimage caravan to Arabia, which departed from this area.

Maq'ad Ridwan Bey (No. 208) 1650. About ten meters beyond the covered market and opposite the Mosque of Mahmud al-Kurdi (below), there is a gate on the right that leads into a courtyard, the busy scene of various activities: carpentry, appliqué work, leather tanning. In the southern corner is what remains of the maq'ad, the second story loggia that faced north, where in the evenings the men of the household relaxed with their friends. Some of the elegant marble paneling is still visible on the walls.

The history of the site is actually much older than the remains of this seventeenth-century mansion. In the first half of the fourteenth century this site contained a palace occupied by the Amir Algai. At his death the palace became the property of 'Aisha Khatun, one of al-Nasir Muhammad ibn Qalawun's daughters. When she died in 1377, the palace was acquired by Gamal al-Din Mahmud, who built the mosque in front of it. Nothing more of the site is known until it became the house of

Ridwan Bey in the seventeenth century, as part of his extensive development of this area.

Mosque of Mahmud al-Kurdi * (No. 117) 1395/797. Mahmud was ustadar, or major-domo, under Sultan Barquq, and his building is on the left when leaving the bazaar. The interest of the exterior façade lies in several places: the dome is built of stone and the zig-zag pattern is one of the earliest attempts at a genuine stone decoration that did not reproduce an imitation of the brick and plaster ribbing of earlier fourteenth-century stone domes; the rounded form of the minaret is unusual for this period and anticipates the later Ottoman style. The design of the metal door is a particularly fine decorative accent.

Inside, the plan is surprising: a long room with both liwans raised one step above the central area and with a ceiling higher than those of the liwans. There are no liwans on the side walls, just three wooden covered windows. The resemblance here to the qa'a of a house is very striking. There are several instances in Cairo of houses being converted into mosques, so it is possible that this is in fact what has happened here. (See Mosque of Khushqadam, Chapter 8). Restorations, begun in 1979, are still underway.

Madrasa of Inal al-Yusufi or Atabki * (No. 118) 1392–93/ 794–95. This lovely madrasa further down the street on the left is also from the early Burgi period, and was built also by a functionary in the court of Sultan Barquq. The general arrangement of the façade is very similar to that of al-Kurdi except that the placements of the dome and minaret, the main exterior elements, have been transposed. The dome is of stone, but its decoration of molded ribs continues that of earlier brick and stucco domes. At the southern corner of the façade there is a sabil–kuttab, notable for its wooden screen.

Inside, a turn to the left brings one into the sanctuary, one of the first examples of the attenuated Cairene madrasa plan that became typical of the later Burgi period. The central courtyard has been covered with a lantern ceiling; the width of the qibla and the opposing liwan have been extended, while the side liwans are virtually nonexistent. Although there are four main schools of Islamic law, the great majority of Egyptians adhere to only two: the Shafi'i (in Lower Egypt) and the Maliki (in Upper Egypt). This type of plan combines well both madrasa and mosque functions: it offers a place of instruction and a place for prayer. Much of the interior decoration has disappeared but the stained glass windows are very lovely. In 1377, Inal was appointed Amir Silah (armorer) and his blazon (the sword) appears in the stained glass windows, which may, however, be later restorations.

At this point look back toward Bab Zuwayla. The view down the street is picturesque and still relatively medieval. The corbeled upper stories that project over the narrow winding street are an adaptation to the climate. In summer these streets are cooler than the wide, straight thoroughfares of western Cairo.

Zawiya of 'Abd al-Rahman Katkhuda * (No. 214) 1729/ 1142. On the left, at the intersection with Sharia al-Magharbilin, is the façade of a small building for a mystic order. This is all that remains of the first building erected by this Mamluk bey of the Ottoman period who in the next thirty years was to become the greatest patron of architecture of his time. The small balcony over the entrance was used for the call to prayer. The round windows with wooden lattice are unusual decorative innovations.

Madrasa of the Amir Gani Bak * (No. 119) 1426–27/830. Next on the left is this madrasa–mosque of one of the mamluks of Sultan Barsbay. Although the general arrangement of the façade does not deviate much from the earlier examples up the street, the decoration is more elaborate—even though the polychrome marble inlay over the door in the portal and over the windows today is missing. The Amir Gani Bak was bought and raised by Sultan Barsbay. His career began in 1421 and by 1422 he had been appointed an amir of forty. His high and rapid rise created for him a number of enemies: his death at twenty-five was attributed to poison. His tomb is in the Northern Cemetery (see Chapter 13).

The building was restored in 1896, and again in 1990. The street at this point is a lively artery in which it is pleasant to saunter slowly and observe the variety of activities taking place: selling, buying, producing, consuming. There is plenty of action. Here ways of living have not changed radically over the centuries.

Mosque–Mausoleum of Ganim al-Bahlawan ** (No. 129) 1478–1510/883–916. This building on the left-hand side of the street is immediately identifiable by the arabesque tapestry of its beautifully carved dome. The mosque was finished in 1478 and the mausoleum was added later at a slight angle. The view of the dome, façade, and minaret while approaching the mosque is eyecatching. The increased decoration of the minaret as well as the extra details on the façade such as the carved patterns on the cresting, the stalactites, and the spandrels around the upper windows are characteristic of the extension and elaboration of surface decoration at the end of the Mamluk period.

Inside, the plan is unusual, although not unique for the later Mamluk period, and prefigures a type of mosque plan that becomes common in the succeeding Ottoman period: a sanctuary divided by parallel aisles with the lighting coming from the windows and the lantern in the central aisle or ceiling. Here the central aisle leads toward the mausoleum, which is placed on the street side of the building and given prominence by its very visible dome. Much of the interior decoration in both the mosque and the mausoleum is missing. The kursi and the minbar, although both badly in need of a good cleaning, are good examples of the furnishings of the period. The inlay work can be compared with that of wooden boxes that are on sale in the Khan al-Khalili today, which shows how conservative patterns of inlay have been over the centuries.

Gate to the Mosque of Qawsun (Nos. 224 and 202) 1329–30/730. Directly opposite the Mosque of al-Bahlawan is the Gate to the Mosque of Qawsun. The narrow alley leads to Sharia Muhammad 'Ali, built between 1845 and 1870 to connect the Citadel with 'Ataba Square. Here is the entrance to what is left of the original Mosque of Qawsun: a few stucco grilled windows in an open courtyard, behind the imposing and recent structure of the present mosque. The medieval remains are of only passing interest now, because the mosque was practically destroyed in the building of the boulevard; but in the early fourteenth

A medieval street

century the Amir Qawsun, a favorite of Sultan al-Nasir Muhammad ibn Qalawun, was one of the most important amirs of the realm, and the remains of several of his buildings still dot the city.

Takiya of Sulayman * (No. 225) 1543/950. On the left, just beyond Ganim al-Bahlawan, a trilobed portal marks the entrance to this Ottoman-style khanqah. A vaulted staircase leads up to the courtyard. This open space is framed by a shallow-domed arcade whose arches are supported by antique columns. People today continue to live in the cells originally built for the sufis. There is a small mosque on the southeast wall. The mihrab is on an axis with the entrance.

The plan is that of an Istanbul takiya. It was built by Sulayman Pasha, governor of Egypt from 1524 to 1534, who built the first Ottoman mosque in the Citadel and continued to build in Cairo even after he had relinquished his official duties.

B. Sharia Muhammad 'Ali to Sharia Saliba

Mosque–Mausoleum of the Amir Ilmas * (No. 130) 1329–30/730. Continuing across Sharia Muhammad 'Ali, this is the first medieval building on the left. The mosque was built during the reign of al-Nasir Muhammad ibn Qalawun, a period in which the sultan was not only a great builder, but in which he gave active encouragement to his leading amirs to do likewise. The canopy entrance is covered with 'dripping' stalactites, so called because of the pendant shape of the niches. Worthy of special notice are the windows with their centralizing arabesque wooden screens and the bronze covering of the door in geometric shapes. The minaret collapsed in 1713, and was rebuilt, reusing the same stone. This was an attempt, in Ottoman Cairo, to build a minaret in the Mamluk style, but the decline in craftsmanship is obvious.

The interior plan is of the regular congregational-mosque type, but it is not on an axis with the line of the main façade, which is aligned with the street. The interior is angled so that the correct orientation toward Mecca is established. Courtyards of mosques were often shaded to protect the devout from the sun and here an awning is still in place. The mihrab, with its softened colors of juxtaposed marbles and the graceful scrolls in the spandrels, is a particularly lovely example of an early Mamluk mihrab. The Amir Sayf al-Din Ilmas, first ustadar (major-domo) and then Viceroy of Egypt, was executed in 1333. He is buried in the mausoleum whose dome is visible on the street side of the mosque.

Tomb of the Amir al-Muzaffar 'Alam al-Din Sangar * (No. 261) 1322/722. This little tomb on the left about two blocks down from Ilmas was once attached to a mosque. It is noteworthy now because of its monumental stone dome, one of the first in Cairo. Stone domes probably came from Syria, where they were plain. In Egypt the earliest stone domes tended to be ribbed, in imitation of the earlier brick domes. The corners of the tomb have been accented by turning them into pseudo-pilasters.

Sabil–Waqf of Yusuf Bey (No. 262) 1772/1186. Across the side street is what remains of this little water dispensary. The chain molding on the façade is characteristic of the eighteenth century.

Mausoleum–Madrasa of Amir Sunqur Sa'di * (No. 263) 1315–21/715–21. Known today as the Tomb of Shaykh Hasan Sadaqa (the name used on map 4), this complex stands on the left side of the street. The amir was chief of the royal mamluks of Sultan al-Nasir Muhammad, and this foundation originally consisted of a madrasa, the founder's mausoleum, and a type of convent for women. The exterior façade with its richly carved stucco accents is very handsome. A portion of the paneled crenelation survives over the door. The stucco decoration of the dome is lavish and uncommon. Each stair-step shoulder of the transition zone is framed, and marked with stucco medallions. Windows with stucco grills in geometric patterns provide light for the interior. The minaret is a good example of the early Mamluk type: tall square base, octagonal transition zone, and mabkhara finial consisting of fluted cap with keel-arch profile. Inside, only the northwest liwan of the madrasa survives. Next to the minaret is a bakery that produces the best shami (flat white) bread in Cairo.

Excavations in connection with the Italian-sponsored restorations of the dervish theater to the rear have revealed this later complex to be a mawlawiya, a Mevlevi dervish hostel. The Mevlevi were followers of Jalal al-Din Rumi, the thirteenth-century Turkish mystic. It is known that Mevlevi dervishes (in the West known as whirling dervishes) were in Egypt in 1630 but it is not known exactly when they came. The theater building dates to 1810, but the decorations belong to 1857. The ritual dances involved as many as thirty-eight people: dancers, orchestra, prayer-reciters. The theater was in use until 1942. Another one of Cairo's surprises is the Turkish-style garden, with its birds, trees, and flowers, which one finds within the precinct.

Khanqah al-Bunduqdariya * (No. 146) 1284–85/683. Also known as the Zawiyat al-Abbar. This small tomb lies on the corner of the next intersection on the left. The inscription around the dome is chiefly interesting because it contains the first example in Egypt of a blazon: it is that of the bunduqdari or crossbowman. This one belonged to an officer of al-Salih Nagm al-Din Ayyub. The blazon was a badge of office, which was used only in Mamluk times, i.e., 1283–1517. In the early period it was a simple representation of the symbol of office, but later it became more complex.

Sabil–Kuttab and Rab' al-Qizlar (No. 265) 1618/1027. This is located on the opposite side of the street. The sabil–kuttab is next to the entrance. On the right façade there are three shops; on the left, two shops and a staircase, which leads up to the living units on the upper floors. Although still a place of work and residence, today it is the façade that is least changed.

Palace of the Amir Taz (No. 267) 1352/753 (see map 2). N.B. This monument was largely destroyed by the October 1992 earthquake, but we mention it as an indication of the area's historical and architectural chronology.

The Amir Taz was a mamluk of Sultan al-Nasir Muhammad ibn Qalawun. He built the palace in celebration of his marriage to the sultan's daughter Khwand Zahra, whom he had married the year before when he was grand dawadar or executive secretary of the chancery. The palace was remodeled several times, most notably in the seventeenth century. In the nine-

teenth century during the reforms of the Khedive Isma'il, it
became a girls' school. It has more recently been used as a
storage depot by the Ministry of Education.

Sabil–Kuttab of 'Ali Agha Dar al-Sa'ada (No. 268) 1677/
1088. At the far corner of the ex-palace is this structure of 'Ali,
the chief black eunuch, who supervised not only the imperial
harim but also the waqfs or endowments of the two holy cities
of Mecca and Madina.

Many monuments in Cairo, usually small, were built by the
black eunuchs in charge of the harim. Perhaps this was because
they diverted funds for this purpose from the waqfs of the holy
cities in Arabia that they also supervised. It was most probably
'Ali Agha who acquired the palace of the Amir Taz and remodeled it in 1678. Around the window frame of the sabil there is
a rather elaborate decor and the inserts in the window grills are
in the name of God, الله . Today the kuttab is still in use as an
elementary school.

Sabil of Umm 'Abbas * 1867/1284. This lovely structure was
built by the mother of 'Abbas, who succeeded his grandfather
Muhammad 'Ali and ruled Egypt from 1848 to 1854. His
mother, the wife of Tusun, built a sabil on this corner. The best
view of this ensemble is from the west, i.e., from the direction
of the Citadel. In this view the sabil sits nicely focused beyond
the canyon-like walls of the hyphenated complex of the Amir
Shaykhu. The sabil's façade is animated by its flowing lines and
growing forms: fronds, garlands, leafy sprays, and full-blos-
somed flowers. The water unit is on the corner with subsidiary
units curving away from it. The inscriptions, historic and
poetic, on blue and red backgrounds provide color accents for
the white marble faces.

The walk along the continuation of this street to the Southern
Cemetery is described in Chapter 8; the walk east–west along
Sharia Saliba in Chapter 4.

8 ◇ The Southern Cemetery

A. Sharia Saliba to Maydan Sayyida Nafisa:
Mosque of Khushqadam al-Ahmadi ✱✱
Tomb of Shagar al-Durr ✱
Tombs of Sayyida 'Atika and Muhammad al-Ga'fari ✱
Tomb of Sayyida Ruqayya ✱✱✱
Tomb of Fatima Khatun ✱
Tomb of Sultan al-Ashraf Khalil ✱
Mosque of Sayyida Nafisa ✱✱
Tomb of the Abbasid Khalifs ✱
Cenotaph of Khadiga

B. The Middle Area—South of the Citadel:
al-Sultaniya ✱
Khanqah–Mausoleum of the Amir Qawsun ✱
Tomb of 'Ali Badr al-Din al-Qarafi
Tomb of Sudun ✱
Tomb of al-Sawabi ✱
Tomb of Amir Tankizbugha
Mosque of al-Lu'lu'a
Mausoleum of the Ikhwat Yusuf ✱✱
Mosque of al-Guyushi ✱✱

C. The Lesser Qarafa:
Mosque of Sayyida 'Aisha
Zawiya and Mausoleum of Zayn al-Din Yusuf
Mausoleum of 'Abdallah al-Dakruri
Mausoleum of Imam al-Shafi'i ✱✱✱
Gate and Liwan of Isma'il ibn Tha'lab
Tomb of Umm Kulthum
Mashhad of Yahya al-Shabihi ✱✱
Sabil–Kuttab of Ridwan Bey al-Razzaz
Tomb of al-Hasawati
Hosh al-Basha or Tomb of the Family of Muhammad 'Ali ✱✱
Tombs of 'Ali Bey al-Kabir and Isma'il Bey al-Kabir ✱

See maps 2, 5, 6 and 7

117

The Southern Cemetery, or the Qarafa, is the great cemetery
that stretches east of the Mosque of Ibn Tulun, south of the
Citadel, and beyond almost to the outskirts of Ma'adi. A very
long day is necessary to visit all the monuments. For the sake
of convenience, therefore, the main areas of this great burial
ground have been divided into three parts.

A. Sharia Saliba to Maydan Sayyida Nafisa (see maps 2 and 5)
Just northeast of the Mosque of Ibn Tulun, Sharia Saliba
intersects with Sharia Suyufiya at the Sabil of Umm 'Abbas
(see map 2 and Chapter 7). Sharia Suyufiya is the continuation
of the Qasaba, the main street of the medieval city that begins
at Bab al-Futuh and as Sharia al-Khalifa continues into the
Qarafa, the great necropolis of al-Fustat. This is a poor area of
Cairo, not very prepossessing, but it does offer a different aspect
of Cairene life.

   At its interesection with Sharia Saliba, follow Sharia Suyufiya
or al-Khalifa south for about three hundred meters. You will
pass on the left a small domed tomb of the Mamluk period,
Qubba Safi al-Din Gohar (No. 270) 1315/714.

Sabil–Kuttab and Wikala of Mustafa Bey Tabtabay (No. 272)
1637/1047. A little further on are the remains of this Ottoman
period monument, recognizable by the tile decoration in the
lunettes over the windows. The tiles are nice examples of so-
called Iznik tiles in cobalt and turquoise. They feature the long
serrated leaf with blossoms associated with this sixteenth- to
seventeenth-century Ottoman decoration. All that is left of the
wikala is the ground story, but it must have been a large one
for it extends a fair distance.

Mosque of Khushqadam al-Ahmadi ** (No. 153) 1366 or
1377/768 or 778. A visit to this monument involves a detour, but
it is worth it. After a slight jog, a street running parallel to
Sharia Saliba intersects Sharia al-Khalifa to the left. Take it
and follow it. Along the way are some buildings with late
nineteenth-century mashrabiya windows. The ruined remains
of the *Sabil–Kuttab of Hasan Katkhuda* 1701/1113 will be on
you left. Further on is a minaret with a missing finial, the
landmark for this mosque.

The mosque is interesting because it is the qa'a of a four-teenth-century palace, which in the fifteenth century was converted into a mosque. The palace was built by the Amir Tashtimur, who was dawadar or executive secretary to Sultan Sha'ban and who died in Jerusalem in 1385. To his house belong the entrance vestibule, the first corridor with its ceiling decoration of interlocking rosettes and the penbox blazon of the dawadar, and the qa'a. To the period of the Amir Khushqadam al-Ahmadi belong the minaret and the second corridor with its composite blazon, and the conversion of the qa'a. Khushqadam, a black eunuch, was a high functionary under Sultan Qaytbay. From 1468 until he fell from favor in 1484 he occupied cumulatively the following positions: chief of the corps of cupbearers, wazir, great treasurer, and warden for the princesses. His tripartite blazon perhaps reflect these charges: white napkin on a red field over a blue cup between red 'horns' on white over a white cup on a blue field. In 1489 Sultan Qaytbay confiscated his goods and Khushqadam was exiled and died in Suakin (Sudan).

The qa'a of the palace/mosque is magnificent. The decoration is basically fourteenth-century: the wide inscription band, the large stucco medallions and roundels in the walls, the mashrabiya-covered galleries in the sides. The mihrab, the minbar, and the convex collar of wooden merlons around the arches in the qibla liwan are fifteenth-century. It has been argued that the plan of the madrasa in its earliest two-liwan form originated from the qa'a of a house, where in early Islam professors used to give instruction. In the late Mamluk period there are plenty of examples of mosque–madrasas whose plans have been reduced to a qa'a-like form. This qa'a mosque offers a succinct statement of this development and of the flexibility and durability of Islamic ground plans.

Return to Sharia al-Khalifa, and continue south for another 150 meters. On the left there is a large mosque with fancy green and white striping around the entrance. This is the *Mosque of Sayyida Sukayna*, built by the family of Muhammad 'Ali in the late nineteenth century over an apocryphal tomb of the daughter of al-Husayn.

Tomb of Shagar al-Durr * (No. 169) 1250/648. See map 5. This tomb lies behind an iron fence one hundred meters further along on the left. Shagar al-Durr's story is very romantic. Although not in a class with Zenobia and Cleopatra, she was one of the rare female rulers of the Middle East and as such she is unique in Islamic Egypt. She was the Armenian slave–concubine of al-Salih Nagm al-Din, the last ruler of the Ayyubid Dynasty, who died in 1249 in a campaign against Louis IX of France in the Delta.

Shagar al-Durr ('Tree of Pearls') concealed al-Salih's death for three months to permit his son and successor, Turan Shah, to return from Mesopotamia and inherit the throne. Al-Salih's mamluks, who had just defeated the Crusaders under St. Louis at the Battle of Mansura in the Nile Delta, refused to accept Turan Shah and murdered him, with Shagar al-Durr's help. She then proclaimed herself Sultana and ruled in the name of an Ayyubid child-prince for eighty days before marrying and sharing power with Aybak, the leader of the mamluks. In 1257, when she heard that he was considering another marriage, she had Aybak murdered. The slave women of Aybak's first wife avenged him by beating Shagar al-Durr to death with wooden bath clogs. Her body was then cast from a tower of the Citadel and left for the jackals and dogs. After a suitable period, her remains were retrieved and buried in the tomb she had constructed for herself.

Her tomb is the last Ayyubid building in Cairo and among the first built within the owner's lifetime. It is small and simple, of plastered brick with carved stucco decoration in the style of earlier Fatimid tombs in the Qarafa. To protect the tomb from neighborhood encroachment it is kept locked by the Department of Antiquities and special arrangements must be made to see it. Once inside, note the prayer niche, which is decorated with glass mosaics in the Byzantine style, an example of the architectural influences from Syria, which were especially strong during the thirteenth century. The mosaic decoration is in the form of a branching tree of life with roundels of mother-of-pearl, a poignant allusion to the owner's name. The carved wooden panels that support the mihrab belong to the Fatimid period. It seems probable that they were reused when discovered in the construction of her husband al-Salih Ayyub's tomb on the Bayn al-Qasrayn (see Chapter 11), which she commissioned. The tomb, repaired by the Comité, is once more in urgent need of care.

Tombs of Sayyida 'Atika and Muhammad al-Ga'fari * (No. 333) c.1122/516. Across the street from Shagar al-Durr's tomb, and on the western edge of the great Southern Cemetery, a green and white striped doorway leads into a compound that contains several tombs in which members of the Prophet's family are buried. These tombs are of great architectural interest. They are among the largest single category of surviving monuments from the Fatimid period, and also the largest related group of surviving funerary monuments from the first six centuries of Islamic history. They are also of continuing interest because they are still places of visitation and prayer.

The tombs on the right are the oldest: the one with the plain dome belongs to a great-great-great-grandson of the Prophet, i.e. the son of Ga'far al-Sadiq, the sixth Shi'i Imam; the one with the ribbed dome belongs to 'Atika, an 'aunt' of the Prophet. Today much of the original decoration of these tombs has disappeared, but still of interest is the form of the squinch that supports the dome. The one-niche-over-three is the first step in the evolution of the elaborate dome-support systems of the Mamluk period.

Tomb of Sayyida Ruqayya *** (No. 273) 1133/527. This is the tomb on the left of the compound. Sayyida Ruqayya was the daughter of 'Ali, the fourth khalif, who was the husband of the Prophet's daughter Fatima. She was not the daughter of Fatima, however, but was born of another of 'Ali's wives. Although Ruqayya died and is buried in Damascus, her shrine in Cairo is still used as a mashhad or oratory, a place where people make vows and pray for the saint's intercession. Sayyida Ruqayya and two other holy women, Sayyida Nafisa and Sayyida Zaynab, were traditionally considered the patron saints of the city. This tradition has not yet wholly died away, and miraculous cures are still attributed to them.

The shrine is well preserved. The green baize-covered cenotaphs in the entrance porch belong to 'Uthman, an agha of the janissaries and a follower of Sulayman Agha al-Silahdar, d. 1824/1239, and his wife Hafiza, d. 1826/1241. They restored Ruqayya's shrine. In 1916 it was restored by the Comité.

Inside the sanctuary, with just enough room to walk around it, is the saint's tomb. The wooden screen that protects it reputedly came from the shrine of Sayyida Nafisa. For a small consideration the custodian will lift the layers of skirting that cover the original twelfth-century cenotaph. The carving of the wood is very fine. A wooden mihrab from the shrine, now in the Islamic Museum, is considered one of the finest late Fatimid examples extant.

The mihrab that dominates the sanctuary is a magnificent example of a late Fatimid mihrab, and is one of the few that remain from this period,. A fluted conch with a triple-scalloped edge is framed by a keel arch—the form inspired by the main arch over the entrance at the Mosque of al-Aqmar, and imitated in the Ayyubid period. The design of the central medallion is a series of linked 'Muhammads' around a central "Ali.'

The support system for the central dome consists of a further elaboration of the stalactite squinch system. Here in addition to the one-over-three niche in the corner there are blind niches that fill up the central area.

Tomb of Fatima Khatun (Umm al-Salih) * (No. 274) 1283–84/682–83. One hundred and twenty-five meters to the south of the Fatimid tombs, on the left (east) side of the street is the Mausoleum of Fatima Khatun. The building was built for a wife of Sultan Qalawun, the mother of his eldest son and first heir, Malik al-Salih 'Ala al-Din 'Ali. This building, and probably the Mausoleum of al-Ashraf Khalil next door, was built by the Amir 'Alam al-Din Sangar, who was the superintendent in charge of construction for Sultan Qalawun's funerary complex in Bayn al-Qasrayn (see Chapter 11).

The original entrance to this enclosure, which once contained a madrasa and garden, was through a tunnel-vaulted gateway next to the minaret. The square shaft of the lower story of the minaret and the fact that it is built of stone shows strong influence from Syria. The mausoleum was originally preceded by a porch, as in the nearby mausolea of Sayyida Ruqayya and Shagar al-Durr. The window has a fine floriated Kufic stucco inscription around it; its form of one round light over two panels is new at this time, probably imitating the Gothic windows of Syria.

The interior of the building is quite plain. Of interest is the support system of the dome, which foreshadows the descending or pendentive stalactite dome supports that also become current in the Mamluk period.

Tomb of Sultan al-Ashraf Khalil * (No. 275) 1288/687. Thirty meters south, on the same side of the street, is this mausoleum built for Sultan Qalawun's son, who reigned from 1290 until 1293, when he was assassinated on a hunting trip in the Delta. Sultan al-Ashraf is primarily remembered for his decisive victory over the Crusaders at Acre in 1291, which drove them from the Syrian mainland. Victorian historians judged him harshly: "His only virtue was courage and his only exploit Acre." Recent assessments, however, view the sultan as an able and creative ruler.

The mausoleum cube is of stone—recent restoration accounts for the differences in the color of the blocks—but the dome and its base are of brick. The interior of the building is in very poor shape: all of the marble with which it was originally faced to a height of three meters has disappeared. In the zone of transition between the round dome and the square base one can see what the one-over-three Fatimid niche system was heralding: here the whole intermediate zone consists of several rows of blind niches, which give to this area a real decorative interest. The windows originally contained stained glass, some fragments of which remain.

These two Mamluk buildings clearly point out the change in scale and decoration from the Fatimid to Mamluk periods, from the small to the monumental, from one in which the ornamentation was concentrated on the mihrab to the increasing complexity and variety of surface embellishment.

Mosque of Sayyida Nafisa. ** Continuing south 150 meters and arriving at the maydan, on your left you will see the Mosque of Sayyida Nafisa.

Sayyida Nafisa is an authentic saint of the city. She was a great-granddaughter of al-Hasan, one of the Prophet's two grandsons. She emigrated from the Hijaz to Egypt and settled in al-Fustat. She had a great reputation for baraka ('blessing from God') and for performing miracles. Among the people who visited her was Imam al-Shafi'i, a great authority on Sunni law whose tomb is further south. After her death in 824 many people were buried near her grave to benefit from her baraka. Over the succeeding centuries her shrine, whose prominence' dates to the Fatimid period, has been embellished and rebuilt many times. The present mosque dates to 1897, ordered by 'Abbas II when the mosque rebuilt by 'Abd al-Rahman Katkhuda in the eighteenth century was damaged by fire.

More recently, in the late 1980s, a whole new extension wing was attached to the mosque to serve as a center for Quranic and religious instruction. Next door to the tomb shrine is an office-cum-reception room in which the contracts for Islamic marriages are signed.

Although nothing remains from the medieval period, the tomb is still well worth a visit. It offers a moving glimpse of a shrine mosque in daily use, and of the part that saints or 'intercessors' still play in the daily lives of the people.

Tomb of the Abbasid Khalifs * (No. 276) 1242/640. To the rear of and adjoining the Mosque of Sayyida Nafisa (via a passageway skirting the mosque on its northwest side) is the cemetery of the Abbasid khalifs, dating from the thirteenth century. The Abbasid khalifs were reestablished in Egypt by the Mamluk sultan Baybars al-Bunduqdari in 1261, following the fall of Baghdad to the Mongols under Hulagu in 1258. A succession of these khalifs was kept by the Mamluks as a symbol of legitimacy, although it was a pale and dwindling one. They were without power or substance, but they lasted until the sultans of Turkey assumed the khalifate in 1538.

The tomb was built in 1242 by Abu Nadla, the ambassador to Egypt of the Abbasid khalif of Baghdad before his fall. Sultan Baybars took it over for the burial of his two sons, probably building at that time the great hosh or courtyard with a vaulted entrance hall. Baybars himself is buried in Damascus, where he died in 1277. The exterior of the shrine, with its ribbed and cusped keel arches and its champfered corners, harks back to the decoration introduced in the Fatimid period and continued in the Ayyubid period.

Inside there are eight cenotaphs, which belong to Abu Nadla, Baybars' sons, and children of the Abbasid khalifs. Masonry epitaphs of seventeen members of the Abbasid family in Egypt are on the wall. The mihrab is similar in style to those

Tomb of the Abbasid Khalifs and Mosque of Sayyida Nafisa

of the late Fatimid period, but the stucco carving is much finer, almost lace-like.

Inscription around the Cenotaph of Khadiga. d. 959. Under a wooden shed in front of the Tomb of the Abbasid Khalifs is a white marble cenotaph of the tenth century. The inscription is in three lines and is a handsome example of foliate Kufic. Until the twelfth century, Kufic script was used exclusively for monumental purposes in Egypt. Here the incorporation of lovely leaf forms and lotus-like designs is the first step toward the elaborate arabesque background emanations with which the Kufic script was ornamented in the Fatimid period. The inscription is in three lines and begins with a section of the Throne verse (2:255).

> (1) God, there is no god but He, the Living, the Everlasting. Slumber seizes Him not, neither sleep; to Him belongs all that is in the heavens and the earth. (2) This is the tomb of Khadiga, daughter of Muhammad, son of Ahmad, son of Bark the Tara'ifi, deceased the 19th (3) of the month of Shawwal in the year 347 [3 January 959], may God have pity on her."

B. The Middle Area: South of the Citadel (see map 6)

Sharia Salah Salim has arbitrarily cut through the Qarafa, separating its parts. Monuments there, mostly from the fourteenth-century Bahri Mamluk period, can be visited before going on to the cluster of tombs in the lesser Qarafa. Take Sharia Salah Salim north after joining it five hundred meters south of the Maydan of Sayyida Nafisa. An overpass will carry you over a large traffic intersection. On the right, more or less parallel with the descending ramp, is the *Mosque of Nur al-Din* (No. 160) 1575, with its recognizably Ottoman minaret. A little beyond this mosque a dirt road to the right leads into the cemetery area.

Al-Sultaniya * (No. 289) c.1350/751. Follow the road into the necropolis toward a nicely restored building with two ribbed stone domes and a gracefully arched liwan between. Around this interesting double tomb structure, which may originally have included a khanqah, all the inscriptions are Quranic. The only literary reference to this complex is in the waqfiya or endowment deed of the Mosque of Nur al-Din, which alludes to its geographical position in relation to the 'Sultaniya' and mentions that it belonged to the mother of Sultan Hasan (ruled 1347–61). While this attribution may be questionable, stylistically a dating to the mid-fourteenth century is reasonable, since a similar kind of bulbous dome on a high drum is found in the Madrasa of the Amir Sarghatmish.

The plan of the Sultaniya, a rectangular complex, was inspired by that of the adjacent khanqah of Qawsun and has antecedents in Anatolian monuments, where the tradition of a central liwan flanked by two identical domed structures is found. Here the central liwan has a cloister vault, which is unusual in Cairo. The minaret, on a line with the northern dome, is free-standing now; however at one time it was linked by a wall to the domed area.

The period between 1346 and 1400 is a period of great inventiveness in ribbed stone domes. These domes are double, which was probably an imitation of a feature common to brick domes of Persia. The outer dome allowed for a high visible exterior profile, while the inner dome provided an interior covering proportionate with the chamber. The ribbing on the domes is not new. It goes back as far as the Fatimid period mausolea more than two hundred years earlier, but the stalacite corbeling at the base of the dome, which gives it a lightly bulbous aspect, is new and is probably inspired by the stalactite substructure of the ribbed mabkhara of the Fatimid–Ayyubid minaret finial. Ribs ending in stalactite corbels, a Cairene development, were probably carried by Tamerlane from Mamluk Damascus to Central Asia in the fifteenth century.

Khanqah–Mausoleum of the Amir Qawsun * (No. 291) 1335/735. The Amir Qawsun was one of the wealthiest and most powerful amirs of Sultan al-Nasir Muhammad. He married a daughter of the sultan, who in turn married one of Qawsun's sisters. After al-Nasir's death Qawsun, as atabak or viceroy for Egypt, was the real power behind the rule of several of the minor sons until he was arrested and murdered in Alexandria in 1341. Qawsun's body was brought back to Cairo for burial.

His tomb complex was the first major complex built by Bahri Mamluks in this area of the necropolis. The minaret, fifty meters to the northwest, is dated to 1336. It is a good example of the early Mamluk style of minarets: keel-arched ribbed finials and rows of stalactite niches. The saw-tooth or spiky collar formed by projecting niches is distinctive.

What is left of the stucco decoration on the outer wall above the entrance is very fine. The raised relief of the roundel and the tightly packed quality of the decoration suggests the presence of Persian craftsmen.

Tomb of 'Ali Badr al-Din al-Qarafi (No. 292) 1300/700. To the west and a little south of the tomb of Qawsun is this rather plain tomb. The ribbed dome is plaster over brick, typical of the early Bahri period. This is the earliest monument in this area.

Southern minaret (No. 293) 14th/8th century. What is now a free-standing minaret originally belonged to a complex.

Tomb of Sudun * (No. 294) c. 1505/910. Continue southeast along the street that fronts al-Qarafi's tomb. Seventy-five meters on the right is the tomb of Sudun, the Amir Majlis, a commander of one thousand men and guard of the council chamber in the reign of Sultan al-Ghuri. He was a courageous soldier renowned for his equestrian skills. He met his death in 1516, at Marj Dabiq in Syria, leading the cavalry charge against the Ottoman sultan prior to his invasion of Egypt.

The building is a typical example of late Mamluk work: built of stone; a chevron-patterned dome; fenestration with a pattern of one round light over two arched panels; a concave–convex moulding of the upper corners. In the inscription the amir is not named but his blazon indicates his office. It is typical of the more complicated blazons of the late Mamluk period, and represents in the upper field a napkin, in the middle a cup between two 'horns of nobility,' and in the lower field a cup.

Tomb of al-Sawabi * (No. 296) 1286/684. Adjoining is the tomb of a retainer of Sultan al-Nasir Muhammad ibn Qalawun. This is a nice example of an early brick Bahri Mamluk building.

Tombs of Sudun and al-Sawabi

The ribbed dome has an attractive inscription band. The tombs of al-Sawabi and of Sudun, at the beginning and end of the Mamluk period, present in a visual summary the evolution of style and form over two hundred years.

Tomb of Amir Tankizbugha (No. 298) 1359/760. About 175 meters further down the street is a tomb built by Tankizbugha ('Sea Bull'), an amir of one hundred and Amir Majlis, as well as a brother-in-law of Sultan Hasan. Not much more is known of him. The amir is not buried here but in another tomb at the southern end of the Northern Cemetery (Chapter 13).

The amir was reported to be of Greek origin, which may account for some of the unusual features of this tomb, or they may simply illustrate the experimentation with forms of the Bahri period. The alternation of concave and convex fluting of the dome is unusual, as is the twelve-sided drum upon which it rests, and the windows that do not have the round opening above the arched panels. But most unusual is the sharp-toothed collar around the base of the dome, perhaps an idea taken from the stalactite balconies of minarets. The interior of the tomb is plain except for the faience roundel in the center of the dome and the shell forms over the squinches in the corners.

Mausoleum to the north of Tankizbugha. (No. 299) 1320–50/ 721–51. This monument is undated and unidentified, but from stylistic analysis—the stalactite canopy over the door, the convex fluting of the dome, the interlaced arcading around the mihrab hood—it probably belongs to the second quarter of the fourteenth century.

Mosque of al-Lu'lu'a (No. 515) 1016/406. This monument is one of several that lie closer to the Muqattam range. Return to Salah Salim and proceed north. Take the first road leading off to the right and toward the square apartment complexes that lie at the base of the range. The mosque is about one kilometer southeast of Salah Salim.

The monument was built during the reign of the Fatimid khalif al-Hakim, who was addicted to nocturnal wanderings and in fact met his end mysteriously upon the Muqattam range, for only his dagger-rent cloak was found by searching attendants. The limestone base upon which the mosque seems so precariously perched was once attached to the adjacent range. The name means 'pearl' and may have referred to its lustrous beauty. The structure has three arched openings on two floors with a mihrab on each.

Visible from this point, to the south and north, are two other interesting monuments.

Khanqah and tomb of Shahin al-Khalawati (No. 212) 1538/945. To the south, upon the limestone slopes, with minaret and arcades dramatically silhouetted against the sky, stand the remains of a monument built by three members of the Khalawati order of mystics from Iran. It is, however, inaccessible.

Mausoleum of the Ikhwat Yusuf ** (No. 301) 1125–50/519–45. One hundred meters to the north is a rather large domed tomb that was built during the later part of the Fatimid period. It is ascribed to the 'brothers Joseph,' but who they were or whether indeed there was a real burial here is a matter of debate. The original tomb chamber under the dome is definitely worth visiting for the splendid carved plaster mihrab that occupies the whole of the qibla wall. The central niche is joined to two side niches to form a triple mihrab. The carving is very fine in both the floriated Kufic inscription of the Quranic verses and in the punched, stamped leaf forms that fill the spandrels of the arches.

Mosque of al-Guyushi ** (No. 304) 1085/478. Another 150 meters to the north, high up on the plateau of the Muqattam, is the sanctuary of Badr al-Gamali or the Amir al-Guyushi, the powerful Fatimid wazir who ruled Egypt from 1074 to 1094 and who rebuilt al-Qahira's defenses. To reach it one must take the road that turns right off Salah Salim to Muqattam City, opposite the eastern entrance to the Citadel.

The true purpose of this monument continues to puzzle and intrigue. The inscription over the entrance calls it a mashhad, a shrine, but nobody is known to be buried there, while its setting is quite isolated from the main pilgrimage centers of the Southern Qarafa.

One theory is that it was a watch tower disguised as a mosque; another that it was built as a memorial to the victories of Badr al-Gamali over the insurgent tribes in Upper Egypt; while a third theory suggests that it was a shrine associated with the saintly antecedents of the Shi'i rulers.

The minaret over the main entrance is the oldest surviving minaret in Cairo. The inspiration is Syrian: tall base, square second story, octagonal third story surmounted by a dome. The cornice of niches in a double row around the first story marks the first appearance of stalactite decoration. It is a feature that will appear often in Cairene buildings.

The glory of the building is its beautiful mihrab of carved stucco. The niche, painted with later Ottoman flowers, is framed by a rectangular panel in which bands of Quranic inscriptions alternate with arabesque leaf patterns. The deep and assured carving is outstanding.

C. The Lesser Qarafa (see maps 6 and 7)

To reach this area start at Salah Salim and the street that runs beneath the overpass oposite the southeast corner of the Citadel. This street, known as Sharia Imam al-Shafi'i, leads south along old trolley tracks to the tomb of the great Imam and the tombs that surround it in a great mixture of styles ranging from Fatimid period to Muhammad 'Ali.

Around the intersection are the following monuments:

Mosque of Sayyida 'Aisha (No. 378) 1762/1175 (see map 6). This lovely mosque stands to the left on the north side of the overpass. 'Aisha, a descendant of Sayyidna al-Husayn, came to Egypt in 762, and died here. Over the centuries various patrons embellished her tomb. The mosque built by 'Abd al-Rahman Katkhuda in the eighteenth century was completely rebuilt by the Comité in the early twentieth century.

Bab al-Qarafa (No. 279) 1494/900. Built by Sultan Qaytbay, at the beginning of Sharia Imam al-Shafi'i. Nearby is the *Tomb of Timurbay al-Husayni* (No. 161) 16th/10th century.

Zawiya and Mausoleum of Zayn al-Din Yusuf (No. 172) 1298/697. This complex is visible from the street on the right

Mihrab of the Mosque of al-Guyushi

just before the street jogs. It is a rare example of a unit endowed by a patron who was not a member of the ruling class. He was the chief qadi, or judge, under Sultan Qalawun. The isolated portal in the courtyard is all that remains of the zawiya built in 1325, forty years later than the mausoleum. Its inscription traces Zayn al-Din Yusuf's genealogy back to the Umayyad khalifs and the Quraysh tribe to which the Prophet Muhammad belonged.

The entrance is noteworthy for being the earliest surviving one to use stalactites. The madrasa has four tunnel-vaulted liwans arranged in a cruciform plan around an oblong court, and is chiefly notable for the band of carved stucco Quranic inscription that completely encircles the interior. The inscription is in cartouches separated by medallions and is very handsome. The tomb is in the south corner, to the right of the mihrab. The dome is unusually high and rests on a triple-tiered stalactite-squinch system that alternates with a triple tier of windows with stained glass insets.

Mausoleum of 'Abdallah al-Dakruri (No. 280) 1466/871 (see map 7). After the street jogs to the right it continues south. Six hundred meters farther down, on the right, is this little tomb chamber noticeable for its ribbed and fluted stone dome. This is the tomb of a pastrycook from Bab al-Luq who in his old age lived in the cemetery and performed pious works. When he died 1466/871 his mausoleum became a place of pilgrimage.

Mausoleum of Imam al-Shafi'i *** (No. 281) 1211/608 (see map 7). Continuing south, you will arrive after six hundred meters at a small square from which there is no apparent egress except by the street you have been following. The entrance to the mausoleum is on your right, beyond the façade of the mosque erected in 1891 by the Khedive Tawfiq upon the eighteenth-century mosque built by 'Abd al-Rahman Katkhuda, which in turn was built on the ruins of the original twelfth-century madrasa.

The Imam al-Shafi'i was the founder of one of the four rites or legal schools, of Sunni Islam. He was a descendant of the Prophet's uncle, Abu Talib, and came to Egypt in the ninth century. He died in 820. The present complex is a mixture of

Mausoleum of Imam al-Shafi'i

epochs, but the mausoleum itself was built in 1211 by Salah al-Din's nephew al-Malik al-Kamil. It is the largest free-standing mausoleum in Egypt.

The large dome, which is visible from afar, is built—like that of the Dome of the Rock in Jerusalem—of two wooden shells covered with lead. The present dome dates from 1772, and we do not know how closely it corresponds to the shape of the original. On its peak, like a weathervane, is a famous metal boat that is supposed to hold grain for birds, although little grain seems to go into it these days. The decoration of the exterior has carry-overs from the Fatimid period—step crenelation, interlacing strapwork frieze on the cornice, blind arches with ribbed hoods, separating rosettes and lozenges.

The interior of the tomb is colorful and airy. It is a popular shrine and has a quality of contemporary vitality that is missing from monuments that are no longer in daily use. The interior is a mixture of periods. Behind the sandalwood lattice-work screen dating from 1911, a gift of the Khedive 'Abbas, lies the Imam's cenotaph, made of teak imported from India. It was carved by Ubayd ibn Ma'ali in 1178–79 and is a superb piece of Islamic woodwork. It was ordered to be placed over the grave by Salah al-Din. Muslims when buried are placed on their sides, facing toward Mecca. In the Ayyubid period the marble column marked the position of the Imam's head; the green baize bulb representing the turban was added much later (1892). The cenotaph immediately adjacent to the saint's belongs to Sayyid Muhammad 'Abd al-Hakam, in whose burial ground the Imam was originally interred. The other cenotaphs mark the burial places of Sultan al-Kamil Ayyub and his mother. The original entrance to the tomb is on the north wall. It is recognizable by the coffered ceiling above the bay leading to the carved door.

The mausoleum was restored by Sultan Qaytbay in the fifteenth century, and to this period are due the marble panels along the walls and a new dome with its squinch systems of stalactite niches. In the eighteenth century, first under 'Abd al-Rahman Katkhuda, and then under 'Ali Bey al-Kabir, further restorations took place that are apparent in the polychrome inlay at the tomb entrance and in the painted decorations of the stalactite squinches and dome.

Although this mausoleum is of considerable architectural interest and is the largest Islamic mortuary chamber in Egypt, its historical and religious significance is perhaps even more interesting. It was here that Salah al-Din founded the first madrasa in Egypt as part of his effort to combat the Fatimid Shi'a. This was a center of a successful missionary effort based on the Shafi'i rite, which is still predominant in south Arabia, Bahrayn, the Malay Archipelago, and East Africa, as well as other places. The Imam himself is revered as one of the great Muslim saints, although no such institution was provided for by the Quran. One of the holiest shrines in Cairo, since medieval times it has been regarded as a source of healing emanations, of baraka. Visitors flock here from all over the Muslim world to recite prayers while circumambulating the cenotaph of the great legal doctor; the sick and infirm congregate here either to be cured or to die at the holy site. Every year a mulid, or religious fair, is held here on the Imam's anniversay. One of many such mulids held at various tombs of saints in Cairo, this is one of the more famous. The tomb is a quiet place in which to observe popular Islam. The Imam's baraka, or blessing, continues to be sought by a steady stream of supplicants.

The small mihrab in the left corner was added in the eighteenth century when it was discovered that the main triple-arched mihrab did not give the true orientation to Mecca.

Gate and Liwan of Isma'il ibn Tha'lab (No. 282) 1216/613. Upon leaving the entrance of the tomb of Imam Shafi'i, turn right and continue south, following the 'main' road. On Fridays this road becomes a lively small livestock market and is lined on either side with people selling rabbits, chickens, ducks, geese, and goats. The street is also lined with burial court-yards. Some of the grave stelae go back to the ninth century. One hundred and thirty meters on the right there is a gate. Over the years the ground level has risen about three meters which accounts for the disparity between street and entrance levels. The gate of stone is very handsomely carved. Of special note are the joggled voussoirs, or the interlocking panels which form the flat arch, and the inscription in Naskhi script, which is used in architecture in Egypt for the first time in the Ayyubid period. This is a cursive, more informal, more flowing type of script than the Kufic and it looks well on the arabesque background.

Over the top of the gate one can see the remains of the liwan, the oldest in Egypt, which was built for a madrasa for the Shafi'i rite to which the mausoleum was attached. The mihrab, keel-arched with a quadruple cusped edge, follows Fatimid models. Isma'il, son of the grand Amir Hisn al-Din Tha'lab, was an amir of the pilgrimage. The Prophet appeared to him in a vision, whereupon the amir abandoned his wordly goods for his sake.

Tomb of Umm Kulthum (No. 516) 1122/516. Continue another 120 meters south and turn right. A small building ten meters along on the left contains the tomb of Umm Kulthum. She was a ninth-generation descendant of the Prophet through his grandson al-Husayn. She came to al-Fustat from Madina with her father and her brothers in the early ninth century. There is literary evidence that her tomb was restored in 1122, along with seven others in the Qarafa, by the Wazir Ma'mun al-Bata'ihi, the same man who built the Mosque of al-Aqmar. All that is left of this restoration now is the lovely mihrab. It is interesting both for its fluted shell hood and for the rows of eight-pointed stars in the niche that contain the name 'Muhammad' or the words 'and Ali.'

Mashhad of Yahya al-Shabihi ∗∗ (No. 285) 1150/545. This tomb with its dome of convex ribs is about thirty meters from the tomb of Umm Kulthum, whose custodian also has the key for it. The interior plan is of a central domed chamber with an ambulatory on three sides. In the main room under the dome there are several cenotaphs, the most interesting of which are the two nearest the mihrab on the right. They belong to 'Abdallah and Yahya, brothers of Umm Kulthum, who died in 875 and 877. This is recorded in the panels of plain Kufic at the ends of their cenotaphs. The floriate Kufic script on the wood frame around the cenotaph belongs to the later rebuilding of the tomb in the twelfth century by the Fatimids. The northeast wall of the tomb opens into a rectangular space, an annex that has been added much later, since it contains the tomb of Isma'il 'Asim Pasha, a high official of Muhammad 'Ali.

Outside and behind the tomb of Yahya al-Shabihi ('the Resembler'—so called because of his physical resemblance to the Prophet) are the remains of the tomb of Qasim al-Tayyib, the father of Yahya and Umm Kulthum.

Sabil–Kuttab of Ridwan Bey al-Razzaz (No. 387) 1754/ 1168. Return to the tomb of Imam al-Shafi'i and on leaving it turn right (south) and right again (west). The alley opens up for a good view of the exterior of the Imam's tomb after a few meters. In front, and slighly to the right as one looks at it, is what is left of Ridwan's sabil–kuttab. The loggia of the kuttab, with parts of its wood roofing in geometric patterns, is easily recognizable. To look at the sabil enter through the wall into the courtyard beyond. Traces of tile as well as closely worked geometric patterns and rosettes mark the sabil façade. The family who live there are very friendly.

Tomb of al-Hasawati (No. 315) c.1150/545. This is a small tomb, recently restored by the Egyptian Antiquities Depart-ment, which lies further along the same alley, on the south side of the tomb of Imam al-Shafi'i. Nothing is known of al-Hasawati, but he is presumed to have been a descendant of the Prophet through 'Ali and hence a Shi'i saint, for the words 'and 'Ali' appear on the colonette on the left side of the mihrab. The mihrab of carved stucco that completely dominates the shrine's interior is quite handsome and is like that of Sayyida Ruqayya. The tomb was originally a 'canopy tomb,' i.e. an open-domed pavilion. Today its 'sunken' appearance is due to the fact that the ground level has risen dramatically over the centuries.

Hosh al-Basha or Tomb of the Family of Muhammad 'Ali ** c.1820/1236. From al-Hasawati a five-domed complex will be visible to the right, directly behind the tomb of Imam al-Shafi'i. Continue along the same alley and turn right at the corner. Twenty meters further along, on the right, is the entrance, a portal with a shallow dome flanked by two posts. The courtyard, now barren and dusty, was once a lushly planted garden. Inside lie the sons of Muhammad 'Ali by his first and favorite wife—Tusun, Isma'il, Ibrahim—surrounded by their wives and children, as well as by devoted servants, distin-

Cenotaphs in the Hosh al-Basha

guished statesmen, and counselors. The first memorial, straight ahead from the entrance, in a room by itself, is the towering white marble tomb of the mother of the Khedive Tawfiq (ruled 1879–92). Turning left on entering, the tomb surrounded by an immense bronze grill belongs to Tusun. Under the central dome and radiating into chambers from it are another thirty or forty multilayered cenotaphs.

They are exuberantly carved with flowers, garlands, and fronds and are gilded and painted in bright colors. A stela at the head topped by a distinctive coiffure or head-covering indicates the rank and sex of the deceased. These turbans, fezzes, tresses, and coronets give to the tombs a funereal reality that is quite poignant. One visitor in the nineteenth century likened the experience of visiting this tomb to one of walking through a "petrified crowd." The custodian will point out the white marble tomb of King Faruq (1920–65), the last of the line. In an outer room, several to a cenotaph, lie the mamluks or retainers of Muhammad 'Ali, who is buried in his mosque at the Citadel.

Tombs of 'Ali Bey al-Kabir and Isma'il Bey al-Kabir * (No. 385) 1773/1187. On leaving the Hosh al-Basha turn right, and right again at the next corner. Halfway up the block is a three-story building on the right. The tombs are located in its courtyard, three cenotaphs under two adjoining open canopy tombs. The carved stone sheathing of the tombs lies about and the place has an air of 'suspended restoration,' but it is worth a stop. This is the final resting place of a man and his general who played a dominant role in eighteenth-century Egypt. The third tomb is not inscribed. Al-Jabarti, the main historian of the period, says it belongs to Murad Bey, one of the ruling duumvirs who lost Egypt to Napoleon Bonaparte.

'Ali Bey was one of 'Abd al-Rahman Katkhuda's mamluks, an extraordinarily ambitious and ruthless man. In 1760 'Abd al-Rahman made the mistake of backing 'Ali as Shaykh al-Balad (chief of the mamluks). Once securely in power, 'Ali Bey banished 'Abd al-Rahman on trumped-up charges to the Holy Cities of Arabia and began to isolate and destroy all possible rivals. He was assisted in this by his own mamluks. One of these, whom he raised to the office of bey or prince, was Muhammad Bey Abu Dhahab (see Chapter 10). Another was

Isma'il Bey, who lies beside him (d. 1786 or 1791). 'Ali Bey aimed at the restoration of the Mamluk Empire and soon began to intervene in the affairs of Arabia and Syria, former provinces of the Mamluks. The Ottoman government was engaged in a desperate struggle with Russia, and a Russian fleet was operating in the Mediterranean. To avoid 'Ali Bey's allying himself with Russia, the Ottoman sultan was forced to acquiesce while 'Ali Bey drove out his viceroys, claiming they were unworthy of the sultan's trust, and ruled Egypt as acting viceroy "until a suitable man should be sent." 'Ali sent Abu Dhahab to conquer Damascus in 1771 and began negotiating an alliance with the Russians. Just as it seemed that 'Ali Bey was indeed becoming "the mighty one of Egypt" ('Aziz Misr), a title he had used in the inscription recording his restorations to the tomb of Imam al-Shafi'i, Abu Dhahab—fearful of the Ottoman reaction and ambitious himself—withdrew from Syria, turned on 'Ali, and assumed power in Egypt. During 1772 'Ali raised another army in Palestine and in 1773 returned to Egypt to confront Abu Dhahab at Salihiya in the Delta. Mortally wounded in battle, he died on the field in May 1773.

9 ◇ Sharia Port Said—
On and Off

Mosque of al-Qadi Yahya *
Mosque of Assanbugha *
Mosque of 'Abd al-Ghani al-Fakhri *
Mosque of Yusuf Agha al-Hin **
Mosque of Malika Safiya **
Mosque of al-Burdayni *
Ribat of al-Qadi Yahya *
Madrasa of Sultan Mahmud *
Mosque of Sitt Hadaq *
Minaret–Portal of Amir Bashtak and Mosque of Mustafa
Fadil Pasha
Mosque of Dhu al-Fiqar Bey
Mosque of Timraz al-Ahmadi
Mosque of Sayyida Zaynab *
Sabil–Kuttab of Sultan Mustafa III *
House of Ibrahim Katkhuda al-Sinnari *
Museum of Islamic Art ***

See map 8

Sharia Port Said or Sharia Khalig al-Misri, as its old name attests, was the site of the canal that was dug during Pharaoh Necho's rule to link the Nile with the Red Sea. Forming the western boundary of the city of al-Qahira, in 1898 it was filled in. When the Belgian industrialist Baron Empain, who built the satellite city of Heliopolis, was granted a concession to establish a tramway system for Cairo, one of the first lines laid down was the north–south route along the old khalig from the Husayniya quarter beyond the north walls to Sayyida Zaynab.

There are many monuments located along and just off this street, and some of them seem to fall into clusters. Sharia Port Said can be reached from al-'Ataba Square, from Salah Salim via Sultan Hasan and Muhammad 'Ali Street, and from the south via Sharia Lazughli, which is east of and parallel to Sharia Qasr al-'Ayni.

Mosque of al-Qadi Yahya * (No. 182) 1444/848. This mosque is a beleaguered landmark. It lies in the midst of a newly-constructed traffic flyover at the intersection of Sharia Port Said and Sharia al-Azhar. It is the first of three monuments built by the Amir–Judge Zayn al-Din Yahya, the Grand Ustadar or major domo of Sultan Gaqmaq. The penbox blazon appears in small panels to either side of the stalactite hood of the window over the southern entrance.

As his name Zayn al-Din ('Ornament of Religion') implies, Yahya was a mamluk of the pen, of the civil and religious orders. Mamluks of the sword, of the military order, were generally called Sayf al-Din, 'sword of religion.' Yahya acquired a great fortune and an exceptional position, which he enjoyed for twenty-five years, until 1470, when Sultan Qaytbay, succumbing to an old grudge, had this octogenarian thrown into prison and cruelly tortured.

The main features of this complex both externally and internally are those of the late Burgi mosque–madrasa: an attenuated ground plan and increasingly ornate surface decoration. The alluring view of the mosque from Sharia Port Said looking north, with merlons and minaret outlined against the sky, is marred by the double row of traffic lanes. The main entrance is underneath the minaret. The mosque was extensively restored by the Comité in 1894, who also rebuilt the southern façade. The ceilings in the liwans and in the sahn with its eight interlacing rosettes around a radiating inscription are especially attractive.

Sabil of Umm Husayn Bey, 1851–52. This nineteenth-century fountain lies behind the Mosque of al-Qadi Yahya. See below, under Mosque of al-Ghani al-Fakhri, for details.

Mosque of Assanbugha * (No. 185) 1370/772. This mosque was built by the Amir Assanbugha ('Strong Bull') ibn Baktamur, who was made an amir of one hundred and commander of a thousand by Sultan al-Nasir Muhammad ibn Qalawun and

Mosque of Assanbugha

who eventually became Amir Kabir. He died in Cairo in 1375 at the age of seventy.

His mosque–madrasa has a very charming exterior façade. One block south of al-Qadi Yahya on Sharia Port Said turn left and go to the end of the street that makes a T-junction with Darb Sa'ada. Turn right on the latter and continue south for two blocks until this structure appears on the left. The exterior is accentuated by the wooden mashrabiya screen across the sabil (with the emblems of the silahdar, or armorer, in the corners) and the projecting mashrabiya window on the second story. The interior has been restored and has no medieval interest.

Mosque of 'Abd al-Ghani al-Fakhri * (No. 184) 1418/821. This mosque lies on Sharia Port Said opposite the bottom of the ramp to the north–south flyover. This amir rose to the rank of wazir and served the Sultans Farag and Muayyad Shaykh. Little else is known of the builder of this mosque, nor why in 1851–52/1267–68 it was extensively restored by the mother of Husayn Bey, one of the sons of Muhammad 'Ali. The bronze door facing of geometric pattern is very handsome. Along the baffled corridor, on the left, the wooden lattice screen hid the well that supplied water for ablutions. The sanctuary liwan, with its flat ceiling and two black Ptolemaic columns, is similar to that of Sultan Barquq. The tomb chamber lies off the qibla on the left. The mother of Husayn Bey included a lovely sabil among her restorations, opposite the mosque. When Sharia Port Said was widened in the 1930s the sabil was relocated behind the mosque of al-Qadi Yahya (above). This mosque was restored by the Comité in 1895.

Mosque of Yusuf Agha al-Hin ** (No. 196) 1625/1035. This mosque sits on its own little island at the intersection of Sharia Muhammad 'Ali and Sharia Port Said, not far from the southwest corner of the old Fatimid royal residential city of al-Qahira and within sight of the Islamic Museum. Yusuf Agha al-Hin was a Mamluk bey who built his mosque in the Mamluk tradition with an Ottoman minaret. There have been two major constructional changes to the mosque, which have altered its original character. A domed mausoleum originally part of the complex was demolished when Sharia Muhammad 'Ali was constructed in the nineteenth century, and the prominent sabil–kuttab was added to the northwestern corner of the mosque in about 1900 following restorations necessary after the khalig was filled in to become Sharia Port Said. Although this sabil–kuttab is a fabrication, it is patterned on the sabil of 'Abd al-Rahman Katkhuda in the Bayn al-Qasrayn (Chapter 11).

It is worth the time to notice carefully the detail and variety of the decoration around the sabil-kuttab: the carved wooden frames around the sabil windows, the iron grill, the ablaq voussoirs, the inlaid marble spandrels, the silhouette cut-out form of the stalactite niches, the mashrabiya railing in front of the loggia, and the wooden eaves.

Inside, apart from the painted inscriptions around the ceiling and the stained glass windows in the shape of a ten-petaled flower, the decoration is subdued—the decoration of the mihrab is very recent. The most interesting feature of the interior is the large gallery in the northwest liwan. A lovely mashrabiya window extends along the whole wall, imparting to it a lightness and delicacy not often encountered. This is one of the few mosques in which this kind of fenestration has survived. From the openings there must have been a good view of the canal and the gardens planted along its length. The cenotaph in the north liwan belongs to the patron, who died in 1646/1056.

Mosque of Malika Safiya** (No. 200) 1610/1019. Turn right into Sharia Muhammad 'Ali (toward the Citadel) and continue about three hundred meters along its length. On the left an Ottoman minaret will become visible behind the arcades, down an alley leading off Muhammad 'Ali called Sikkat al-Malika.

During the Ottoman period the principal religious foundations were mosques; but only one mosque, this one, was a royal foundation, and this more by appropriation than by real design. It was started by 'Uthman Agha, the Agha Dar al-Sa'ada or black eunuch in charge of the harim, a post that also included the supervision of the Egyptian waqf estates of the holy places in Arabia. 'Uthman Agha was the agent and slave of the noble Venetian beauty Safiya, of the Baffo family, who had been captured by corsairs and presented to the imperial harim, where she became chief consort of Sultan Murad III (ruled

1574–95) and virtual regent for her son Muhammad III (ruled 1595–1603). 'Uthman died before the mosque was completed, and it went to her as part of his estate. She endowed the mosque with a deed that provided for thirty-nine custodians, among whom were a general supervisor, the preacher "pious and learned," the *khatib* (orator) "learned, proficient, ascetic, of noble morality," two imams "to supervise the cantillations of the Quran and rites and reading," "a pious and honest time-keeper," "a neat, decent man to incense the mosque, neither wastefully nor parsimoniously," "a man handy with repairs and construction," and "two men understanding plants, trees, herbs, and their improvements and irrigation, charged with the care of the garden," etc.

The plan of this mosque comes closer to the plan of an Istanbul mosque than any other Ottoman building in Cairo. Originally it was set in a garden enclosure. One enters it by the imposingly high steps on the south side. They lead to a courtyard surrounded by domed arcades. Inside the sanctuary, the internal arrangement of space is also thoroughly Ottoman and closely related to the plans of several Istanbul mosques: a central dome rests on six arches supported by red granite Ptolemaic columns. There are small domes in each corner. The one Cairene feature of this plan is that the prayer niche protrudes on the back wall. The mihrab, except for the blue Iznik tiles, is in the Mamluk style of polychrome marble panels. The minbar of carved and pierced marble, with its pointed conical top, is also in the Ottoman style. The decoration, subdued and concentrated primarily on the mihrab and in the colored glass roundels in the windows, does not detract from the magnificent sense of space and volume.

Only one of the gateways to the original, walled, enclosure remains, that on the north side. The ruined sabil–kuttab that stands within the precincts is that of *Muhammad Mustafa al-Muhasibgi* (No. 329) of 1716/1129. Walk under the trefoil arch with its stalactite squinches and out onto the street. Turn right and walk to the end. On the left at this point you will see the minaret and entrance to the:

Mosque of al-Burdayni * (No. 201) 1616–29. The mosque was begun by a religious Shafi'i scholar Karim al-Din al-Burdayni and completed in 1694 by a wealthy merchant. Perhaps for this reason its minaret, uncharacteristically, is not in the Ottoman style. It is a beautful little pastiche of Mamluk art. A small mosque, in form no larger than a square room with a raised gallery at the northwest end, it is richly decorated. The walls are covered with marble panels, marble and mosaic arcading, marble roundels; the ceiling shimmers softly with gilt; the stained glass windows glow with color. In short, the contrast with the somber mosque of Malika Safiya is noticeable.

Once outside again, follow the curve of the façade along the street, heading back toward Sharia Muhammad 'Ali along Sharia Mukhtar Pasha. The sabil–kuttab one passes on the left belonged to *Shahin Agha Ahmad* (No. 328) 1675/1086. When the road forks, bear right. It will take you to Sharia Muhammad 'Ali. Cross it, turn left, i.e. toward the Citadel, and follow it a few meters until you reach Sharia Habbaniya. Enter to the right and continue south until you reach, on your left, a mid-fifteenth-century Burgi Mamluk mosque.

Ribat of al-Qadi Yahya * (No. 204) 1452/856. This is the last of three monuments that this amir–judge left in Cairo. The outer façade with its trilobed portal, sabil–kuttab, and mashrabiya window is attractive. The inscription identifies this buildings as a ribat or hospice in which the poor could find shelter. There are not many of them in Cairo, since their functions by the end of the fifteenth century were absorbed by the zawiyas. Just inside the entrance are stairs on the left that lead to the upstairs rooms. Otherwise the plan is that of a small congregational mosque. Two palm trees grow in its courtyard, which give it an air of peace and fertility. A double arcade sets off the sanctuary and there is a domed area over the mihrab. The minbar is very fine: the inlay is delicate and in some places tinted green, which gives it additional interest. The blazon of the penbox, the emblem of the dawadar or executive secretary, appears on it. The mosque was restored by the Comité in 1905.

Madrasa of Sultan Mahmud * (No. 308) 1750/1164. Continue west along Sharia Habbaniya, which eventually joins Sharia Port Said. On the right, the corner is dominated by a handsome sabil–kuttab that belongs to the madrasa ordered

built in 1750 by the Ottoman sultan Mahmud I (ruled 1730–54).
His tughra or royal cipher appears over each window. This sabil
introduces a new style to Egypt: the curved or bow-front sabil,
and evidences a new interest in local monuments by Ottoman
sultans. Unfortunately, the window grills are obscured by brick
walls, but the undulating roof of the upper floor is very graceful.

Although there is an elaborate entrance on Sharia Habbaniya,
with Iznik tiles, entrelac frames, and engaged columns, the
main entrance to the madrasa is on Sharia Port Said. The
façade above the row of little shops is plain except for the leaf
scrolling meander that runs across it at about mid-point. The
portal is given prominence by its height and by the blue and
white tiles that embellish it. Stairs from the entrance lead up
to a courtyard, defined by a shallow domed arcade in which
there are cells or rooms. The inscription calls the monument a
madrasa. Not many madrasas were built during the Ottoman
period. The only other such building was that of Sulayman
Pasha (Chapter 7), which this one resembles except for the
sabil–kuttab. The plans of both resemble those of Ottoman
madrasas in Turkey.

Today this buildings is used for a variety of neighborhood
purposes: child care center, sewing school for teenage girls,
religious instruction center for girls and boys, and a women's
club from 6 to 8 p.m. It is closed on Fridays.

Sabil–Kuttab of Bashir Agha Dar al-Sa'ada (No. 309) 1718/
1131. Directly opposite, across Sharia Habbaniya, is this monument in the more traditional style of square sabil with square
kuttab above. Bashir was a black eunuch who became Kizlar
Agha or Agha Dar al-Sa'ada (Lord of the House of Joy, i.e. the
imperial harim in Istanbul). He was the longest lived and
arguably the most powerful Kizlar Agha in Ottoman history.
His small sabil in Cairo was built before he was appointed to
this post.

Mosque of Sitt Hadaq * (No. 252) 1339–40/740. Off Sharia
Port Said, on the east side, opposite the monument complex of
the Amir Bashtak, is an unnamed alley. Walk into it for about
250 meters, until it comes to a dead end at a shop. The mosque
is on the right. This is a modest congregational mosque whose

main interest lies more in the person of its patron than in the importance of its location or the architectural quality of the building. This is the only mosque built by a woman that survives from the period of Sultan al-Nasir Muhammad ibn Qalawun, whose reign from 1310–41 was the most brilliant period of medieval Cairo, especially in architecture. Sitt Hadaq, also known as Sitt Miska ('Lady Musk') was a lady of power, influence, and wealth in his court. She was a slave who became the nursemaid in charge of the affairs of the harim and of the training and education of the royal children. She was also Stewardess of the Royal House. In 1328 she made a pilgrimage to Mecca, an event she commemorated in the inscription of the façade.

For many recent years the mosque has been under restoration and access is difficult. A noteworthy feature of the inside is the mihrab, whose hood is decorated with glass mosaics.

Minaret and Portal of the Amir Bashtak (No. 205) 1336/ 736 and **Mosque of Mustafa Fadil Pasha** c.1863/1280. Further along Sharia Port Said, and visible on the left, is what remains of the Mosque of the Amir Bashtak, built in the reign of Sultan al-Nasir Muhammad ibn Qalawun. These remains have been incorporated into the mosque built by the mother of Mustafa Fadil Pasha. He was the younger half-brother of the Khedive Isma'il who, after being exiled for plotting, became an important wazir and cabinet minister in Istanbul. As you enter the mosque, look up at the fourteenth-century canopy portal with its dripping stalactites that end in rosettes. The tomb of Mustafa Fadil, who died in 1875, is on the right. Although it is locked, it can be seen through mashrabiya windows to be very ornate.

Opposite the mosque is a sabil built by Elfat Hanim, his mother, in 1863. It is small, simple, but charming with its rounded front, three grilled windows, wooden eaves and acanthus scrolls. The blue background of the inscription, which added color and zest to the façade, is faded now but still discernible.

Mosque of Dhu al-Fiqar Bey (No. 415) 1680/1091. Farther on the left on Sharia Port Said stands this small, simple mosque from the Ottoman period. The minaret seems squat, the façade is plain. The sanctuary is an oblong room with four columns that support a lantern opening over the center.

Mosque of Timraz al-Ahmadi (No. 215) 1472/876. Still on the left, this monument is near the corner in the next block. It can be idenfified by the small, domed tomb chamber that huddles next to the minaret over the entrance. The sabil–kuttab on the other side was completely restored and rebuilt in 1701/1113 and 1766/1180. Sayf al-Din Timraz was a secondary master of the horse, an amir of forty, and thus a lesser functionary at the court of Sultan Qaytbay. His mosque is a rare example of a monument built by a junior official. It was built near a bridge that crossed the canal at this point. The inside plan is quite unusual, and it is possible that it was amended in the eighteenth century. The left side has an arch spanning it, while the right side has a central skylight with a gallery opposite the qibla.

Mosque of Sayyida Zaynab * 1884/1303. Sharia Port Said curves slightly to the west and this mosque, an imposing monument on the left, becomes a dominant landmark. The cult of Zaynab goes back to Fatimid times. It is generally believed that this Zaynab is the valiant sister of al-Husayn, who was with him at the battle of Karbala; however, she may never have come to Egypt. There is a mausoleum in her name in Damascus. Nevertheless, she is one of the patron saints of Cairo. Another Zaynab was the cousin of Sayyida Nafisa and her faithful companion for forty years—perhaps it is she who is buried here. There has been a shrine at this location since Fatimid times, but tangible architectural documentation does not commence until the sixteenth century, when a series of builders beginning with 'Ali Pasha in 1549 and ending with Sa'd Pasha in 1859 contributed to it. The present neo-Mamluk building is a new mosque on the site of the old shrine. It was sponsored by the Khedive Tawfiq and finished in 1884. The mosque was enlarged and the south annex added in 1942. Women are not allowed in the main sanctuary area. They are, however, allowed to enter into the tomb by a special entrance on the north corner. The saint's cenotaph is protected by a magnificent silver screen provided by the Bohra Isma'ilis of India. The faithful come to pay their respects, to voice their petitions, and to seek the saint's blessing, but they are not encouraged to linger. Non-Muslims are not welcome in the mosque.

Sabil–Kuttab of Sultan Mustafa III * (No. 314) 1759/1173. Across the street and slightly south is this very handsome fountain of the late Ottoman period, a high point of the Ottoman style in Cairo. The overall use of colored marble—its marble window frames, carved columns, and the tughra or official signature of the Ottoman Sultan in the center above the windows—is particularly noteworthy. There is an elegant entrance on the street side, one whose square shape contrasts neatly with the rounded form of its dependency, but the 'working' entrance is to the left in the side alley. The sabil, with inlaid marble panels, a splendid but faded wooden ceiling, and blue and white Delft tiles, is being used by a shaykh. The kuttab is being used as an elementary school.

House of Ibrahim Katkhuda al-Sinnari * (No. 283) 1794/ 1209. Follow the curve of the street north. The east bank of the Nile was nearby in the ninth century. Access to the house is down an alley, off Sharia Lazughli, thirty meters beyond the curve of Sharia Port Said, on the right (east) side, near Number 27 (between a Dalia shoe store and a sweet shop). Walk down the alley until a magnificent second-story mashrabiya window signals the house.

   In 1911 this house was identified as one of three (the other two have since been destroyed) that were requisitioned in 1798 by the French to house members of the Committee of Sciences and Arts, who had come with Napoleon Bonaparte's military expedition to make a methodical study of the country. The house had been built a few years earlier by an amir of Murad Bey who had started as a humble black doorman from southern Nubia. Today it is being used as an arts and crafts center, producing works of wood, stained glass, silk screen, and batik. It is closed on Fridays, but open on other days from 9 to 1:30 p.m.

   The house is oriented toward the north (to catch the prevailing breezes). In front of the house there was once an extensive garden. The mashrabiya window of the main qa'a of the harim is over the main door. All the features of a medieval Cairene house are here: the inner courtyard with maq'ad; the qa'a of the harim that stretches from the street view in front to the maq'd view in back, with a malqaf over it that keeps it cool.

The Museum of Islamic Art.*** This is on Sharia Port Said, near its intersection with Sharia Muhammad 'Ali, in Maydan Ahmed Maher. It is open daily, but closed at the time of the noon prayer on Fridays. This museum contains nearly 80,000 items, a representative selection of which are on display in galleries newly refurbished and reorganized. The collection is a superb supplement to the monuments and should not be missed. From the Fatimid period, for example, there is a fine collection of wooden panels depicting the merry life of the court, the only surviving fragment of the Western Palace of al-Qahira. There are also movable, wooden mihrabs from the tombs of Sayyida Ruqayya and Sayyida Nafisa, and an extensive display of luster ceramics. From the Ayyubid period there is the handsomely carved wooden tabut of al-Husayn, as well as fine inlaid brass candlesticks. The collection of enameled mosque lamps from the Mamluk period, as well as inlays of metal, wood, and marble on objects and furnishings, should not be missed, nor should the minbar from the Madrasa–Mausoleum of Tatar al-Higaziya, nor the Quran boxes and inlaid tables in the name of Sultan Sha'ban. The museum also contains a large assortment of artifacts from.other areas of the Islamic world, such as ceramics and metal from Iran and carpets from Turkey, which offer interesting comparative material. The courtyard–garden area contains a lovely nineteenth-century salsabil (fountain) from the al-Monastirli Palace on Roda Island, as well as some extraordinary marble panels that have survived from the palace of the Fatimid wazirs. One visit to this museum will seem hardly enough, but one at least should be made.

10 ◇ Bab Zuwayla to the Mosque of al-Azhar

See map 9

To get to Bab Zuwayla, go to Maydan Ahmad Maher (site of the Islamic Museum) via Sharia al-Qal'a (Muhammad 'Ali) from 'Ataba Square, or take Sharia Port Said south from its intersection with Sharia al-Azhar. From Maydan Ahmad Maher, turn east on Sharia Ahmad Maher, a street bordered by the shops of parasol-makers and tombstone-carvers, among others. There are also several shops specializing in the tin lanterns that children carry on Ramadan nights.

An alternative approach to Bab Zuwayla, starting from the green pedestrian overpass over Sharia al-Azhar, is to walk south from the complex of Sultan al-Ghuri for 350 meters until reaching Bab Zuwayla, in effect reversing the itinerary outlined in this chapter.

As one walks along Sharia Ahmad Maher one passes the *Mosque of al-Mar'a or Fatima Shagra* (No. 195, 1408–69/873) on the right and the *Sabil of Hasan Agha Arzingan* (No. 420, 1830/1246) on the left.

Gate–Tomb–Takiya of al-Gulshani * (No. 332) 1519–24/ 926–31. On the right, opposite a long wall, behind a scene of great lumber activity, a flight of steps leads to a rather imposing portal. Ring the bell and somebody will let you in.

Ibrahim al-Gulshani was a Turk who came to Egypt in 1507 and founded the first takiya of the sufi Khalawati order in Cairo. As well as being an intellectual and author of philosophical treatises and poetical works, al-Gulshani was a man of substance and position. His son married the widow of Tumanbay (see below). The major part of the monument has since disappeared—only the mausoleum in a large courtyard remains. The structure is Mamluk in style—a domed cube with triangular chamfering at the corners of the transition zone—but the decoration of glazed tiles that covers the buildings is Ottoman. Some of the tiles and fragments are examples of sixteenth-century ware. The decoration of the interior is curious: it is a painted facsimile of tiles. Perhaps in the gloom it was hoped the difference would not be noticed; perhaps it was intentionally economic; perhaps there was a great deal of breakage in the consignment of tiles from Istanbul.

Bab Zuwayla (Bab al-Mitwalli) ** (No. 199) 1092/485. Of the three Fatimid gates that remain standing, this is perhaps the least interesting structurally, because it was from the north that the attack from Syria was expected. Visually, however, with its crowning fifteenth-century minarets, it is the most dramatic and it gives into a bazaar quarter that is as full of life today as it was in the Middle Ages.

Bab Zuwayla, also called Bab al-Mitwalli, dates from 1092. It was part of the city fortifications put up by the Armenian wazir Badr al-Gamali and his Anatolian or Mesopotamian Christian architects. The gate was named after Fatimid soldiers from the Berber tribe al-Zawila, who were quartered in the vicinity after the building of the original gate in 969, when al-Qahira was founded. The name Bab al-Mitwalli dates from Ottoman times when the wali of the janissaries, or commander of the police force charged with maintaining public order, had his residence and headquarters near here. The gate was a place of public execution, and the heads of criminals were exposed above the gate on spikes. In the nineteenth century the name was associated with a local saint, Mitwalli al-Qutb, who had lived by the gate and worked miracles. The gate became a resort for those in need of the saint's intercession. When a person was sick, a piece of clothing or some hair or other token was hung on the doors of the gate and the saint responded directly to the owner.

In the early Mamluk period the sultans used to watch the start of the *mahmal* procession from the platform extending between the two towers on the inside. This was the annual caravan that took the new kiswa or cloth covering for the Ka'ba, woven in Egypt, to Mecca. This platform was also used by the ceremonial drummers who played there every evening and who signaled the entrance into the city of amirs who commanded forty or more mamluks. In the early fifteenth century al-Maqrizi described the place as being notoriously unlucky. It was here that the last of the independent Mamluks, Tumanbay, was hanged by the Turkish sultan Selim the Grim in the sixteenth century. Tumanbay's rope broke on the first two attempts. He was a gallant and appealing ruler, but his luck ran out early.

The gate's projecting, rounded towers connected by a covered passageway over the large, arched opening are north Syrian or Byzantine, not Arab, in inspiration and spirit. The two minarets that spring from the towers belong to the Mosque of al-Muayyad, just inside the gate, which forms the wall to the west. East of the gate the ruins of the Fatimid city wall extend for about one hundred meters, but are concealed by modern buildings and debris. The objects hanging on the east tower, looking like weights and bar bells are exactly that and were used in the medieval period by members of special fraternal societies to keep fit.

Mosque–Mausoleum of Sultan al-Muayyad *** (No. 190) 1415–22/818–23. This is the first building on the left as one passes through Bab Zuwayla. Al-Muayyad Shaykh, a Burgi or Circassian Mamluk, was sultan from 1412 to 1421. Al-Maqrizi relates that during the reign of Farag ibn Barquq, al-Muayyad, a great intriguer during a time of great intrigues, was captured and thrown into a prison on this site. He suffered terribly from the lice and the fleas, and vowed then that if he ever came to power he would transform the infested prison into a "saintly place for the education of scholars." Sultan al-Muayyad spent 40,000 dinars on its construction. The madrasa, due to the sultan's lavish endowments, became one of the prominent academic institutions of the fifteenth century. A large library was collected; the most eminent scholars of the day filled professorial chairs; and the most famous specialist in Quranic exegesis in Egypt, Ibn Hagar al-'Asqalani, was installed as lecturer in Shafi'i jurisprudence.

The exterior façade of this monument provides an excellent example of how Mamluk buildings were intended to dominate the urban setting, both physically and visually: as one looks north through the arched opening of Bab Zuwayla the massive façade ending in the portal and the dome fills the vista; as one looks south it is the twin minarets soaring over the gate that catch the eye. The portal, with its red and turquoise geometric frame around the door, the nine-tiered stalactite fall from the hood, and the carved arabesque patterns of the upper frame, is particularly beautiful. The panels on either side are an example of square Kufic and are an arrangement of the *shahada*, the first pillar of Islam: "There is no god but God; Muhammad is the Messenger of God." The magnificent bronze door originally belonged to the Madrasa of Sultan Hasan and was purchased for five hundred dinars, a relatively paltry sum. Over the portal and on the bays to either side is a Quranic inscription often used in religious buildings:

> Only they shall visit God's sanctuaries who believe in God and the Last Day, and perform the ritual prayer and pay the poor-tax and fear none save God; it may be that such are rightly guided. (9:18)

From the entrance vestibule one passes into the mausoleum, where the sultan and his eldest son are buried. On the largest cenotaph there is a beautiful reused panel of tenth-century Kufic script, a verse from the Quran (15:45–46): "Surely those who keep from evil will be among gardens and fountains: Enter them in peace, secure." The graceful leaf forms that emanate from the vertical letters and fill the empty spaces over the horizontal letters are characteristic in early Islamic art of the desire to fill voids. These 'foliate' beginnings lead subsequently to very lush arabesque backgrounds for scripts.

From the mausoleum one enters into the sanctuary of the congregational mosque, which is a late example in Cairo of the open courtyard plan on a large scale. The mosque originally had four façades. But in the late nineteenth century it was in such a bad state of disrepair that the Comité rebuilt the western façade, and turned the courtyard into a garden. On the opposite side of the courtyard, on its northern side, there is a hammam, a bath, that is worth seeing. The decoration of the interior is also of a richness and scale that scarcely occurs later in the Mamluk period. The mihrab and the minbar are both fine examples of the style of the period, while the ceilings, which were restored in the early twentieth century, seem like aerial carpets.

A tomb chamber at the southwest end of the sanctuary was for the female members of the sultan's family. Today it is kept locked and the dome that once stood over it has disappeared. The Turkish tiles inset in the qibla wall are due to restoration work by Ibrahim Pasha, the son of Muhammad 'Ali, in 1839–40. A door at this end of the sanctuary leads to the second-story platform of the Bab Zuwayla, and to the minarets. The view from the top is well worth the climb since it offers, north and south, a superb perspective on the extent and contours of the medieval city. Above the entrance of each minaret there is a cartouche in which the architect al-Mu'allim Muhammad ibn al-Qazzaz has left his name and the dates of completion, 1421 and 1422. This signature on the part of an architect is rare in Cairo.

Wikala (No. 395) **and Sabil–Kuttab** (No. 358) **of Nafisa Bayda**** 1796/1211. Of this building, just opposite Sultan al-Muayyad's mosque, only the façade with its elegant bank of upper-story mashrabiya windows is still impressive. At the southern end, near Bab Zuwayla, is the sabil–kuttab. Its rounded front is characteristic of a change in the outline of such monuments that was introduced about 1750. At the northern end, next to a jeweler's shop, is the entrance to a bath, for men only, which is still in operation. The fires that heat the water are also used to cook the *ful mudammas* (broad beans) that supply Egyptians of the quarter and beyond with their breakfast fare.

Nafisa Bayda (Nafisa 'the White One') started her career as a slave. She was married first to 'Ali Bey, "the mighty one of

Egypt" in the mid-1700s (see Chapter 8), and then to Murad Bey, a mamluk of the Qazdughli faction, who rose to power at the end of the eighteenth century. From 1784 he shared power with another mamluk, Ibrahim Bey. Twice he was driven to Upper Egypt: firstly by a newly appointed and determined Ottoman viceroy and secondly by Napoleon Bonaparte. He died there in 1801. Nafisa was a woman of beauty, wealth, charity and great culture. During Murad Bey's resistance she acted as intermediary between him and Napoleon. She is the only female patron to have a monument survive on the main ceremonial way of al-Qahira.

Sabil–Kuttab of Tusun Pasha * (No. 401) 1820/1236. A little further north the street bends to the right, and behind the stalls on the right selling hardware items is this charming monument of the early Muhammad 'Ali period. Ahmad Tusun died in 1816 after contracting the plague in the course of a successful campaign against the Wahhabis of Saudi Arabia.

The structure is similar to the commemorative sabil–kuttab of Isma'il built in the Bayn al-Qasrayn. The rooms of the kuttab are to either side of the round-fronted sabil. Today these rooms are being used as an elementary school. The ornamentation of the sabil—acanthus garlands, fronds, grills, seals, sunbursts, poetic verses—are characteristic of the Muhammad 'Ali period.

Mosque of al-Fakahani * (No. 109) 1735/1148. One hundred yards further north on the right-hand side of the street is the Fakahani ('Fruit-Seller') mosque, built by the Fatimid khalif al-Zahir in 1148. Nothing remains of the original mosque except the doors, which are notable examples of Fatimid woodwork. Take some time to admire the finely carved arabesque panels. Arabesque is decoration based on an unending, moving, twisting, vibrant design of leaves and stems that flow from one to another in a pattern that is rhythmically repeated and covers the whole surface of the panel or object. In Egypt, the arabesque patterns of the late Fatimid period are especially beautiful.

The rest of the structure dates to 1735, when it was rebuilt by Ahmad Katkhuda al-Kharbutli, and is of interest primarily as an example of a small Ottoman Cairene congregational mosque.

House of Gamal al-Din al-Dhahabi * (No. 72) 1634/1044.
Turn right (east) at the northwestern corner of Fakahani
Mosque onto Sharia Khushqadam. It turns left almost immediately and then right again. The house of Gamal al-Din is on
the left about one hundred meters down the lane, which is
quite narrow at this point and gives one a nice sense of a
medieval street.

Gamal al-Din was the chief of the corporations of gold
merchants in Cairo and the wikala–sabil–kuttab that he endowed in the same year still stands (just off the Qasaba behind
the stalls selling gold jewelry, see Chapter 11). His house is an
example of a mansion of the seventeenth century, built in the
Mamluk style. It now houses the Documentation Center of the
Egyptian Antiquities Organization's Islamic section, which is
open from 9 a.m. to 2 p.m. Perhaps the most charming part of
this old house is the interior courtyard ensemble, with its
central fountain and finely decorated door leading to the maq'ad
or second story loggia with its double-arched opening. To the
east of the loggia is a splendid qa'a with a high dome in the
center and handsome inlaid marble dadoes on the wall. The
ceiling is beamed, coffered, and painted and there are
mashrabiya screens at the second-story level at the northern
end to permit the women of the harim to witness the activities
below.

The Ghuriya *** (Nos. 189, 65, 66, and 67) 1503–05/909–10.
Proceed up the main street another two hundred meters and
you will find yourself between two Mamluk buildings just
before the intersection with the modern Sharia al-Azhar. These
belonged to Sultan Qansuh al-Ghuri, the last but one of the
Mamluk sultans and the last to enjoy a reign of any duration
(1501–1516). Al-Ghuri died fighting the Ottoman Turks outside Aleppo, following the defection of Amir Khayrbak in the
midst of the battle (see Mosque of Khayrbak, Chapter 6). His
body was never found.

The madrasa–mosque, on the left, is in late Mamluk cruciform style. It is the last flowering of Mamluk art. The effect is
of a pleasant, robust building, with strong features and func-

The Ghuriya (drawing by Prisse d'Avennes)

tional design. This is a quiet place to rest one's feet and look down upon the bold designs of the marble panels of the courtyard, or up at the arches with their intricately carved geometric and arabesque surfaces, and at the lantern ceiling, a wonderful interlace of lobes and roundels. The interior also provides a vantage from which to contemplate the bazaar scenes behind the madrasa. Look down through the barred windows upon the sellers of spices, herbs, perfumes, and textiles.

With luck you can get someone to take you up to the roof. The ascent is worthwhile on two counts: as a behind-the-scenes glimpse into the warren of rooms along the way, and as a panorama of the main area of the Fatimid medieval city, north and south. It is disappointing to discover when up there that the red and white checkerboard squares that are such a distinctive feature of the minaret are actually painted on, and very crudely at that. The minaret is square and represents a reversion from the circular–octagonal shape that had become standard by this time. The present top with five bulbs is a misrepresentation of the original, which had four bulbs covered with green tiles.

The mausoleum–sabil–kuttab is across the medieval street. The dome of the mausoleum, huge and covered with green tiles, was unstable from the beginning and was rebuilt three times. Finally, in 1860 it was replaced with a wooden ceiling. The building is now used as a neighborhood cultural center, with adult education classes and lectures. The people who run it are eager, helpful, and very proud of what they are doing. It is heartening to see the structure being put to good use. One enters into a vestibule. To the right is the mausoleum, which is now being used as a library. Perhaps the most interesting feature here is the carved surface of the wall. From just above the marble wainscoting to just below the springing of the dome (now missing) the whole wall is carved in an arabesque pattern which gives it a curious look of stone brocade. Al-Ghuri himself was not buried in his mausoleum, although others were before his death. The first was a daughter of his in 1505, followed by his son Nasir al-Din Muhammad, aged thirteen years, and his concubine mother. The latter were victims of the plague. Tumanbay, his successor, after he was hanged by orders of the Ottoman sultan Selim, also found his final resting place here. To the left, the vestibule leads to a little theater. This T-shaped room with a mihrab was originally part of a khanqah. The sufis did not reside here but were expected to be present at the time of the hudur, the service during which the sufis perform the dhikr. The theater has been newly restored and it provides an attractive setting for popular theatrical performances.

Adjoining the mausoleum is a rare enclosed maq'ad, overlooking a court that is accessible through an entrance on Sharia al-Azhar around the corner from the mausoleum. It is the first entrance one encounters and is easily identifiable because it is below street level.

We have a full, contemporary account of al-Ghuri's reign and the building of these structures in the chronicle of Ibn Iyas. Al-Ghuri emerges as an energetic (he was still playing polo in his 70s) and arbitrary despot, cruel and superstitious, and thoroughly human in his weaknesses. Time and again we read of someone who was savagely tortured to extract money from him, or of someone else who was hanged or cut in two for some offense real or imagined. On the other hand, al-Ghuri loved flowers, was fond of music, wrote poetry, and was attracted to sufis and other pious men. He was a great patron of architecture. Ibn Iyas has this to say: "How amazing that al-Ghuri is not buried in the magnificent tomb on which he had spent 100,000 dinars, but else was destined and he lay stretched out in the wilderness the prey to wolves and leopards."

The madrasa was inaugurated on the eve of the Feast of the Sacrifice ('Id al-Adha) in May 1503, with a great banquet attended by the Abbasid khalif Mustamsik, the chief judges of the four orthodox rites, and the principal military and civilian officials. The illuminations were prodigious. All the shops from Bab Zuwayla to the Bazaar of the Tarboush-sellers around the madrasa were decorated and illuminated.

Ibn Iyas notes that:

The new building was richly decorated and garnished with profusion of marble. It was a splendid construction of sumptuous elegance, to which one could compare no contemporary monument. Nevertheless, the Sultan was generally reproached for having built with the aid of illicit confiscations, not to mention the fact that most of the marble had been taken from other buildings and bought at ridiculous [forced] prices. . . . Muayyad was also criticized in a similar fashion for the mosque which he had built at Bab Zuwayla. The Egyptians are unable to hold their tongues when it comes to slanging a neighbor.

The beautiful marble slabs that once decorated the madrasa, having been confiscated by al-Ghuri from someone else, were in turn confiscated and taken to Istanbul by Selim I in 1517.

The mausoleum and the madrasa together form one of the most impressive hyphen or double ensembles in Cairo. What makes these buildings especially interesting is the configuration that they give to the Qasaba at this point. The projection of the sabil–kuttab at the northern end of the mausoleum on the right and of the minaret at the southern end of the madrasa on the left means that the thoroughfare narrows at the ends and that between the buildings there is a rather spacious area. The shops built into the lower levels on the Qasaba façades show that this space was intended to be a commercial square, which in fact it was.

The street between the two buildings was once roofed over, and it was at this point, the site of the Silk Bazaar, that David Roberts did a famous drawing in 1839. Today the silk merchants have gone, but the sale of textiles, stacked as bolts of colorful yard goods or as finished articles floating like banners above the crowds, was still lively here until damage done to the monuments in the October 1992 earthquake and the need for extensive restoration led the local authorities to evict the traders and remove the stalls from both sides of the street. The façades of both buildings were cleaned in 1989. The result, a new tawny beige sandstone with black and white marble accents instead of the uniform grungy-gray, is eye-catching.

Wikala of al-Ghuri ✳✳ (No. 64) 1504–05/909-10. After emerging from the Ghuriya onto al-Azhar street, turn right (east) and walk a further hundred meters up the street. You will find yourself in front of another unmistakably Mamluk building with protruding upper-story mashrabiya windows and strong, square lines. It is the wikala (khan or caravanserai) of al-Ghuri. It has been converted into a cultural center, with ateliers for artists, a handicrafts school for boys, and displays of native handicrafts

of the desert tribes. The personnel of the establishment are glad
to show you around and it is well worth an hour of your time. It
is closed on Fridays.

This wikala is the best-preserved example of a prosaic,
commercial hotel. Merchants would keep their animals on the
ground floor and themselves and their wares in rooms on the
upper floors. The structure is solid and functional. One has to
imagine its courtyard as a scene of movement, with sacks and
bales and boxes of merchandise being unloaded from pack
animals by sweating porters, while buyers and sellers sat and
bargained just as their descendants do today in the nearby
bazaar. Cairo was a major spice entrepôt, and great quantities of
eastern spices were shipped and traded in such khans all over the
city—there were two hundred of them in 1835. Today there are
only twenty, and only this one has been restored. This particular
wikala was built just as the spice trade was falling on bad times
because of the Portuguese discovery of an alternative route to
the East around the Cape and across the Indian Ocean.

Mosque of al-Azhar *** (No. 97) 970–1894. One hundred
yards to the east of the Wikala of al-Ghuri is the Mosque of al-
Azhar, the foremost center of theology in Islam and the oldest
university in the world (although the latter claim is disputed by
the Qarawiyin mosque in Fez, which dates to 933). Founded by
the Fatimid conqueror Gawhar al-Siqilli in 970 as the congregational mosque of the new city of al-Qahira, it soon became a
center for teaching Isma'ili Shi'i theology. It has played an
important and continuous role in the religious and political life
of Egypt and the surrounding Arab states ever since. Its
religious teaching methods and subject matter are essentially
unchanged since the time of Salah al-Din. The traditional
religious subjects, which include exegesis, traditions, jurisprudence, rhetoric, and grammar, are still taught.

In recent years it has been modernized by the addition of
schools of medicine, science, commerce, etc., to make it competi-
tive as an institution of higher learning. It now has a separate
faculty for women, the Kulliyat al-Banat al-Islamiya. In 1991/
92 al-Azhar University had a student body of over eighty
thousand and a teaching staff of 5,381. In addition to the main
Cairo campus, it has nine other campuses throughout Egypt.

Al-Azhar is a great mixture of styles and periods, all of which blend together in a comfortable, if confusing, whole. The color-coded plan by the entrance vestibule shows this. For example, as you face the main façade, the left half is the work of the Khedive Tawfiq (late nineteenth century); the right wing was added by the Khedive 'Abbas Hilmi in 1894, while the central portion, the double-arched gate, belongs to the mid-eighteenth century. In March 1983 al-Azhar celebrated its one-thousandth anniversary as a teaching university. The panels on its façade were repainted.

The double-arched Gate of the Barbers (so-called because this was where students used to have their heads shaved) leads into a wide, marble-paved enclosure formed by two Mamluk madrasas originally built in the ziyada or outer enclosure of the mosque. On the left is the **Aqbughawiya Madrasa** of 1340/740 with its handsomely decorated portal in red and black marble inlay. This madrasa was built by the Amir Sayf al-Din Aqbugha ('White Bull'). He was not a pleasant man—in fact al-Maqrizi, the fifteenth-century historian, writes that there was "nobody meaner, crueler, nastier nor harder of heart." The land for his complex he took by extortion, and the madrasa, described as gloomy, was built with materials illegally seized or stolen, and by laborers and artisans who were not only under-paid, but beaten and whipped as well. Aqbugha was greatly esteemed by the Sultan al-Nasir Muhammad, perhaps because his sister was the Princess Tughay, the sultan's favorite wife. Aqbugha was promoted to major-domo or chief steward of the sultan's household and Commander of the Royal Mamluks. To build his madrasa the sultan lent him the court architect Mu'allim ibn al-Suyufi.

Since 1898 this madrasa has housed al-Azhar's valuable collection of manuscripts and Qurans. The mihrabs in the tomb chamber and in the east wall of the library are interesting because of their decoration. They are both done in glass mosaic with mother-of-pearl, and depict branching sprays emerging from a cup, a technique and design that was brought to Cairo from Syria.

On the right-hand side of the entrance enclosure is the **Taybarsiya Madrasa**, 1309–10/709, built by the Amir 'Ala al-Din Taybars al-Khazindar, the commander-in-chief of Egypt for the Maliki and Shafi'i schools of law. Now it contains the

Courtyard of the Mosque of al-Azhar

most precious manuscripts in al-Azhar's library and it has to be specially opened (although not on Fridays). The façade belongs to the additions that 'Abd al-Rahman Katkhuda made to the mosque in 1753/1167. Thus only the qibla wall dates from the fourteenth century. It is worth the effort to have a look at the mihrab, perhaps one of the handsomest of the early Bahri period, for its combination of glass mosaic and polychrome inlaid marble.

The main courtyard is entered by passing through the **Gate of Sultan Qaytbay**, 1469/873, a superb example of the carved-stone surface decoration of the later Mamluk period. Against an embroidered and tessellated surface, the stalactite niches give the impression of stone lace. The minaret above the gate was also added by Sultan Qaytbay, in 1475.

The sahn or central court belongs to the Fatimid period; the dimensions are according to the original tenth-century plan, but the decoration of roundels and keel-arched panels are from a restoration by the khalif al-Hafiz in 1138/532. On the right-hand side, behind the mashrabiya screens of the portico colonnade, are the riwaqs or residential units that provide rent-free lodgings for students, Egyptian and foreign, who need accommodations.

When reaching the sanctuary look up into the small dome in the porch at the entrance. The pierced windows illuminate the richly carved stucco surface added by the khalif al-Hafiz in 1138/532. The original structure of al-Gawhar begins inside, although it too consists of a mixture of subsequent decoration and restoration. The central aisle of the sanctuary is both higher and wider than the aisles that flank it to right and left. This rather basilican feature is reminiscent of certain mosques in North Africa, where the Fatimid dynasty originated. The stucco carving in the clerestory and on the interior façade, though 'restored,' are original in spirit. The Kufic inscriptions and foliate stucco carving in the hood of the mihrab are also original. The delicate stucco panels above the niche belong to a restoration by the Amir Salar to repair damage wrought by the earthquake of 1303. The gleaming marble below the niche was added recently by the Bohras, a sect of Isma'ili Shi'is.

Al-Azhar has always been a center of learning. When the Fatimid dynasty was overthrown, Shi'a teaching was abolished. Under the Mamluks all four Sunni rites were added. During the Ottoman period students came from all parts of the Islamic world to study at al-Azhar. Here today's students in the Faculty of Arabic and Islamic studies sit on the floor at the feet of their shaykh, in a halqa or circle much as they did in the medieval period; or they sit by themselves with lips moving, memorizing the texts they are expected to know by heart. The long runners of red and white niche-patterned carpeting in the sanctuary were a gift from the Pakistani president Zia ul-Haq.

The area four arcades deep behind and one step up from the mihrab is the enlargement made to the mosque by the great builder of the Ottoman period, **'Abd al-Rahman Katkhuda** in 1753. At the west or right side of the extension, up a flight of stairs, is his tomb. He was an unusual man, who in spite of his great wealth and prestige had little personal ambition. He preferred instead to dispense charity and to beautify the city with elegant buildings. His additions to al-Azhar almost doubled its original size. One can leave the mosque from this area through the Bab al-Sa'ida, which also belongs to 'Abd al-Rahman's restorations.

At the east end or left side of the Katkhuda extension is the **Tomb–Madrasa of the Eunuch Amir Gawhar Qunqubay**, the treasurer of Sultan Barsbay, built in 1440/844. The door from the sanctuary is now locked, so one must enter it by leaving the building from the courtyard through the lateral entrance on the north side. The mausoleum was restored in 1980–82 as a collaboration by the Egyptian Antiquities Organization and the Royal Danish Academy of Fine Arts. The marble paving, inlaid wooden doors, and stained glass windows provide a charming example of the Mamluk style of the mid-fifteenth century. The dome of this madrasa, with its arabesque pattern formed by interlacing scrolls and floriate motifs, marks a new step in the evolution of the carved stone domes of the Mamluk period.

Al-Azhar has three minarets near its main entrance: one belonging to the Aqbughawiya madrasa, one donated by Sultan Qaytbay, and the third with the double finial donated by Sultan al-Ghuri, 1501–1516. The Qaytbay and al-Ghuri minarets have double staircases beginning with the second story: one for ascending, the other for descending. This strengthens the shaft.

An excellent view of the area that comprised the medieval city of al-Qahira can be obtained from either minaret. A fourth minaret, that of 'Abd al-Rahman Katkhuda, stands next to the Bab al-Sa'ida entrance.

Sabil–Kuttab and Wikala of Sultan Qaytbay * (Nos. 75, 76) 1477/882. Exit from the Bab al-Sa'ida of al-Azhar onto Sharia Shaykh Muhammad 'Abduh. Take some time to look at the rich carvings that enliven the surface of the double-arched entrance. Opposite and slightly to the right is the Wikala and Sabil–Kuttab of Qaytbay.

This wikala is one of three that survive from the Burgi Mamluk period and is sited in one of the most important commercial districts of old Cairo. To either side of the richly decorated portal are fourteen shops on the main façade. Inside, the ground floor contained twenty-eight locked storerooms and three stairwells leading to thirty-seven living units above, which provided lodgings for travelers, merchants, and lower-income residents. A sabil–kuttab with rich decorative details over the entrance and windows, as well as a watering trough for animals, takes up the corner.

The structure has suffered grievously over time, but its main glory, the profusion and variety of decorative panels and lintels, can still be appreciated. Stanley Lane-Poole wrote in 1900: "In its original state this wikala must have been a noble building; even as it is, one may call it almost a text-book of Saracenic decoration."

Mosque of Abu Dhahab ** (No. 98) 1774/1188. Opposite the main gate of al-Azhar, on property that originally extended to the Wikala of al-Ghuri, is the mosque built by Muhammad, a mamluk of 'Ali Bey al-Kabir. His reign from 1772 to 1775 fell between that of his master 'Ali Bey (1768–72) and that of his own two mamluks Ibrahim Bey and Murad Bey (1775–98). At his investiture as a bey or prince, because he distributed "without counting gold instead of silver as no single amir had done before," he was nicknamed Abu Dhahab or 'Father of Gold.' The mosque is all that remains now of a great religious complex that also included a madrasa, a library, a takiya, latrines and fountains, begun in 1774 and completed a year later. The

Façades of al-Azhar and Abu Dhahab

complex represents the last of the great religious complexes built by mamluk beys for the benefit of Islam. The minaret of this mosque–madrasa is a notable departure from the Ottoman type and resembles more closely that of the Mosque of al-Ghuri. This was probably no conicidence, since the mosque was built after 'Ali Bey al-Kabir and Abu Dhahab had sought to restore the empire of the Mamluks. When they failed, Abu Dhahab professed great loyalty to the Ottoman sultan, an allegiance that is expressed in the mosque's plan (see Chapter 8).

At ground level there is a row of shops, a common source of income for the maintenance and upkeep of the building and its personnel. The plan of the mosque is very similar to that of Sinan Pasha at Bulaq: a covered portico with shallow domes surrounds the mosque on three sides; the interior is a large room whose dome is supported by a squinch arch over two corner windows. The ablutions area is separated from the mosque by a fine mashrabiya screen, and tiles decorate the tympanum over the doors.

The novel feature here is the incorporation of the tomb in the northeast corner where the founder and his sister are buried.

This is common Mamluk practice but it appears here in the Ottoman period for the first time. Abu Dhahab built the mosque when he was at the height of his power, and included a large endowment for teaching. When he died in Palestine in 1775 while attacking the governor of Acre in the service of the Ottoman sultan his body was brought back and buried in the tomb he had built for himself.

Khan al-Zarakisha (No. 351) 16th/10th century. To the east, with its attractive and harmonious arrangement of windows, lies this building whose name commemorates the embroiderers who worked in it.

11 ◦ Al-Azhar Square to Bab al-Futuh and Back

A. *Sharia al-Mu'izz li-Din Allah to Bab al-Futuh:*
Madrasa–Khanqah of Sultan al-Ashraf Barsbay **
Mosque–Sabil–Kuttab of Shaykh Mutahhar
Wikala of Gamal al-Din al-Dhahabi
Madrasa–Mausoleum of al-Salih Nagm al-Din Ayyub **
Sabil–Kuttab of Khusraw Pasha **
Madrasa of Sultan al-Zahir Baybars I *
Hospital, Madrasa, Mausoleum of Sultan al-Mansur
Qalawun ***
Qa'a of Muhibb al-Din al-Muwaqqi' *
Sabil of al-Nasir Muhammad *
Madrasa–Mausoleum of al-Nasir Muhammad **
Sabil–Kuttab of Isma'il Pasha *
Madrasa–Khanqah of Sultan Barquq **
Qasr Bashtak **
Madrasa of the Amir Mithqal **
Madrasa of al-Kamil Ayyub
Sabil–Kuttab of 'Abd al-Rahman Katkhuda **
Mosque of al-Aqmar ***
Bayt al-Sihaymi ***
Mosque–Sabil of Sulayman Agha al-Silahdar **
Mosque of Abu Bakr Muzhir **
Mosque of al-Hakim **
Bab al-Futuh, Bab al-Nasr, and the Northern Walls ***

B. *Bab al-Nasr to Sayyidna al-Husayn:*
Wikala of Sultan Qaytbay *
Wikala of the Amir Qawsun
Sabil and Wikala of Oda Bashi
Khanqah of Sultan Baybars al-Gashankir **
Madrasa–Mausoleum of the Amir Qarasunqur
Sabil–Kuttab and Wikala of Oda Bashi *
Mosque of Gamal al-Din al-Ustadar *
Mosque of Mahmud Muharram *

174

Mosque of Marzuq al-Ahmadi
*Musafirkhana Palace ***
*Madrasa–Mausoleum of Tatar al-Higaziya **
*Maq'ad of Mamay al-Sayfi **
*Mosque of Sayyidna al-Husayn **
*Sabil–Kuttab of Ahmad Pasha **

———————

See map 10

This area was the heart of Fatimid Cairo. It contains the highest and most varied concentration of medieval monuments in the city. The most logical way to see it perhaps is by walking up Sharia Mu'izz li-Din Allah (the Fatimid Qasaba or High Street) to Bab al-Futuh, along the north walls to Bab al-Nasr, and from there down Sharia al-Gamaliya to Maydan Sayyidna al-Husayn. Interesting monuments are also located on cross streets and alleys between these two north–south arteries. To be seen thoroughly the monuments listed in this chapter should be visited over several days. It is possible, however, to walk the combined routes in a long morning, with brief visits to main monuments, and still have a little time for shopping in the bazaar.

Muski and Khan al-Khalili: These two terms are used interchangeably by foreigners and Egyptians alike, but they are actually two different, adjoining bazaar areas. The Muski, properly speaking, lies astride the eastern part of the nineteenth-century city. Sharia al-Muski, also called Sharia Gawhar al-Qa'id, runs from 'Ataba Square to Sayyidna al-Husayn Square. The name comes from 'Izz al-Din Musk, one of Salah al-Din's followers.

Khan al-Khalili is a large bazaar bounded on the east by Sayyidna al-Husayn, on the west by Sharia Mu'izz li-Din Allah, and on the south by Sharia al-Muski. The original khan or caravansarai was built in 1382 by Sultan Barquq's master of the horse, the Amir Jarkas al-Khalili. You can still see vestiges of the Mamluk structure and early additions here and there. In particular, take a look around the tourist police post in the middle of the bazaar on the street leading from the western façade of the Mosque of al-Husayn. It is situated in a courtyard;

the rooms opening off it are occupied by sellers of old furniture, among other things. This is a classic khan, like al-Ghuri's wikala, but much more modest. In the bazaar street outside the courtyard look up to the stonework and the heavy iron grills through which merchants rooming in the khan could watch the traffic outside. This was the gate of the original khan. Opposite it is a domed gateway from Sultan al-Ghuri's time. A little further down this same street is a gate (Bab al-Badistan, no. 53), also from al-Ghuri's time (1511).

Historically, Khan al-Khalili has always been a resort of foreign merchants—Armenians, Jews, Persians, and non-Egyptian Arabs. In recent years, however, many of these merchants have moved away and its composition has changed. A considerable variety of souvenirs, antiques, and jewelry are offered for sale here. Except for gold and silver, which are sold by weight, bargaining is usually possible.

The famous Fishawi's teahouse, gathering-place of entertainers and intellectuals, just beside the al-Husayn Hotel, is sadly truncated today. Half of it has been removed to make way for a modern building erected in the name of civic improvement, but one can still have a cup of mint tea there while contemplating the passing scene.

The al-Husayn Hotel, on the south corner of the square, is a good place to stop for rest and refreshments. The fifth-floor roof restaurant provides beverages, brewed or bottled, and a meal, as well as an excellent view of the square and the domes and minarets southward over al-Azhar to the Citadel. Other authentic places for nourishing snacks in this immediate area are Dahan, a white restaurant with red lettering just west on Sharia al-Muski, which specializes in grilled meats (kufta and kebab), and the Egyptian Pancake (*fatir*) House where the cook puts on a wonderful show of stretching the pancake dough by twirling it in mid-air.

A. Sharia al-Mu'izz li-Din Allah to Bab al-Futuh

To get to Sharia al-Mu'izz li-Din Allah (the Qasaba) start at the green pedestrian overpass on Sharia al-Azhar, in front of the hyphenated complex of Sultan al-Ghuri, which dominates the south corners of the street.

Madrasa–Khanqah of Sultan al-Ashraf Barsbay ** (No. 175) 1425/828. This monument stands on the southwest corner of the intersection of Sharia al-Muski and Sharia Mu'izz li-Din Allah. It dominated the spice bazaar, where heaped mounds of herbs, roots, and spices still beckon to the buyer visually and aromatically. By turning the trade in certain spices into state monopolies Sultan Barsbay used the profits to subsidize much of his building and foreign campaigns. He conquered Cyprus in 1426 and forced the Lusignans—descendants of the Crusader kings of Jerusalem—to pay him tribute.

The monument is not well preserved but it is worth visiting. It is of the classic madrasa plan with attached mausoleum on the street side. The sabil–kuttab is next to the portal entrance at the southern end of the façade. In the long corridor that connects the main entrance with the courtyard on the left is an alcove faced with a mashrabiya screen. This hides the cistern wherein water for the sabil–kuttab was stored. The main inscription around the vaulted liwans inside is interesting because it is a rare example of a waqf (or endowment) deed carved in stone as a perpetual reminder to its overseers as to how the monies reserved for the maintenance and personnel of this building were to be spent. Of special note are the ceiling in the northwest liwan, partially restored, a rich tapestry of gold and blue; the inlaid minbar; the specially created room in front of the mausoleum for Quran readers; and the high and narrow tomb chamber, in which are buried Fatima Ashrafiya and Muhammad, wife and son of the sultan.

Mosque and Sabil–Kuttab of Shaykh Mutahhar (No. 40) 1744/1175. This building stands on the northwest corner of the intersection of Sharia al-Muski and Sharia Mu'izz li-Din Allah. The lunette of tiles over the door and the minaret over the entrance belong to the mosque, which was attached to the pre-existing sabil–kuttab built here by 'Abd al-Rahman Katkhuda. This lovely fountain–school is virtually identical with a twin whose main features are fully described further up the street.

Wikala of Gamal al-Din al-Dhahabi (No. 411) 1637/1047. One block north from the corner, i.e. from Shaykh Mutahhar, turn left into Sharia al-Maqasis for a look behind the façade of the Gold Street, as the main street is known at this point. The wikala is at the end of the street, a small building with a sabil-kuttab at the left end of the façade. It was built by the same gold merchant whose house is described in Chapter 10; its interest today lies in the fact that it is still a lively place of work, in which gold and silver jewelry continue to be produced.

A large metal-plated door (opposite the right end of the wikala's façade) leads into the courtyard of another wikala, and back onto the Qasaba. Turn left and proceed north. The small shops of the Goldsmiths' Bazaar with the glittering array of bangles, necklaces, and earrings gradually give way to the metal and aluminum pots and basins of the Coppersmiths' Bazaar (al-Nahhasin) from which at this point the street gets its popular name.

Madrasa–Mausoleum of al-Salih Nagm al-Din Ayyub **

(No. 38) 1242–50/641–48. The façade of this structure is hidden by the fronting stalls, but the minaret rising above them on the right provides a skyline landmark. Except for the façade and the minaret, not much of the building remains, but it is one of the more important monuments historically because it repre-sents a transition, both politically and architecturally, between those of the preceding Fatimid period and subsequent Mamluk complexes.

Al-Salih Nagm al-Din Ayyub, son of al-Malik al-Kamil, was the last of Salah al-Din's dynasty to rule Egypt. He was the husband of the famous Shagar al-Durr (see Chapter 8), who ruled the country with Aybak, the first of the Mamluk sultans, after al-Salih's death in 1249 while fighting the crusading Louis IX of France. His madrasa was the first to be built for all four Sunni legal schools or rites and his tomb was the first to be built within the city instead of in the necropolis. The monument thus marks the introduction of what became a basic Mamluk mau-soleum formula: tomb and theological school. Later this madrasa came to be more than just a center for worship and scholarship. Here the four chief religious justices or qadis heard cases referred to them from lower courts. Throughout much of the Mamluk period it was the supreme judicial tribune of the state. This was the center of the town—the courthouse square of Cairo.

*Madrasa–Mausoleum of al-Salih Ayyub and Sabil–Kuttab
of Khusraw Pasha*

The minaret is a rare survival from the Ayyubid period and displays the evolution of minaret forms from late Fatimid to early Mamluk (c.1340). It is composed of three stories: square, octagonal, and a fluted keel-shaped cap, known as a mabkhara or 'incense burner.' The minaret's decoration of blind-keel and open S-curving arches derives from the Fatimid period. The stalactite collar below the ribbed finial is new. The minaret stands above a richly decorated doorway. This decoration, and that of the façade to right and left—keel-arch panels with ribs and cusps, panels of stalactites, niches with shell-motif hoods, the shallow relieving arch over the joggled voussoirs of the door transom—stems from prototypes originating in the late Fatimid period (see the Mosque of al-Aqmar further along).

Walk in under the minaret and you find yourself in Harat al-Salihiya, an alley on the edge of the Khan al-Khalili bazaar. Turn left after a few paces and walk into a courtyard. This was the madrasa. One arched liwan still stands on the east (Nahhasin Street) side. A small mosque has recently been built into it. On the opposite side of the open yard one can distinguish remnants of another arch. This is all that remains of the original school, which was once two blocks of buildings, each containing two arched liwans: one on this (north) side and one on the other (south) side of Harat al-Salihiya.

Return to the Street of the Coppersmiths and turn right. The tomb of al-Salih is in the domed mausoleum attached to the north end of the façade in 1250 by Shagar al-Durr, the first instance in which a secular ruler's tomb had been given such prominence. The mausoleum contains an early example of a dome supported by a stalactite squinch system so characteristic of later Mamluk architecture, and a fine wooden cenotaph marking the tomb. There are two carved wooden Quranic friezes around the chamber. The chamber and mihrab were once enriched with slim marble panels, a new decorative style brought to Egypt from Syria by the Ayyubids. Another influence from Syria, which no longer survives, is that the hood of the mihrab was decorated with glass mosaics.

Sabil–Kuttab of Khusraw Pasha ** (No. 52) 1535/942. Khusraw Pasha, governor of Egypt from 1534 to 1536, was a great patron of architecture, but this is the only building he commissioned in Cairo. It protrudes from the wall of the Madrasa of al-Salih between the minaret and the mausoleum. In the Ottoman period the sabil–kuttab became the most frequently built commemorative foundation, because it was the most economical for a patron, yet dispensed the two mercies most highly praised by the Prophet Muhammad: water to the thirsty and religious instruction to the ignorant. As a building type it harks back to the free-standing fountain–school of Sultan Qaytbay (Chapter 7). This early Ottoman structure, in which both plan and decoration are appropriated from the Mamluk repertoire, and which is located on the old processional way of Cairo, also serves to point out some of the continuities in Cairene architecture.

Madrasa of Sultan al-Zahir Baybars I (al-Bunduqdari), al-Zahiriya * (No. 37) 1262–63/660–62.

Next to the tomb of al-Salih once stood the Madrasa of Sultan Baybars. Aybak, who married al-Salih Ayyub's widow Shagar al-Durr in 1250, was one of al-Salih's slaves and was the first Mamluk ruler, but the Mamluk empire really began with Baybars al-Bunduqdari (Baybars of the Crossbow), who ruled from 1260 to 1277. A great leader, organizer, and builder, he defeated the Mongols of Hulagu at 'Ayn Jalut (Goliath's Spring) in Palestine in 1260, after they had destroyed Baghdad in 1258, and carried on a series of successful and almost overwhelming campaigns against the Crusaders. His madrasa, the Zahiriya, was built on the site of the Hall of Tents and the Hall of the Lotus of the great Eastern Palace of the Fatimids, next to the tomb of his former master al-Salih Ayyub.

The Madrasa of Baybars existed until 1874, when it was destroyed in the building of the road from the Suq al-Nahhasin to Maydan Bayt al-Qadi. In 1882 the minaret fell. All that survives today is the block of stones that was once the lower part of the west corner. Over the windows on the south side are carved stone relieving arches, under which are two panthers carved in stone. Bay-bars means 'Lord Panther,' and the animal appears on several of his works. The bronze-plated door from this madrasa is now at the main entrance of the French Embassy in Cairo, on Sharia al-Giza.

Bayn al-Qasrayn (see page xii). This area on the Qasaba, the central avenue of Fatimid and medieval Cairo, was known as Bayn al-Qasrayn, 'between the two palaces.' It was a ceremonial ground between the great Eastern Palace and the lesser Western Palace of the Fatimid khalifs. Of these Fatimid palaces, only richly carved remnants of woodwork on display in the Islamic Museum survive, but Figure 2 gives one an idea of their relation to buildings now standing. Bayn al-Qasrayn was the center of al-Qahira, the court city founded by the Fatimids. Its importance as a ceremonial way persisted into medieval times— the variety of monuments that are still clustered upon it show that it was a favorite building site for those who held power. It is in this area of Cairo that Naguib Mahfouz, the 1988 Nobel prizewinner, set the first volume of his 1957 *Cairo Trilogy*. In Arabic it is called *Bayn al-Qasrayn*; in English it is available as *Palace Walk*.

Hospital, Madrasa, and Mausoleum of Sultan al-Mansur Qalawun *** (No. 43) 1284–85/683–84. Sultan al-Mansur Qalawun (the last name means 'duck') was a Tatar or Mongol from the Qipjaq region of the lower Volga, which was ruled by the Golden Horde. Al-Salih Ayyub was the first importer of slaves from this region, and he made them his bodyguards or mamluks (literally, 'chattels'). Since they were quartered at his river citadel on the Island of Roda in the Nile, the name Bahri (or 'riverine') was applied to them. Qalawun, one of al-Salih's mamluks became sultan in 1279 and founded a dynasty that ruled for almost a century. He died at the age of seventy while en route to attack the Crusader fortress of Acre in 1290. His complex of buildings in the Bayn al-Qasrayn provide the earliest monumental examples of the new styles and techniques brought to Egypt from Syria, and dramatically illustrate what is to become the hallmark of Mamluk architecture: imposing scale and profusion of ornament.

   The Hospital. Opposite the Sabil of Khusraw is a gateway leading to the maristan or hospital of Qalawun. Go through the gate and down the wide, tree-shaded walk. At the end is a clinic for eye diseases that occupies the site of the original hospital and madhouse. The hospital was built on the cruciform plan, with four central liwans or bays and numerous adjoining chambers and halls. The liwans were equipped to handle specific disorders: one each for fevers, eye diseases, surgery, and dysentery. There was a separate hall for women. Three high-arched liwans remain; the carved stucco work around the windows of the eastern liwan is worthy of attention. There has been a hospital on this site ever since the time of Qalawun. Open to all, the institution founded by him was one of the wonders of the age: it was staffed to treat every known illness and had every convenience then known, including musicians and story-tellers to entertain the patients.

The Madrasa. Return to the main street and turn left, or north. The façade on the left is that of Qalawun's madrasa. At the corner, the building line retreats from the street and turns left into the main entrance of the complex. The corridor into which the entrance opens is now blocked at the rear, but originally it was the entrance to the maristan. It runs between the madrasa on the left and the mausoleum on the right. The main door, covered with bronze polygons, is an early example of the geometric patterns preferred by the Mamluks. The beamed and coffered ceiling of the passage has suffered over time but still bears traces of former beauty.

The plan of the madrasa is that of a courtyard with a liwan at either end. The sanctuary liwan, at the eastern end, is strongly reminiscent of a north Syrian basilican church, with three aisles, classical columns, and a clerestory of double-tiered arches. The stucco carving is partly original and partly restoration. The mihrab, at the far end of this liwan, has a hood decorated with glass mosaics, a feature also imported from Syria, strong in Byzantine influences.

The Mausoleum. From the main corridor one enters, on the right, the vestibule court or atrium of Qalawun's mausoleum. Above the entrance is a handsomely carved stucco arch; below this is a doorway of mashrabiya. This is an early example of a wood shaping and joining technique that has beautified many Middle Eastern buildings.

The tomb chamber, with its plan of an octagon in a square and its arches on square piers and ancient red granite columns, is reminiscent of the Dome of the Rock in Jerusalem. One is at once struck by the height of the chamber and almost overwhelmed by the profusion and variety of the ornament: marble strips on the

walls, panels of polychrome stone inlay in geometric patterns
(with the name Muhammad in square kufic), capitals and inscriptions rich with gilding, a mashrabiya screen around the cenotaph,
carved stucco around the arches, painted decorations on the
square supports of the arches, stained glass windows, and a
painted, coffered ceiling. Against the qibla is the mihrab, which
exemplifies a new style. Its hood is entirely decorated with
polychrome marble and its niche is divided into registers of mosaic
inlay and blind arcading. The ornamental profusion, rich hues
and shadowy stillness imparts an impression as near as possible
to what the original grandeur of Mamluk architecture must have
conveyed. Sultan Qalawun and his son Sultan al-Nasir
Muhammad are buried under the tabut or cenotaph in the center.

One more thing to notice while in the mausoleum is that the
eastern or qibla wall is of varying thickness. This is apparent in
the difference in depth of the window embrasures on the left
and right. This allowed the façade to be aligned with the street,
while the interior orientation was angled so as to conform with
the direction of Mecca.

Back on the street, note the doorway with its interlacing
strapwork of polychrome masonry, or ablaq, a design imported
from Syria. Also look at the façade. Note the carved stair-step
crenelations of the parapet; the dramatic band of thuluth
inscription, the monumental script favored by the Mamluks;
and its division into arched bays with triple double-tiered
windows. This arrangement of the façade marks a new emphasis on vertical rather than horizontal space. Foreign influences
are also present in the minaret. The square bottom and middle
stories recall the shape of Syrian minarets, but the interlacing
arcades filled with carved stucco forming a network around the
top story (restored in 1303 after the great earthquake) recall
Spanish and North African wall decoration and were perhaps
the work of craftsmen from Andalusia or Morocco. During the
Muhammad 'Ali period, the entire exterior of the mausoleum
was painted in a red and white checkerboard pattern, now
fortunately faded; although traces are visible on the rear or
west side of the minaret as can be seen from the courtyard of the
adjoining Madrasa of al-Nasir Muhammad.

Qalawun's complex has a gothic cast in its outside façade
and in its interior sumptuousness that was probably no acci-

dent, since he was familiar with Crusader churches of Syria, and many artisans of that region displaced by war were attracted to Cairo by the patronage of the new ruling elite. The whole complex, with its three components, was built in thirteen months, from June 1284 to August 1285, and visitors continue to agree with al-Maqrizi's comment of the fifteenth century: "When a spectator contemplates this huge edifice and hears it was built in such a short space of time he often will not believe it."

This is indeed a worthy place of interment for a ruler whose inscription on the façade, in part, reads:

This noble dome, this magnificent college, and blessed hospital was ordered by our Lord and Master, the August Sultan al-Malik al-Mansur, the Wise, Just, God-assisted, Victorious, Champion of the Faith, Conqueror, Sword of the World and True Religion . . . Lord of Kings and of Sultans, the Sultan of the Length and Breadth of the Earth . . . King of the Two Continents and the Two Seas, King of Kings of Arabs and Non-Arabs, the Guardian of the Two Qiblas, the Servant of the Two Sanctuaries, Qalawun al-Salihi, the Associate of the Commander of the Believers—may God prolong his glory, glorify his victories, elevate his beacon, and double his power—the incomparable among contemporary kings, the treasure of those destitute of resources, he who renders justice to the oppressed against the oppressor. . . . The beginning of all this took place in 1284 and its ending in 1285.

Qa'a of Muhibb al-Din al-Muwaqqi' * (No. 50) 1350/751. This house was restored and used as a residence by 'Uthman Katkhuda, chief amir in Cairo from 1730 to 1736 and the father of 'Abd al-Rahman Katkhuda. It was restored again by the Comité in 1911. The house is about halfway along the left-hand side of Sharia Bayt al-Qadi, the street that debouches into Bayn al-Qasrayn opposite the Mausoleum of Qalawun. The doorway is that of an ordinary dwelling. The only clue to its location is the little green and white plaque marking Islamic monuments. The qa'a or main reception hall, which is all that remains of the palace, is an outstanding example of Mamluk domestic architecture on a grand scale.

It is an unexpected sight—a long, narrow room that is about sixteen meters high. This was a reception room and diwan, where guests sat in the raised portion of the south end. The woodwork is partly original and partly sixteenth-century addition, i.e. the consoles that replace the original, larger arches. There was once a marble wainscoting around the room but it is gone. The fountain in the floor is of a later period.

There is about this place a feeling of lonely anachronism. It is as though one has stumbled suddenly through a bricked-up doorway and found oneself in a room that has been hidden and unsuspected for centuries. Its decorations still look fresh and one can imagine it being put to use tomorrow. One even expects the old Katkhuda himself to come gliding in with an invitation to coffee. This is a good place to rest a few minutes and look at your surroundings.

See if it is possible to get up to the roof on the way out. Aside from a view of the quarter, there is an example of a malqaf, or ventilator, which was once a standard feature of Cairene houses. It is a rectilinear airscoop, looking like the head of a stairway and designed to capture the cooling wind from the north. It does not rotate because other winds are unwelcome. The design is pharaonic.

Sabil of al-Nasir Muhammad ibn Qalawun * (No. 561) 1326/726. Located on the northern corner of the façade of the Madrasa of Qalawun, this little fountain, in very poor condition, is the earliest example of an architectural form given to the free distribution of water in Cairo. The noteworthy feature is the band of faience mosaic at the base of the little cupola. This type of tile decoration, usually associated with Persia, is rare in Cairo but not unique at this period.

Madrasa and Mausoleum of al-Nasir Muhammad ** (No. 44) 1296–1304/695–703. Sultan al-Nasir ('the Victorious') Muhammad was one of Qalawun's five sons. He ruled for a total of forty-two years in three different stretches from 1293 to 1341. Variously described as despotic, enlightened, cruel, shrewd, deceitful, suspicious, tasteful, and vengeful, he was a man of courage and intellect and his reign marked the high point of Mamluk culture and Islamic civilization in Egypt. Al-Nasir was

Minaret of the Madrasa of al-Nasir Muhammad (detail)

an active builder who also encouraged his amirs to build, and his reign is credited with some thirty surviving mosques, the aqueduct from the Nile to the Citadel, and a canal from the Nile to Khanqah, twenty kilometers north of Cairo.

The complex was begun in 1296 by al-'Adil Kitbugha, an interim sultan, and finished by al-Nasir, during his second reign. The monument was restored in 1985–86 by the German Archaeological Insitute. The Gothic doorway comes from a Crusader church at Acre, which was captured by al-Nasir's older brother and predecessor, al-Ashraf Khalil, in 1291 (see Chapter 8). The minaret is covered with an exceptionally fine, closely-patterned, carved stucco surface, probably North African workmanship. It was built at about the time Qalawun's nearby minaret was restored. The dome fell in 1870 and has not been replaced. Only the zone of transition next to the minaret remains.

The general plan is the same as that of Qalawun's. The madrasa lies on the left (south) and the mausoleum on the right as you enter. The madrasa was the first cruciform madrasa in Cairo and has four liwans or vaulted halls around the same court, one for each of the schools of Sunni jurisprudence: Shafi'i, Maliki, Hanbali, and Hanafi. In the eastern one there is a fine stucco mihrab. Its style is derived from Mongol Iran, evidence of the better relations that existed between the two courts in the early fourteenth century. The mausoleum is locked. Al-Nasir Muhammad's favorite son Anuk and mother Bint Suqbay are buried here. Al-Nasir himself lies next door in the mausoleum built by his father.

Sabil–Kuttab of Isma'il Pasha * (No. 402) 1828/1244. Opposite the Madrasa of al-Nasir, this fountain commemorates the youngest of Muhammad 'Ali's three sons by his first wife. The style of this one-story sabil is derived from imperial fountains of Istanbul. Above the windows is the tughra or official seal of the Ottoman sultan Mahmud II. The rounded bow front, the iron grills over the windows, and the elaborately carved wooden roofing with its sunburst motif are characteristic of the exuberantly baroque style of the Muhammad 'Ali dynasty. The kuttab is in the rooms to either side of the sabil.

Sabil of Isma'il Pasha

Madrasa–Khanqah of Sultan Barquq ** (No. 178) 1384–86/
786–88. This building stands beside the Madrasa of al-Nasir.
Barquq was the first Circassian Mamluk sultan. The
Circassians, from the Caucasus, were subjects of the Tatar
Golden Horde and were first imported to Egypt as slave troops
by Qalawun in the thirteenth century. In Cairo these troops
were lodged in the Citadel, from which they were known as
Burgi ('tower') Mamluks. Barquq established their dominance
in the Mamluk government in 1382, when he seized power
through a series of intrigues and assassinations. Although his
reign was necessarily full of action in order to maintain his
throne against fractious Mamluk amirs and governors in Syria,
it contributed little to Egypt's glory.

The Burgi or Circassian Mamluks bring about a racial and
political change in the mamluk cadre, but architecturally a real
change in plan or style is not evident until the mid-fifteenth
century. Sultan Barquq consolidated his social position by
marrying the widow of the Bahri sultan Sha'ban, and the style
of his complex, as those of the late Bahri period, is dominated
by the grandeur of the mosque–madrasa of Sultan Hasan.

This structure was built to contain a khanqah and a madrasa,
and the monumental inscription across the façade names
Jarkas al-Khalili as the superintendent in charge of construction; it is also known that Ahmad ibn al-Tuluni was the court
surveyor who acted as architect. It was built a century later
than Qalawun's complex but the continuity in styles is striking.
Qalawun's complex set the monumental architectural style
that was continued throughout the Bahri and early Burgi
periods. Characteristic of this style is the counterbalancing and
contrast of massive forms: the horizontal façade, whose breadth
is given additional emphasis by its division into tall, shallow
recesses; the semi-spherical canopy of the dome; and the vertical thrust of the minaret.

The high, rectangular, slightly offset entrance is next to al-
Nasir's madrasa. Under a panel of black and white marble one
enters through bronze-plated doors whose geometric star patterns are inlaid with silver. Barquq's name (meaning 'plum' in
Arabic) is visible on the raised boss of the central star. Inside,
a vaulted, bending passage leads to an open court, which is
paved with marble mosaic and which features large porphyry

Façades of Qalawun and Barquq

disks, presumably sawn from classical columns. The plan is that of a cruciform madrasa. Four doors set in the angles led upstairs to the accommodations and facilities for the sixty sufi and 125 student inmates. These doors exhibit a new form of decoration. Instead of an overall covering, the main design is a central medallion, with four quarter circles in the corners. This provides a graceful pattern, but one that needs less bronze. The qibla or sanctuary liwan is to the right of the courtyard entrance. It was used for the Hanafi school of law. The iwan is divided into three aisles by lateral arches, an arrangement reminiscent of the Madrasa of Qalawun next door. Its beautiful ceiling, which was restored in this century, is supported by four columns of porphyry. The ancient Egyptians and the Romans maintained porphyry quarries in the hills above Safaga on the Red Sea coast, and it is a tribute to their engineering skill that they could move such large pieces of it overland through some of the most forbidding territory in Egypt. These particular columns are pharaonic. Enameled mosque lamps, examples of which are to be seen in the Islamic Museum, were once suspended from the chains. The minbar was presented by Sultan Gaqmaq in 1440.

Entrance doors of the Madrasa of Barquq

One enters the great domed tomb chamber by the courtyard door to the left of the qibla iwan. The small vestibule chamber was used for Quran recitations. The decorative ensemble of the tomb chamber is splendid. Look at the marble floor, the bands of inscription, the gilt arabesque stalactites of the transition zone, and the stained glass windows, all of which were renewed by the Comité. Fatima, one of Barquq's daughters, is buried here. The sultan and other members of his family are buried in the complex in the northern cemetery described in Chapter 13. The rich gilding of the stalactite pendentives supporting the dome was renewed in the early twentieth century.

Qasr Bashtak ** (No. 34) 1334–39/735–740. Just past Barquq's complex on the opposite side of the street are the remains of the palace of the Amir Bashtak. It is recognizable by the projecting mashrabiya windows in an otherwise plain façade. At ground level there are openings for shops. The rents added to the amir's income. They also provide an example of cultural continuity from Roman precedents. The entrance is the second door off the Darb al-Qirmiz, the alley that begins at the north corner of the façade. In small roundels to either side above the entrance are the diamond-shaped napkin blazons of the jamdar, the sultan's master of the robes, an exalted court position that Bashtak held. Inside, pass through a courtyard, up the stairs and into a great qa'a or reception hall. This was the main reception hall of the palace. The mashrabiya screens along the galleries on the north and south sides of the room permitted the unseen ladies of the house to look down upon and enjoy the festivities below. Through the lattice windows at the end of the hall you can look out and see the life in the streets below. High in the walls of the main hall are stuccoed windows with colored glass. The blazon of the jamdar is obvious. The coffered wooden ceiling is typical of the early Bahri period. A fountain, of inlaid polychrome-marble geometric shapes, once stood in the center of the room. (A beautiful fountain from this period is on display in the Museum of Islamic Art.) By comparing the decoration of this hall with that of the mausoleum of Sultan Qalawun one notes that there is great similarity between the decoration used for secular and for religious architecture. It is easy to imagine how grand this room must have been when one passed through the latticed screens that originally spanned the arches—the slots in the stone to which the screens were fixed are still visible—and entered the paved inner court, with the fountain playing as musicians and dancing girls, in rich fabrics and glittering jewelry, prepared to entertain the guests.

The Amir Bashtak, one of the most powerful amirs of his time, was married to a daughter of al-Nasir Muhammad. His palace, built on the site of earlier structures, originally stood five stories high and had running water on all floors. This great hall gives some idea of the scale of the original building, which remains today a rare example of fourteenth-century Islamic medieval domestic architecture, and a point of origin for subsequent domestic arrangements of the sixteenth, seventeenth, and eighteenth centuries, many examples of which are still standing. The palace was restored in 1983 by the German Archaeological Institute as one of a cluster of monuments revived in this immediate angle formed by the Darb al-Qirmiz and Sharia Mu'izz li-Din Allah.

Tomb of Shaykh Sinan (No. 41) 1585/994. On leaving Bashtak's palace follow the alley north, turning right at the small tomb of this holy man, part of the restoration program of the German Archaeological Institute.

Madrasa of the Amir Mithqal ** (No. 45) 1361–63/763. This is located further along on the right side of the alley. Sabiq al-Din Mithqal al-Anuki, an Abyssinian, was chief of the eunuchs of the royal palace in charge of rearing the young mamluks, a post to which he was appointed by Sultan Sha'ban in 1363 and kept until his death in 1374. This structure, established to teach the Shafi'i rite and built at the high point of his career on part of the original site of the eastern Fatimid palace in the center of Mamluk Cairo, speaks for Mithqal's importance. It is unusual for being suspended over an alley, and is thus a 'hanging madrasa'—the alley leads to Maydan Bayt al-Qadi. On the ground floor are storerooms.

The building was first restored by the Comité in 1913–16, and again by the German Archaeological Institute in 1973–76. Of the interior, apart from its good condition, the most unusual feature is the mashrabiya facings of the upper parts of the lateral liwans and at the sides of the northwest liwan. Behind them were the rooms for students and professors, five in all. The mihrab in grey, red, and white marble with turquoise accents is very attractive. The stained glass windows and marble panels on the floor make up the other decorative features.

Madrasa of al-Kamil Ayyub (No. 428) 1229/626. Back on the Qasaba, directly opposite the Qasr Bashtak on the west side of the street, lies this Ayyubid fragment, part of a liwan of a madrasa built by Sultan al-Kamil, the nephew of Salah al-Din. It was established to train scholars in the traditions of the Prophet and during the thirteenth and fourteenth centuries was the most respected center for this study in Egypt. After the famine of 1403–04 it suffered a severe decrease in revenues and entered a prolonged decline. Today it is interesting primarily because relics of the Ayyubid period are so few. The doorway and bank of mashrabiya windows belong to an Ottoman period restoration of 1752, as does the mosque through which one walks. Turn left in the ablutions courtyard, then right into the vacant lot beyond. From here the arched vault of the liwan is visible to the right.

Sabil–Kuttab of 'Abd al-Rahman Katkhuda ** (No. 21) 1744/1157. This amir, a senior officer of the powerful Qazdughli regiment of Mamluks, was noted for his high style of living and his liberal patronage of the arts. He restored and built more than thirty-three monuments around the city. This building occupies the slim point of a triangular block that separates the main street into two branches, and fully exploits the advantages of its situation at an important street junction.

The joggled voussoirs around the arch of the window, the polychrome mosaic patterns in the arch spandrels, the engaged corner columns, and the stalactite cornice are derived from Mamluk architectural precedents. However, the style of this sabil reveals Ottoman influences that are quite new to Cairo at this time—for example in the simulated joggling pattern of the stone façade and in the carved area, between the arches, of very realistic flowers: peonies, asters, and chrysanthemums. These floral forms were brought by the Mongols from China, and became particularly popular in the art of Turkey in the sixteenth and seventeenth centuries.

Sabil–Kuttab of 'Abd al-Rahman Katkhuda

One may gain access to the monument by inquiring for the custodian at the Qasr Bashtak. The interior of the sabil is faced with tiles imported from Syria, among which the representation of the Ka'ba at Mecca in the northwest corner is interesting. From the porch of the Quran school above, one gets a good view of the Bayn al-Qasrayn looking south.

Mosque of al-Aqmar *** (No. 33) 1125/519. Facing the Sabil–Kuttab of 'Abd al-Rahman, take the left-hand street and continue north. The mosque, which will be on your right, was originally sited at the northeast corner of the great eastern Fatimid palace. The Fatimids were Isma'ilis, a sect of the Shi'a. They believed that the true leadership of the community passed from Muhammad to 'Ali (his son-in-law), to Hasan and Husayn (his grandsons), and then to the descendants of al-Husayn through his son 'Ali Zayn al-'Abidin. With the death of the sixth Imam, Ja'far al-Sadiq in 765/148, there was a split in the Shi'i community. Those who followed the eldest son Isma'il became the Isma'ilis or Seveners; those who followed his younger brother and his descendants became the Twelvers. Today, the spiritual head of the Isma'ilis is the Aga Khan.

Al-Aqmar, 'the moonlit,' was built by Ma'mun al-Bata'ihi, grand wazir to the khalif al-Amir from 1121–25, during a time of great political and spiritual crisis for the Fatimid regime. It is one of the seminal monuments in Cairo's architectural history. It was the first mosque in Cairo whose entrance is not on an axis with the qibla wall, i.e. the façade follows the alignment of the street, while the qibla wall is oriented toward Mecca. This is thus the first example in Cairo of a ground plan being adjusted to an existing urban street plan, a phenomenon that over the ensuing centuries was to become increasingly common and complex.

It was also the first mosque in Cairo to have a decorated stone façade. A wing to the right of the entrance salient, balancing that to the left, has been destroyed by later buildings. The ribbed shell hood of the entrance salient, with its pierced medallion, appears here for the first time, and was the prototype of all the later cusped, ribbed, blind, keel-arch decoration that is still in vogue on Cairo's buildings and in the ornament of Egyptian buildings elsewhere. The panels of stalactites, the

Detail of the façade of al-Aqmar

shell-topped niches, appear for the first time. The historic
inscription below the cornice is also a first. It states, in summary, that "its construction was ordered by the servant of our
lord and master Imam al-Amir bi-ahkam Allah, son of Imam al-
Musta'li . . . the most illustrious lord al-Ma'mun, commander of
the armies, sword of Islam, helper of the imam, surety of the
judges of the Muslims, and guide to the propagandists of the
believers . . . in the year 519 [1125]." The decoration of the
façade is charged with an iconographic composition that is rare
and unusual in Islamic buildings. It is explicitly Shi'i in its
content. The name 'Ali, through whom Shi'i rulers claim descent, coupled with that of Muhammad, figures prominently in
several places. The various decorative panels on the left wing,
such as the star below the mosque lamp (upper left), the
representation of a closed door where Qurans are kept (upper
right), and the herb growing out of the pot (lower left), taken
together can be understood to be a visual allusion to
Muhammad's words at the Farewell pilgrimage: "I leave to you
two precious legacies, the Book of God and my posterity, the
members of my family." Furthermore, the major and minor
niches on the façade can be grouped into numerical combina-

tions that have Shi'i meanings, such as three for 'Ali, Hasan, and Husayn; five for Muhammad, Fatima, 'Ali, Hasan, and Husayn—the People of the Cloak; and seven for the Isma'ili Imams.

The level of the street over the centuries has risen dramatically, which is why one must descend stairs in order to enter the building. The plan is that of a small congregational mosque. The interior is original and bands of Quranic verse in Kufic script on an arabesque background still survive around the keel arches of the courtyard. Restorations to the mosque—the mihrab, minbar, ablutions area—were made by the Amir Yalbugha al-Salami, the dawadar to Sultan Barquq, in 1393. The stump of the minaret is later. Now, six hundred year afterward, the mosque is being given a total and inventive restoration by the Bohras, an Ismai'li Shi'i sect from India, who claim spiritual descent from the Fatimid Imams. One of the few Fatimid structures to have survived the centuries more or less intact, this mosque has been 'spruced up' by the Bohras, who have added new inscriptions and new windows to the sanctuary area.

Bayt al-Sihaymi ∗∗∗ (No. 339) 1648 and 1796/1058 and 1121. One block up from al-Aqmar, turn right into a street called Darb al-Asfur. Immediately on your left is the doorway that leads into the *House of Mustafa Ga'far* (No. 471) 1713, a trader in coffee at the Wikala Dhu al-Fiqar. Today the premises are being used to instruct neighborhood girls in sewing. Further along, on the left hand, is the Bayt al-Sihaymi, perhaps the best, certainly the most charming, example of an old Cairo house—well worth a visit. It is also a place in which to sit down and rest, and take in the living arrangements, both gracious and practical, of the medieval Islamic world.

The doorway, in a plain and solid façade, except for the overhanging second-story mashrabiya windows, is marked only by its monument number. The entrance passage, turning to provide an indirect barrier betwen the public and private worlds of the owner, leads into a delightful courtyard, of shrubs, birds, and a central fountain. For an appreciation of the Islamic medieval house there are two things that are helpful to keep in mind. The first is the strict division between male and female spaces, between the salamlik ('greeting') or public areas and the

Courtyard with Maq'ad of Bayt al-Sihaymi

haramlik ('forbidden') or private areas of the house. The second point is that these houses were skillfully adapted to climatic conditions: space was used according to climatic rather than utilitarian purposes, and in them the movement tended to be from day to night, from summer to winter. Living spaces often had no specific functional designations.

The courtyard is not only a place of beauty and surcease, but served the house as light source and as temperature regulator. During the evening, cold air was trapped within its confines; during the day this air was dispersed into adjoining rooms and spaces.

The ground floor and open spaces belonged to the men. The large benched area at the far end of the courtyard was the tahtabush, an area where the owner of the house, in the cool of the morning, could transact business affairs or meet with acquaintances; or, when no outsider was about, the women of the house could gather. The second story loggia, the maq'ad, above the courtyard entrance, was where the owner could relax in the evening with friends. The maq'ad always faced north to catch the prevailing breezes. The tahtabush and the maq'ad reflect an increasing openness to light and air, which the Ottomans introduced to the basic Mamluk house plan. The arched openings below the maq'ad are storerooms for extra household supplies. On more formal occasions, or in the winter, the owner entertained in the qa'a, which one approaches through a door at the northwest corner of the courtyard. The small atrium just in front of it was where, upon the benches around the walls, special readers sat and recited the Quran. The qa'a itself, though shorn of its splendid furnishings and empty of its former life, is still grand. The central area contains a fountain whose polychrome inlay is typical of the period both for secular and religious usage. Above, the narrow domed opening served more as an escape for hot air than for illumination. The floor on either side is raised and it was here upon richly woven textiles and against thick bolsters that the men reclined, smoking their pipes, eating the food that was brought in, or watching the entertainment by musicians and dancers around the splashing fountain. High ceilings, thick walls, marble surfaces, and the flow of air from the courtyard kept the room cool in summer; in winter, it was heated by brass braziers aglow with charcoal.

A flight of stairs just in front of the atrium leads to the private quarters, the women's areas. First one sees the small rooms of the bath area. It was only the wealthy houses that had their own baths, for one of the acceptable excursions of secluded ladies was to the baths, where they could meet and gossip with other women. When one enters the main reception room of the harim, one is immediately struck both by the richness and the variety of the surface decoration (marble floors and dadoes, wood lattice, stained glass, painted ceilings) and by its similarity with the decoration of religious buildings. The delicate wood lattice of the main window is not only decorative, but also practical in subduing the sun's glare and filtering out the dust from the atmosphere. Through this lace-like barrier, which 'revealed without revealing,' the ladies could look down into the courtyard and across to the maq'ad.

On the way from the qa'a of the harim to the private apartments, one passes underneath the malqaf, the wind scoop. Facing north, to get the desirable prevailing breezes, it channeled the cold night air into the house, from whence it circulated throughout the rooms. Below the malqaf is an oratory where the ladies said their prayers, since women in Islam are not required to go to the mosque to worship.

In the gardens in the back of the house there is a well, a flour mill, and storage areas, which served the needs of the large extended family—owners and servants—who lived here. This outdoor area belonged to the women. It is also from here that the carving of the mashrabiya window can best be studied at close hand.

Mosque and Sabil of Sulayman Agha al-Silahdar ** (No. 382) 1839/1255. This monument is on the left side of the Qasaba just north of, and visible from, al-Aqmar. Its patron Sulayman the Armorer, at one time in charge of the arsenal during the reign of Muhammad 'Ali Pasha, endowed other buildings around the city. This mosque deserves greater study as a rare and fine example of a monument dating from the reign of Muhammad 'Ali, and as a mixture of indigenous and imported styles. The innovative feature is the sense of movement, derived from European baroque and rococo forms, imported via Istanbul to Cairo, which gives the basically Mamluk façade new life. The rhythm of the windows, from upper right to lower left, continuing into the rounded form of the sabil, is the most obvious expression of this new surface plasticity. Other examples are in the upward slanting wooden eaves, the growing plant forms where sabil and mosque meet, the undulating fronds above the windows, and the patterns of the finely cast grills. The northern end of the façade is set above street-level shops.

Entrance can be achieved either by entering the gate next to the sabil and following the street around to the back, or by the main door at the northern end of the façade. The plan inside is also a blend of Ottoman and Cairene styles. The small forecourt with shallow domed arcades is Ottoman, but the roof with the malqaf (the wind-scoop facing north) over it is Mamluk, as is also the plan of the sanctuary, which is divided into three aisles by four central columns. A railed balustrade over the entrance was for the use of either the agha or his women. The only notable feature of the inside decoration is the large frond spray over the mihrab. The mosque is one level up. At ground level behind the lowest tier of windows is the kuttab, now being used as a storeroom by the Ministry of Education.

Mosque of Abu Bakr Muzhir ** (No. 49) 1479–80/884. Follow the street that leads to the back of the Mosque of Sulayman. It turns left and left again about a block further on.

The Mosque of Abu Bakr, the superintendent of the chancery in the reign of Sultan Qaytbay, is an excellent example of late Burgi Mamluk architecture, one of the few from this period in this part of the city. It is also an admirable example of the architect's ability to make a regular and symmetrical plan out of an inauspicious plot of ground. Although the building is rich in decoration it does not have a stone dating inscription; however, Abu Bakr's blazon of office, the penbox, appears in the wooden inlay on the minbar and on the doors, and the date is on the finial of the minbar.

The main door is very handsome with its bronze facing and geometric pattern based on a twenty-sided star surrounded by ten ten-sided stars. If it is closed, continue around the mosque to the side entrance, just next to the sabil–kuttab. After entering, turn right and climb the stairs (left and down leads to a small oratory and the ablutions area). At the top, on the left, notice the very fine wooden door. Prayer mats were stored in this alcove.

Interesting points in this mosque are the loggia box in the northwest liwan, presumably for the amir or for Quran readers; the triple arcade on two columns of the main liwans; and the red paste and black bitumen arabesque decoration over the windows in the sanctuary. In the arch of the one furthest left there is a signature: "Made by 'Abd al-Qadir al-Naqqash ['the Engraver']". A similar signature by the same engraver appears in the mihrab of the complex of the Amir Qajmas al-Ishaqi (see Chapter 6).

Mosque of al-Hakim ** (No. 15) 990–1013/380–403. Two blocks north of the Mosque of al-Aqmar the steet widens out into a market area (lemons and onions especially), and on the right rise the imposing wall and minaret of al-Hakim's Mosque.

The Fatimid imam al-Hakim bi-Amr Allah (literally: 'Ruler by God's Command') was famous for his eccentricities and arbitrary edicts. He enforced the confinement of women, for instance, by forbidding cobblers to make shoes for them. He forbade the eating of mulukhiya (Jew's mallow), even then an Egyptian favorite, and once had all the honey in Cairo tipped into the Nile. He was given to prowling about the city at night (as was Harun al-Rashid in Baghdad), to see whether his commands were being obeyed. He disappeared one night while riding his donkey in the Muqattam Hills, and was apparently murdered. This was shortly after he had let himself be proclaimed divine. One of his followers, a man named Darazi, fled to Syria where he preached the divinity of al-Hakim and gave his own name to the Druze sect.

Begun by al-Hakim's father al-'Aziz, the structure was an arcaded congregational mosque built outside the original northern wall of the Fatimid court city. It covers about the same area as Ibn Tulun's mosque, is similarly built of brick and plaster, and makes use of pier supports for the ceiling. But new influences from North Africa, where the Fatimids originated, are also apparent: the monumental main entrance with its projecting stone porch on the façade, and the basilican disposition of the main aisle of the sanctuary, which is higher and wider than the lateral aisles.

Over the centuries the building has been used variously as a prison for Crusader captives, as a stable (by Salah al-Din), as a warehouse and fortress (by Napoleon Bonaparte), as a repository for Islamic art (1890), as a boy's school (in the Nasser period), and from time to time as a mosque. The interior, once in a ruinous state, was rebuilt in 1981 by the Bohras, an Isma'ili Shi'i sect based in India. The gleaming marble and shining gilt of the mihrab, while impressive, have little to do with the mosque's original facings or decorations. Remnants of the original decorations remain, however, on the wooden tie-beams, in the stucco carving in the clerestory, and in the Quranic inscriptions. To the right of the main mihrab is a smaller niche faced with polychrome marble, which was added by the merchant 'Umar Makram in 1808.

The most outstanding features of the mosque are the minarets at either end of the façade. Their massive, trapezoidal bases, which project into the street, were added for strengthening soon after the mosque was built. In the great earthquake of 1303, the minarets were damaged. They were restored by Baybars II al-Gashankir, to whom the rubble filling of the casings and the mabkhara finials are due. Enter the northern one and from the staircase that spirals around the free-standing minaret observe the beautiful bands of original Fatimid decoration and admire these masterpieces of stonework.

Bab al-Futuh, Bab al-Nasr, and the Northern Walls ***1087/ 480. The fortifications of the northern Fatimid city run along the northern side of the Mosque of al-Hakim. They were ordered by the Armenian dictator, Badr al-Gamali al-Guyushi, to replace the original sun-dried brick wall of Gawhar, and are the work of Armenian architects and masons imported from northern Mesopotamia. These two gates and the intervening stretch of wall between them constitute one of the most monumental ensembles in Cairo. Great masterpieces of Islamic military architecture, they are important as rare examples of works built before the Crusades.

The wall should be seen from both inside and outside to appreciate fully the skill of the masons and engineers who built it. It is best to enter at Bab al-Futuh, where the custodian is to be found. From there one can walk along the top of the wall to

Bab al-Nasr, return to Bab al-Futuh inside the wall, and then
walk back to Bab at-Nasr outside the wall. This is altogether
about six hundred meters. It is worth it. However, if one wants
a shorter sampling, proceed along the top of the wall until the
first shallow rise beyond the minaret of al-Hakim. Immediately
to the right are stairs that descend to the inside level. From
there walk back to the main entry.

Bab al-Futuh, 'Gate of Conquests,' is at the northern termi-
nus of the street that starts at Bab Zuwayla, also the work of
Badr al-Gamali. These two gates mark the northern and southern limits of the Fatimid city proper. As one can see from the
map, there are also stretches of Ayyubid wall extending beyond
the Fatimid fragment, all that remain of Salah al-Din's plan to
connect the Fatimid city with the Citadel, the political and
military center that he built.

Just inside the entrance gate to Bab al-Futuh and down a
flight of stairs is a huge, vaulted room for the quartering and
gathering of troops. As one mounts the stairs leading to the top
of the wall, notice both the finely joined vault of the stair, and
the sudden appearance of carved reliefs: a hippopotamus under
a window, an offering procession. These are blocks that are
reused from the pharaonic complexes at Memphis.

When one comes to the top of the wall at Bab al-Futuh, or
enters into the northern minaret of al-Hakim and climbs to the
first story, stop to look down the Fatimid main street, lined with
shops all the way to Bab Zuwayla, in the distance. One can also
see the forest of minarets that gives Cairo its Islamic air. The
range in dates and styles is unique to Cairo.

Bab al-Futuh is flanked by two rounded towers, as is Bab
Zuwayla to the south—the two resemble each other. The decorative details and the masonry of Bab al-Futuh are finer,
however, and the total effect is quite different, in part because
a large area in front of the northern wall has been cleared and
one gets a more distinct impression of a walled fortress. The
splayed arch with its diamond pattern of carved motifs just over
the entrance leading into the city is particularly fine. Above it
a cornice supports a protrusion. This was the forerunner of the
machicoulis, the overhang through which defenders poured
boiling oil, lime, etc., upon their enemies below. The end
brackets are ram's heads, a manifestation of Mars among the

signs of the Zodiac, which was in the ascendant when al-Qahira was founded. The walls are solid from the base to two thirds of the way up and the circles visible in the masonry at eye level are the ends of columns that were used to bond the outer, finely dressed exterior face with the rubble core of the interior.

As one moves eastward note how the wall follows the salient of al-Hakim's northern minaret because the walls were built to enclose the mosque. Note also the projecting latrine, of Roman origin.

The eastern gate, Bab al-Nasr, 'Gate of Victory,' is flanked by two square towers, decorated with shields, ancient symbols of victory, but its general plan is the same as Bab al-Futuh's. The inscription over the entrance gives the name of Badr al-Gamali and the date, and reads: "By the power of God, the powerful and the strong, Islam is protected, fortresses and walls are raised up." On arrival at the top one notices that the east tower is marked 'Tour Courbin,' and the west tower is 'Tour Julien.' These inscriptions date from Napoleon's occupation (1798–1801), when these fortifications were garrisoned by French troops, and the names refer to officers in that army.

The interior of the wall is an admirable example of military engineering, with meticulous masonry details in the vaulting and firing embrasures, for example. (Watch for pitfalls. It is

Bab al-Nasr and a minaret of the Mosque of al-Hakim

well to carry a flashlight.) The projecting towers enabled the defenders to deliver flanking fire against attackers trying to scale the wall between the towers. The defenders could move from tower to tower under complete cover, and guard rooms, living quarters, and supply points made each section of the wall a fortress in itself. Cairo was never besieged, however, and these defenses were never put to the use for which they were designed, i.e. to protect Cairo against an attack from the Seljuk Turks in Syria.

B. Bab al-Nasr to Sayyidna al-Husayn

Passing through Bab al-Nasr, take Sharia al-Nasr, subsequently Sharia al-Gamaliya, which runs parallel to the Fatimid main street. The types and chronology of monuments along this street are less grand and varied than those on Sharia Mu'izz li-Din Allah, but are nevertheless interesting. Most of them are commercial establishments. Government control of the spice trade beginning with Sultan Barsbay and the development of Bulaq as the city's main port of the Mediterranean in the mid-fifteenth century, meant that goods shipped up the Red Sea were offloaded at al-Qulzum (Suez) and traveled overland to Bulaq, passing by the north walls, instead of going via Qus and the Nile to al-Fustat as they had in previous centuries. Later wikalas or caravansarais reflect the economic renewal and development that took place in this area during the seventeenth and eighteenth centuries based on the textile, spice, and coffee trade.

Wikala of Sultan Qaytbay * (No. 9) 1481/885. Immediately on your right upon entering the city through Bab al-Nasr is a large wikala, one of the few remaining from the Mamluk period. It is a ruined example of a commercial warehouse whose plan did not change significantly over the following centuries. Although it is now inhabited as a tenement, it still shows the main features of these commercial structures: the façade with its fine doorway contains shops on the ground floor and living units above. Inside, in a large rectangular open courtyard, the animals were unloaded—storerooms were located at ground level. The rooms leading off the gallery on the upper floors lodged travelers and merchants.

Mausoleum of Ahmad al-Qazid (No. 10) 1335/735. Continuing southward, this tiny tomb on the left with its ribbed-plaster-over-brick dome and fine band of inscription is worth noticing. The saint's tomb lies behind the open grill of the window.

Wikala of the Amir Qawsun (No. 11) 1330/730. At the next intersection, the building on your right was built by the favorite of Sultan al-Nasir Muhammad, a great patron of architecture. Qawsun came to Egypt with a merchant in 1320, caught the eye of the sultan, was made his cupbearer, and attained within a short time the grade of amir of one hundred and commander of a thousand. His blazon of office—the cup—appears in the roundels of the gateway, which is all that remains of this monument. It was to this warehouse that merchants on their arrival from Syria brought their goods. From here fruit from Syria was distributed to the markets of Cairo and al-Fustat. Four thousand people in 360 units once lived in this wikala. This is the approximate northern limit of the original Fatimid city.

Sabil and Wikala of Oda Bashi (No. 691) 1673/1084. On the left opposite the Wikala of Qawsun, beginning with the sabil and its lunettes of Turkish tiles, are the remains of what was once an impressive façade and establishment. The top stories have been lost, but people continue to live here. This patron, a great builder along this street, was a high-ranking white eunuch, whose Turkish title means 'Chief of the Chamber.'

Hosh Utay and part of the Wikala of Muhsin Ramadan (No. 499) 1817. Further down the street, on the left, this portal that abuts onto the side of the Khanqah of Baybars al-Gashankir was part of another commercial depot.

Khanqah of Sultan Baybars al-Gashankir ** (No. 32) 1306–10/705–09. About seventy-five meters farther down the street on the left is the Khanqah of Baybars II, who restored the minarets of the Mosque of al-Hakim.

Al-Nasir Muhammad was deposed for the second time by Baybars, who became atabek of Egypt, and by the Amir Salar, who became regent for the young prince they appointed sultan.

They ruled Egypt together until 1309, when Baybars became sultan for a year. In 1310 al-Nasir Muhammad, with the support of the governors of Syria, returned to power and Baybars was captured, flogged, and strangled. His sobriquet al-Gashankir means 'the taster,' a job he held at one point in his career. It is used to differentiate him from his more distinguished predecessor, Baybars al-Bunduqdari, or Baybars of the Crossbow.

The building was erected in 1310 on the site of the Fatimid wazir's palace, fine marble panels from which are displayed in the courtyard of the Museum of Islamic Art. This khanqah (sufi monastery) is the oldest that survives in Cairo. Khanqahs and madrasas were introduced into Cairo by Salah al-Din as part of the institutional accompaniment of the Sunni revival after the ousting of the Shi'i dynasty. Here the khanqah appears in Cairo for the first time as part of a royal tomb establishment. Baybars spent an enormous sum on the interior decoration of the structure. The historian al-Maqrizi, writing in the fifteenth century, considered it to be the most sumptuous khanqah in Egypt. The *waqfiya* or foundation deed has survived and it gives a detailed description of the regulations to be followed by the residents. It provided a living for four hundred sufis and one hundred troopers and children of mamluks. In 1389 Ibn Khaldun, the famous Tunisian philosopher, geographer, and traveler became director of the khanqah.

The sheer mass of the beautiful façade is broken by the imposing, round-arched canopied doorway that projects into the street. The inscription on the façade has a blank section where Baybars' names and royal titles were cut away by order of al-Nasir.

At the entrance a block of pharaonic stone has been used as the sill. This must have been deliberately placed there so that all those entering this religious establishment would step on the pagan gods incised on it. Follow the passageway to the tomb chamber on the left. One enters through an atrium and a fine mashrabiya screen, similar to the arrangement at the Mausoleum of Sultan Qalawun. This is a richly decorated chamber, and the marble paneling is particularly fine. Continue to the courtyard along the corridor, which constitutes a 'baffled' or transitional entrance. This type of entrance was derived from military architecture, but was employed by architects in religious and secular architecture when seeking to avoid a direct and sudden entrance into the heart of the building. The two arched liwans at either end of the courtyard are flanked by cells in which the sufis, or Muslim mystics, of the monastery lived. The plan of the khanqah is one of cruciform iwans, but the lateral ones are hidden behind the side walls of the courtyard. These iwans are each two stories tall. The windows in these façades are decorated with motifs that originated in the Fatimid period: affronted S-curves, ribbed shell niches on engaged columns, and ribbed, keel-arched frames.

Once back in the street look back at the minaret with its mabkhara finial and bunches of stalactites that support the balcony. One can still see bits of green tile on the mabkhara top. These pieces of turquoise faience tile with which it was faced are rare in Cairo. This technique, current in fourteenth-century Anatolian and Persian architecture, shows influences coming from Mongol lands at this time. This view, looking north with the minaret in front of the dome, was one that nineteenth-century European artists were fond of sketching.

Sabil–Kuttab of Qitas Bey (No. 16) 1630/1040. Opposite the khanqah, this modest monument is located on the corner of the Darb al-Asfur, which leads to the Bayt al-Sihaymi.

Madrasa–Mausoleum of the Amir Qarasunqur (No. 31) 1300/700. All that remains of this building, built on the site of the Fatimid wazir's palace, is the mausoleum and part of the façade. Qarasunqur ('Black Falcon') was gukandar or polo master to Sultan Qalawun, and two polo sticks, the badge of his office, are featured above one of the windows of the mausoleum. Intricately carved lintels and handsome stucco window screens are the main decorations of this façade. The tomb is hard to get into as the key is with the Antiquities Department. Since the late nineteenth century the precincts have been the Gamaliya Boys' School, and even to look at the inner façade one must be prepared for the children who, although friendly, are lively and noisy.

Sabil–Kuttab and Wikala of Oda Bashi * (Nos. 17 and 19) 1673/1084. A few meters down the street on the left, on a corner, stand these monuments built by Muhammad Katkhuda and his brother the Amir Dhu al-Fiqar Katkhuda Mustahfizan. The sabil–kuttab is still handsome, with its double projecting wooden awnings and the panels of blue and green Turkish tiles. The L-shaped space from here to the next corner belonged to the wikala, also known as the Wikala of Dhu al-Fiqar. It is in a ruinous state now, but in the eighteenth century it was one of the principal centers of the grand commerce in coffee and spices in Cairo. On the ground floor there were thirty-two storerooms; on the second floor thirty-four apartments for merchants and traders; and on the third floor there was a rab' or tenement that provided permanent rooms at a monthly rent to those who worked in the quarter.

Mosque of Gamal al-Din al-Ustadar * (No. 35) 1407/810. On the opposite corner is the mosque founded by the Amir Gamal al-Din Yusuf, the major-domo of Sultan Farag ibn Barquq. He was an extremely powerful amir, who was responsible for many constructions in this area and from whom the name of this quarter, al-Gamaliya, is derived. His career was a long catalogue of extortions and violations, and he was not mourned at his demise. Gamal al-Din ran afoul of his master the sultan, who executed him, seized his goods, and wished to tear down the mosque. However, he was prevented from doing so by the qadi, and instead erased Gamal al-Din's names.

Wikala of Oda Bashi or Dhu al-Fiqar (drawing by P. Coste)

The once beautiful and still charming stucture is raised above the shops on its lower façade. Shop rents contributed to the costs of maintaining the building and its staff. Although this is called a mosque, the plan is that of a madrasa, one of the few in the area built for all four rites. The master builder or architect has ingeniously solved the diverse demands of the complex, sited on a rectangular plot at the corner of a major thoroughfare. In the arms of the liwans are unobtrusively located from left to right as one faces the qibla: the sabil, the entrance, the tomb designate, and the ablutions area. The northwest liwan is almost one and a half times deeper than that which contains the prayer niche, which is a curious feature of this particular building.

In the qibla liwan the white, blue, and gold panels of arabesque below the ceiling and the small turquoise pilasters that extend across the wall remain as hints to the former richness of the decoration. Gamal al-Din reportedly spent twelve thousand gold dinars on its construction. It was his intention to outfit it like a palace because he planned to retire to it. The courtyard is covered with an awning to protect those praying at noon from the sun's direct rays.

Wikala al-Bazar'a (No. 398) 17th/11th century. This caravansarai adjoins the mosque on the west. It provides a good example of an Ottoman wikala whose plan, except for being larger, has not changed from Mamluk predecessors. One passes through the portal, upon which the decoration is concentrated, through a vaulted passage leading into a large courtyard. The first floor, with its storerooms, is built of stone; the lodging areas on the upper floors are of brick and plaster.

Wikala and Sabil of 'Abbas Agha (No. 396) 1694/1106. Along this same street were located two other seventeenth-century wikalas but only the portal and façade of this one remains.

Mosque of Mahmud Muharram * (No. 30) 1792/1206. About one hundred meters down the Gamaliya, on the left, is this mosque, built by an influential and wealthy merchant. A good example of a mosque of the late Ottoman period, it is built over shops. The arrangement of the façade echoes the main scheme of Mamluk façades. There is a simple but perceptible rhythm: the trilobed form of the portal hood is repeated in the shape of the upper windows of one light over two, and the square of the door by that of the lower windows.

The interior plan is simple: a square chamber with four central columns that support a malqaf for both air and light. A large elevated maqsura over the entrance was presumably for women or Quran reciters. The mihrab is of inlaid marble. The most curious feature is the way the mosque is oriented: the mihrab is set at an angle in the qibla wall.

Mosque of Marzuq al-Ahmadi (No. 29) 17th/11th century. Next on the left, this is a small mosque of the Ottoman period that contains the tomb of Sayyid Marzuq and Mahmud Shams al-Din, both of whom were followers of Sayyid Ahmad al-Badawi, the sufi saint who came to Egypt around 1200 and died here in about 1265. He was a great scholar, leader, and mystic, and he rallied popular opinion against the Crusader states. Over the centuries he has become one of the holy figures whose blessing and intercession is sought by thousands of devotees. Al-Badawi's tomb–shrine is in Tanta.

Musafirkhana Palace** (No. 20) 1779–1888/1193–1203. At the corner of the Mosque of Marzuq al-Ahmadi turn left down the Darb al-Tablawi. Keep following it until it leads to a solid façade on the left. Round the corner to find the entrance to the palace, the residence built by Mahmud Muharram. A very successful merchant, who traded between Egypt and the Hijaz, Muharram was a pious and honest man. His palace and his mosque were once attached to a takiya for sufis. His household became the center of an important social circle, and did much to make this area of the city fashionable. Musafirkhana means 'guest house.' At the beginning of the nineteenth century Muharram's palace was acquired by Muhammad 'Ali and was later used by his family as a royal guest house for distinguished visitors and emissaries. The Khedive Isma'il (ruled 1863–79) was born here in a room above the dining room.

The palace offers a rare and complete specimen of a princely house at the turn of the century—spatial arrangements continue virtually unchanged from the early Mamluk period. In fact this residence is a similar but grander version of the Bayt al-Sihaymi. Areas that should not be missed are the well and the saqiya, or water wheel, off the entrance to the left; the salamlik qa'a, with its beautifully carved ceiling and inlaid fountain; the haramlik qa'a, with its soft marble panels; the bath area, with its insets of colored glass; the courtyard and the handsome second-story mashrabiya window.

The palace once provided studios for artists and some of them will return. The custodian has been at the palace for twenty years and is an informative guide.

Madrasa–Mausoleum of Tatar al-Higaziya * (No. 13) 1348 and 1360/748 and 761. An alley opposite the Mosque of Mahmud Muharram leads to this monument. The princess Tatar was the daughter of Sultan al-Nasir Muhammad ibn Qalawun, the sister of Sultan Hasan, and the wife of the Amir Baktimur al-Higazi. Information about this structure is fragmentary. Tatar built her madrasa on the site of the Amir Qawsun's residence. He had married one of her sisters in 1347. Tatar died of the plague in 1360. The building was restored by the Comité in 1895, and more recently by the German Archaeological Institute.

Once again the interior plan is the result of the two needs of qibla orientation and street alignment. This is a three-liwan madrasa: two of them on the qibla side and one opposite. The various dependencies—such as ablutions, storage, access to the minaret—lie behind doors off the liwans. The tomb is on the corner of two streets and the open window through which passers-by can solicit a blessing or invoke a prayer suggests why this visiblity was desirable. The band of Quranic inscription on the liwans, with its flowing letters upon a blue background, is not only beautiful, but helps to give unity to the interior.

Maq'ad of Mamay al-Sayfi * (No. 51) 1496/901. Continue south around Tatar's mausoleum along the same street until it opens out into a little maydan or plaza. On the south side is the remnant of another medieval palace. This is the maq'ad, literally the sitting place, of the palace built by the Amir Sayf al-Din Mamay ibn Khadad, a commander of one hundred amirs under

Sultan Qaytbay. The palace was finished in July/August 1496, but the amir did not enjoy it for long—he was beheaded in March 1497 after the death of Sultan Qaytbay. During the last hundred years of Ottoman administration this structure was the seat of a court. Bayt al-Qadi, its popular name, means 'House of the Judge.'

The second-story loggia faced north over what was once a lovely garden but is now the Maydan Bayt al-Qadi. Below the graceful five-arched arcade are the storerooms in which staple provisions for the large household were kept. Over the door there is a complex blazon of the late Mamluk period. It shows, in the upper register, a napkin; in the middle, a cup charged with a penbox between a pair of horns; and in the lowest field, a cup. This is the same blazon used by the Amir Qajmas al-Ishaqi (see Chapter 6) and the Amir Khushqadam al-Ahmadi (Chapter 8). It is possible that these complex or composite blazons of the late Mamluk period indicated a grouping of certain amirs or were corps badges of some kind.

The inscription of poetic verses that runs under the ceiling around the room is particularly striking.

Mosque of Sayyidna al-Husayn * (No. 28) 1154/549 and 1237/634. The arched entrance over the street to the east of the maq'ad (once the main entrance to the Amir Mamay's palace) leads back to Sharia Gamaliya. Turn right (south) and follow it to the Mosque of Sayyidna al-Husayn (our Lord Husayn), large and recent (1873–78) with Turkish-style minarets. Egyptians are a courteous people and they ordinarily tolerate visitors in their mosques, but this one contains a holy shrine and it is best to admire it from the outside.

Al-Husayn was the son of 'Ali, the Prophet Muhammad's son-in-law and the fourth and last of the orthodox khalifs. After his father was assassinated, al-Husayn was urged to claim the khalifate; but he was killed at the Battle of Karbala in Iraq in 680, an event commemorated by the Shi'a with yearly rites of flagellation. A head believed to be al-Husayn's was brought to Cairo in 1153 and a shrine built for it on the site of the mosque. All that remains of the Fatimid structure (and even this is doubtful) is the lower part of the gateway at the south corner of the present mosque—the Bab al-Akhdar. A minaret with wonderfully carved arabesque panels in stucco, added by the Ayyubids in 1237, rises above the remains of the Fatimid gateway. Al-Husayn's wooden cenotaph, a magnificent specimen of twelfth-century wood carving, is on display in the Museum of Islamic Art.

The Mosque of al-Husayn is a major center for congregational prayers in Cairo today, and on Fridays at the noon prayer the sidewalks and maydan are covered with mats and rugs laid down by the overflowing congregation. The shrine of Sayyidna al-Husayn is also still a major pilgrimage center. Men and women enter the tomb chamber through separate doors, the men through one in the mosque sanctuary and the women through one beyond the Bab al-Akhdar. The great silver mashrabiya screen that surrounds the grave was a present from the Bohra Isma'ili brotherhood in India. For the Shi'a al-Husayn is the supreme Islamic martyr; for the Sunnis he is the beloved grandson of the Prophet. All therefore continue to come and seek his intercession in many areas of their daily lives, such as academic, professional, marital, procreative. In 1187, Ibn Jubayr, a tourist in Cairo, recorded his impressions of a visit to the shrine: "We observed men kissing the blessed tomb, surrounding it, throwing themselves upon it . . . calling out invocations . . . and offering up humble supplications such as would melt the heart and split the hardest flint." Today, eight hundred years later, the popular devotion to this saint is no less strong. Here the president of the Republic and his ministers come to perform prayers on the principal feasts.

Sabil–Kuttab of Ahmad Pasha * 1864/1278. This stands just opposite the western wall of the Mosque of al-Husayn. It is a neglected, almost impossible-to-describe, and superb memento of the Muhammad 'Ali period. Because the street is narrow the façade of this sabil is convex. Steps lead up to the three grilled windows. Today this space is being used by a sweet-cakes vendor. Look up and notice the elaborate and deep carving of the panels that support the kuttab with its curving roof, and the clock base next to it.

12 ◊ ○The Citadel

See map 3

The Citadel, situated on a spur of the Muqattam Hills, dominated Cairo and was the nerve center of the city and of Egypt for almost seven hundred years. Its rich and varied history deserves fuller treatment than we can possibly give in a book this short; those hungry for more details, particularly about the walls, should consult K.A.C. Creswell and the bibliography.

The Citadel hill had been favored by the early rulers of Cairo as a spot for taking the air, but the first major construction work there was the fortress begun by Salah al-Din in 1176. He also extended the city walls to the river at a point near where the main railway station now stands and as far as Old Cairo to the south. Salah al-Din and his immediate successor al-'Adil did not live in the Citadel, but his nephew al-Kamil used it in the early thirteenth century and, with a few exceptions during the Ottoman Period, all successive rulers of Egypt lived in the Citadel until the Khedive Isma'il built 'Abdin Palace in 1874.

The southern part of the site was covered with a succession of elaborate buildings and palaces, of which very little remains today because Muhammad 'Ali pulled down most of what was there when he built his mosque and the Gawhara Palace in their place. Below the Citadel was the maydan, or parade ground, and stables, where the Mamluks played polo and put on military reviews. From that point one went up to the Citadel to observe or participate in the functions of the royal court. There the Sultan dispensed justice and injustice, rewarded and punished, received ambassadors and supplicants, examined criminals and officials, and carried on the business of ruling personally and arbitrarily in Mamluk fashion.

Salah al-Din ibn Ayyub, founder of the Ayyubid dynasty in Egypt, came to power as the result of a threatened attack by a Crusader force against the Fatimids, whose strength was ebbing in 1168. They appealed for help to Nur al-Din, the powerful Seljuk overlord of Damascus, who dispatched a military aid mission, of which Salah al-Din was the second-in-command. The Crusaders were successfully repulsed, but the rescuers remained and seized control of Egypt. Salah al-Din became the ruler of Egypt in 1169 and in 1171 he suppressed the Fatimid khalifate and Egypt returned once more to the Sunni fold.

Salah al-Din gave orders to build the Citadel as a secure seat of government. He also built the city walls with which he intended to enclose al-Qahira (the residential royal city of the Fatimids), his Citadel-fortress, and al-Qata'i'–al-Fustat, the commercial–economic center of the greater Cairo complex.

The City Walls **: Many parts of these walls still exist and are visible along the northern walls (Chapter 11) and along the Darb al-Ahmar (Chapter 6). The most interesting and easily accessible section is the corner that remains where the extension to the northern Fatimid walls turned south toward the Citadel. One way to get there is to drive east along Sharia al-Azhar to the traffic circle beyond the modern section of the University and make a 3/4 turn around it, and on to Sharia al-Mansuriya. Continue north slowly—five hundred meters or so—until you see four palm trees on the right, just before a left turn that leads to the north gates. Another way is to go east from Bab al-Nasr, along the street that lies just outside the North Walls, until it comes to Sharia al-Mansuriya. The Ayyubid walls will be in front of you.

The corner tower in this section is called Burg al-Zafar. It has an octagonal interior covered by a dome of cut stone supported by spherical pendentives. It is flanked on either side by a postern gate. The fortifications imitate those of Badr al-Gamali, but the long arrow slit is an advance on the eleventh-century ones, since it enabled the archer to get a plunging fire. The vault of the staircase of the right-postern gate is worth noticing for its attractive pattern of stars and hexagons. Proceeding south along the wall, the next gate is called Bab al-Gadid, or the New Gate. This gate contains a most important feature, a bent entrance, in which the idea was to make the enemy expose its non-shielded and unprotected side to the defenders. Bent entrances were later incorporated into both domestic and religious architecture. (The area along the Ayyubid walls is badly in need of a clean-up and is thus perhaps only for the avid or habitual sightseer.)

The Citadel: The Citadel was built on an artificially detached spur of the Muqattam range, with limestone quarried from it and large blocks supplied by the small pyramids at Giza. It consisted of two enclosures, the northern and the southern. The northern half was the military area. With its long thread of curtain wall and half-round towers, it was completed by Salah al-Din between 1176 and 1182. His brother and successor al-'Adil was responsible for strengthening several of the towers in 1207. Two of them, built around Salah al-Din's original corner towers, are the Burg al-Ramla and the Burg al-Haddad. They stand above Sharia Salah Salim as it curves behind the Citadel and passes between it and the Muqattam range.

Walls of the Citadel

The southern half was developed by Salah al-Din's nephew al-Kamil (1218–38) as a royal residence. The buildings—a mosque, an audience hall, private palaces, a library, a mansion for the wazir—were torn down by Sultan al-Nasir Muhammad. His buildings in turn were pillaged and allowed to fall to ruin by the Ottomans and the French and finally demolished by Muhammad 'Ali. There have thus been three major building periods in the Citadel's history: Ayyubid, fourteenth-century Mamluk, and nineteenth-century Muhammad 'Ali. The two enclosures are connected by the Bab al-Qulla, which stands just to the northeast of al-Nasir Muhammad's mosque. Below the Citadel mound were the royal stables, a ceremonial maydan/polo ground, a park, and a camel and horse market. Beyond lay the palaces and endowments of principal amirs and pashas.

For many recent years the Citadel was used as a military installation and much of it was not open to visitors. In 1983, however, the Egyptian Antiquities Organization engaged in a widespread restoration and refurbishing program so that the area is now a major tourist center.

The Citadel is divided into three major sections: the fortress proper on the northeast, the walls of which are largely Ayyubid and Turkish; the southern enclosure with nineteenth-century walls; and the lower enclosure marching down the face of the hill on the west, which is almost exclusively from the Muhammad 'Ali period. These walls are nineteenth-century, except for the Bab al-'Azab, the great lower gate opening onto the maydan, built by Radwan Katkhuda in 1754/1168 (see Chapter 5). This gate leads up to the southern enclosure, and the narrow passageway connecting the two was the scene of a real power coup in 1811. Muhammad 'Ali, originally an Albanian mercenary, came to Egypt as part of the Ottoman military forces sent to oust the French expeditionary troops who had invaded the country in 1798. The mission was successful, and for Muhammad 'Ali, a shrewd and ambitious man, the time and the place were right for his own preferment. In 1805 he was appointed Ottoman wali and pasha. In 1811 he consolidated his position by disposing of the remaining Mamluk beys. He invited them to a celebration banquet at the Citadel. As they were leaving through the narrow defile to the Bab al-'Azab, they were shot down by his Albanian guards. At a fusillade, a ruling class that had dominated Egypt for more than 550 years was finally destroyed, and with them the traditional society they had ruled.

The Western Approach: This is no longer an approach that can be made by car, but it can be walked. The road leads up from Maydan Muhammad 'Ali in front of the Madrasa of Sultan Hasan and curves around almost 180 degrees, circumnavigating the old Daftarkhana or archives building in the process. The wall on the left before the first gate is sixteenth-century in its lower courses and Muhammad 'Ali in the upper. The first gate dates from Muhammad 'Ali and is called Bab al-Gadid, 'New Gate.' The wall from here to the next, or middle, gate dates from Salah al-Din's time, with some courses added on top by Muhammad 'Ali. Passing through the middle gate one finds oneself in the sloping courtyard before Bab al-Qulla.

The Eastern Approach: Driving out to Heliopolis and the airport on Sharia Salah Salim, one approaches closest to the Ayyubid walls just opposite the:

Cistern of Ya'qub Shah al-Mihmandar (Jacob King, the chief of protocol), 1495–96/900. There are two interesting aspects of this building. The first is that the dome does not cover a grave but a cistern; the second is that the inscription, the sole decoration on the façade, commemorates the Mamluks' victory at the battle of Adana in 1486 and their capture of the Ottoman general. Turn left just before this point to enter the Citadel and the parking lot where cars are left. Salah al-Din's Ayyubid wall is characterized by smooth masonry with narrow headers and by small, half-round towers with arrow slits. Al-'Adil's addition is the great square tower that is midway down the stretch from the southwest corner to the inner gate. This leads to the main parking area. On entering that gate, the walls on the right are sixteenth- or seventeenth- century. The Gawhara Palace is on the left and the Mosque of Muhammad 'Ali looms above.

Gawhara (Bijou) Palace (No. 505) 1814/1229. This palace, built by Muhammad 'Ali in a style inspired from Europe, was divided into two wings: the east wing, for administrative offices, is in ruins and closed to the public; the west wing contained the pasha's private apartments and reception halls. This part, burned in 1974, was reopened again in 1983 as a museum where paintings, furniture, curios, porcelain, and glass belonging to the descendants of Muhammad 'Ali can once more be seen. Among the artifacts on display are sections of the silver embroidered black velvet *kiswa,* the covering for the Ka'ba, which was traditionally embroidered each year in Cairo and sent to Mecca. Muhammad Ali's throne, made of carved and gilded wood, is also on view. It was in the Bijou Palace that Muhammad 'Ali waited while the Mamluks were being massacred down below. There is a pleasant cafeteria (with restrooms) just before entering. This area of the Citadel plateau was built up with fill in Sultan al-Nasir's time and the Bijou Palace stands on the southern edge of the site of al-Nasir's Striped Palace (Qasr al-Ablaq). Hereabouts St. Francis of Assisi preached to the Ayyubid Sultan al-Kamil.

Mosque of Muhammad 'Ali ** (No. 503) 1824–48/1246–65. The mosque of Muhammad 'Ali was designed by a Greek architect named Yusuf Bushnaq. Its form was modeled on the Mosque of Yeni Valide (1599) in Istanbul, whose patroness was Safiya Baffo (see the Mosque of Malika Safiya, Chapter 9). The mosque is more impressive at a distance than close up. Built in Turkish imperial style as a statement of sovereignty by Muhammad 'Ali, its size and magnificent location make it a Cairo landmark; irrespective of its artistic merits it is an unparalleled contribution to the skyline. Its great dome and towering minarets eighty-two meters high give the Citadel a romantic, oriental quality that makes up for any shortcomings of detail. Among those shortcomings is the alabaster with which the mosque is sheathed. A gesture of baroque *luxe,* the stone unless frequently cleaned becomes terribly grimy, and the overall effect is cheapening.

In the courtyard front of the sanctuary there is a charming Turkish baroque ablution fountain, which in its individual and collective features is very similar to the sabils of the Muhammad 'Ali dynasty around Cairo. Notice the lush acanthus fronds, and the painted landscape scenes inside the domed roof. The gingerbread clock was a gift from Louis Philippe in 1846 in exchange for the obelisk now in the Place de la Concorde, Paris.

The plan of the interior consists of a great central dome, supported by four semi-domes, one on each side, with four smaller domes, one for each corner. The interior is impressive because of its size, and it shows the wonderful arrangement of mass and space that is characteristic of the Istanbul mosques. But the decoration, which was not finished until 1857, in its profusion and eclecticism, is at odds with the simplicity of the architectural structure itself. Six large medallions around the dome enclose the names of God, Muhammad, and the first four khalifs, the 'Rightly Guided Ones': Abu Bakr, 'Umar, 'Uthman, and 'Ali.

Muhammad 'Ali, who died in 1848, is buried in this mosque, behind the bronze grill to the right of the entrance. A magnificent white marble cenotaph marks his final resting place. There are two minbars or pulpits in the mosque. The larger one of wood decorated with gilt ornament is original. The smaller one of alabaster was a gift from King Faruq in 1939/1358. The mihrab niche is quite deep and protrudes on the exterior wall of the mosque. This is a Cairene feature that goes back to Fatimid times.

Structurally, the mosque has not enjoyed good health. Toward the end of the nineteenth century it showed signs of cracking and the masonry in various parts was reinforced. By 1930, however, major cracks had appeared again, especially in the cupolas, and the condition became so dangerous that a complete scheme of overhaul was drawn up. Between 1931 and 1939 the domes were demolished, rebuilt, repainted and gilded at a cost of LE 100,000.

After a quick look at the mosque, go around behind it to its southwestern side and walk over to the parapet, from which there is a fascinating view of Cairo. Directly in front is the fortress-like Madrasa of Sultan Hasan, flanked by the Rifa'i Mosque. Directly to the west, in the left quadrant, is the great Mosque of Ibn Tulun. Off to the south, one can see the Tomb of Imam al-Shafi'i and on the horizon on a clear day the pyramids of Giza are visible. Looking north one can also see from this point Bab Zuwayla, al-Azhar, and the other monuments of the Fatimid city.

Mosque of Sultan al-Nasir Muhammad ** (No. 143) 1318–35/718–35. The entrance is across the road from the entrance to the courtyard of Muhammad 'Ali's mosque. This mosque is notable for its two different minarets. One is near the main entrance and the other is in the northeast corner so that the call to prayer could be projected into the northern enclosure, where the troops were garrisoned. Stylistically they have no parallel anywhere in Egypt. They differ from other minarets of this period in having fluted bulbous finials and glazed faience decoration on their sides. This was a time of friendly relations between the Mamluks and the Mongols of Persia; a master mason from Tabriz is known to have entered the royal service in Cairo.

Inside, the mosque seems unusually plain. This is so because the Ottoman sultan Selim the Grim carried off to Istanbul all of its marble panels. The qibla wall has been completely restored, but one can see that the other walls once had marble dadoes. The mosque is in the arcaded courtyard style, with a great dome in front of the mihrab. The original dome was covered with green tiles. It fell in 1468, and again during the Ottoman period. The present concrete dome was erected by the Comité in 1935. This mosque, large enough to hold five thousand worshippers, was the principal mosque of the Citadel, serving Mamluk sultans, Ottoman pashas, and autonomous Mamluk beys. The columns have been reused from various sources—Ptolemaic, Roman, Christian—as indicated by their differing capitals and built-up bases. The arcades are double-storied and the arches have ablaq masonry. The ceiling over the arcades is flat and coffered and traces of its light blue and silver/white decoration are still visible.

The architect of this mosque was al-Mu'allim ibn al-Suyufi. He was the court architect and is known to have been responsible for two other buildings in Cairo: the Mosque of al-Maridani and the Madrasa of Aqbugha, both built in 1340.

Sultan al-Nasir Muhammad, the greatest builder of the Bahri Mamluk period, concentrated state power in the Citadel, making it the political, military, and administrative center of the Mamluk regime; however, this mosque is all that is left of his vast building program here. Everything else was demolished by Muhammad 'Ali when he made the Citadel *his* seat of power, as al-Nasir Muhammad himself had destroyed earlier Ayyubid structures.

Yusuf's (Salah al-Din's) Well (No. 305) 1176–93/572–89. On leaving the Mosque of al-Nasir, turn right and go around it, taking the first road to the right on the east of the mosque. This will lead you to a tower that stands over this famous well, which goes down ninety-seven meters to the level of the Nile. Water seeps to the well from the river through natural, rather than artificial, channels. The great central shaft is surrounded by a spiral staircase that gives the well its local name of Bir al-Halazun, 'well of the snail;' the name Yusuf, or Joseph, was one of Salah al-Din's. The well was dug during his time (1176–82) by Crusader prisoners, among others. When in use, the rock stairs were covered with earth so that donkeys could move up and down the ramp carrying the water. The Citadel was also supplied by two aqueducts, which discharged near the base of the hill and from which water was raised to the top by a series of water wheels, but since such provisions would be uncertain during a siege, the well was designed in the first instance as a secure source of water in the event of attack.

Harim Palace * (No. 612) 1827/1243. This is the palace that Muhammad 'Ali built in the northern enclosure. The entrance is through the Bab al-Qulla, which connected the southern (residential) and northern (military) enclosures of the Citadel. During the Second World War this palace was used as a hospital; today it is open to the public as the Military Museum. It is worthwhile just to walk through the acres of rooms, appreciating by doing so both the number and the scale of the various apartments. The palace furnishings have disappeared, but magnificent ceilings remain. One room has been preserved, a downstairs bath area. It contains a marble salsabil, or wall panel, down which water trickled and splashed into various receptacles, eventually reaching to the central bathing basin by a marble channel in the floor. The running water helped the ventilation and cooled the hall in the summer. Hot air moved upward and escaped from the wooden lantern in the roof.

Mosque of Sulayman Pasha ** (No. 142) 1528/935. Near the far (eastern) end of the northern enclosure is a little domed mosque, the first built in the Ottoman period. It was located near the tomb of a holy man Sidi Sarya, built in the late Fatimid

Salsabil from the Monastirli Palace, c. 1830

period. The mosque was built by Sulayman Pasha, a court
eunuch who became wali (governor) for the corps of janissaries
quartered in the northern enclosure. The mosque, though
small, is a good example of early sixteenth-century Ottoman
architecture. It is a center-domed free-standing structure located in a garden enclosure. The minaret has a slender faceted
shaft with a conical finial, typical of the Ottoman style and new
to Egypt.

The entrance used today, which is not the main entrance,
leads directly into the sanctuary. The plan is that of the early
Ottoman inverse-T, in which the mihrab is located in the stem
of the T. The dome in Ottoman mosques was used to cover the
whole sanctuary of the mosque instead of just the mausoleum
annexed to it or only the part in front of the mihrab. A handsome
inscription encircles the dome, a prominent and elevated place
for the written word of God, the basis of the universal law of
Islam, (Quran 3:189–94):

> God's is the kingdom of the heavens and the earth, and
> God is over all things powerful. In the creation of the
> heavens and the earth, in the alternation of night with
> day, are signs for those possessed of minds, who remem-
> ber God standing, sitting, and reclining; who consider the
> creation of the heavens and the earth. 'Our Lord! You
> have not created this for vanity. Glory be to You! Preserve
> us from the torments of the Fire. Our Lord! Those whom
> You cause to enter the Fire You have abased indeed; for
> evil-doers there shall be no helpers. Our Lord! We have
> heard a crier calling us to faith: "Have faith in your Lord!"
> and we have faith. Our Lord! Forgive us of our sins, remit
> from us our misdeeds, and cause us to die among the
> righteous. Our Lord! Grant us what You have promised
> us by Your messengers, and abase us not on the Day of
> Resurrection; You will not go back on the tryst!'

As in the Muhammad 'Ali Mosque, the large medallions that
interrupt the inscription contain the names of God, Muhammad,
Abu Bakr, 'Umar, 'Uthman and 'Ali. Inscribing these names in
dominant medallions, often drawn by famous calligraphers, is
a featue of Ottoman mosques and began at a time when the
Ottoman empire's chief rival was the Shi'i Persian empire of the

Safavids. Their purpose is thus hortatory and religious more
than decorative: they remind the faithful of Sunni orthodoxy.
The central dome is supported by three semi-domes, which,
here as in the Muhammad 'Ali mosque, are supported by
spherical triangle pendentives, a technique adopted by the
Ottomans from Byzantine architecture. The frescoed walls
were restored in the nineteenth century. It is not certain how
faithful they are to the original Ottoman decoration, but a rich
effect is achieved.

Otherwise the decoration harks back to Mamluk precedents: the projecting loggia upon molded corbels, the marble
wall paneling perhaps acquired by appropriation from the
Mosque of al-Nasir Muhammad, the marble decoration of the
mihrab, and the simulated marble veneer made of bitumen and
red paste in the grooved inscription around the walls. The
minbar is composed of panels of marble held together by iron
cleats and is decorated with a geometric pattern based on stars
and polygonal forms, both the material and the pattern inspired by Mamluk work. The conical hood, however, is characteristic of Ottoman minbars, and similar to the conical finials
on Ottoman minarets.

As in mosques built on a large or open plot of land the main
entrance is on an axis with the mihrab. It leads out into a
courtyard with a cloister around it covered with shallow domes.
The vault above the entrance is worth noticing. The stucco
arabesques and half-palmettes act as frames for painted floral
designs, badly in need of restoration. This emphasis on floral
motifs, rather than on geometric or arabesque ornament, was
new in Cairo and was brought in by the Ottomans. Across the
courtyard is the supposed burial place of Sidi Sarya. The
custodian maintains that he was a companion of 'Amr ibn al-
'As, the Arab conqueror of Egypt. However, the cenotaphs with
marble turban toppings belong to various Ottoman officials.

13 ◇ ᕗhe ᕐᖮorthern Cemetery

See map 11

Stretching for some three kilometers on either side of the
Citadel are the great cemeteries of Cairo. To the casual visitor
coming in from the airport via the Citadel road the Northern
Cemetery, lying at the foot of the Muqattam Hills, seems sere
and dusty, a jumble of small houses with innumerable domes
rising up among them. One sees little to indicate that the place
is worth visiting. The Southern Cemetery, which is even vaster,
is skirted at only one point by most visitors, as they start
climbing the ridge south of the Citadel, and few are aware of
what it contains.

Each cemetery is a true necropolis, a city of the dead, once
organically joined but today severed by the modern highway of
Salah Salim; but they are also areas of very lively expressions
of life. Surrounding the tombs of sultans and amirs are thousands of family burial plots. Mostly these are courtyards, open
and closed, containing cenotaphs and burial rooms. On Thurs-
day evening and Fridays, and on major feast days, members of

the family, particularly women, come to the cemeteries to visit the dead. This has always been considered a pleasurable excursion. Today one can still see peasant carts rumbling through the town, loaded with women in black milayas, with blankets, cooking utensils and comestibles, headed for the cemetery. Others will already be there, seated in groups, picnicking among the grave markers.

This practice of picnicking with the dead has been remarked on by many foreign visitors. It is not difficult to see a connection with the ancient Egyptian preoccupation with the afterlife; there is no great distinction between leaving food in a tomb to be consumed after death and preparing and eating food next to the tomb as a gesture to the dead.

As early as the fifteenth century, foreign visitors to Cairo remarked that the city could not hold all the population, so many lived in the cemeteries. They lived here as custodians and caretakers and as inhabitants of the monumental complexes. That people live here today is not new; what has changed is that people choose to do so now because of the great population pressures upon urban facilities.

The Northern Cemetery is often wrongly called the 'Tombs of the Khalifs.' The Abbasid khalifs were not buried here but in the great Southern Cemetery below Ibn Tulun's Mosque (Chapter 8), and the Fatimid khalifs were buried in the Eastern Palace of al-Qahira. The cemetery was primarily developed in the fifteenth century and it is the tombs of the Mamluks that are here. Three of its most outstanding monuments belong to Burgi Mamluk sultans. For ease in pathfinding start with the northernmost and work south; but anybody pressed for time should concentrate on the complexes of Barquq, Barsbay, and Qaytbay, which lie in chronological order and impart a sense of architectural evolution.

Tomb of Qansuh Abu Sa'id (No. 164) 1499/904. Past al-Azhar University on Sharia al-Azhar going east there is a traffic circle, beyond which there are two 'straight ahead' choices: the one on the left leads onto Salah Salim and goes south toward the Citadel; the one on the right leads under and then onto Salah Salim, leading north toward Heliopolis. Take the latter, and proceed northward until you come to a bridge over an intersection. Keep to the right, below the bridge, and take the second turn on the right. The Tomb of Qansuh Abu Sa'id now stands free, between two streets. An arrow on map 11 indicates the direction of its location. Originally the tomb chamber was part of a larger complex that marked the northern limit of the cemetery. The triple-arrow design of the dome and the triangular pattern at the corners of the transition zone are unusual. The story of Qansuh in its general outlines follows the medieval mamluk pattern. As a young Circassian he was purchased by Sultan Qaytbay. When it was discovered that he was the brother of Qaytbay's favorite concubine, Qansuh was elevated to dawadar, became the protector of Qaytbay's heir, and subsequently became sultan for a year, but he was deposed and exiled to Alexandria.

Complex of Sultan Inal * (No. 158) 1451–56/855–60. About two hundred meters south of Qansuh's tomb stands a massive

Mausoleum of Inal

façade that is actually two complexes joined together. That on the north is Inal's.

Inal was a mamluk of Sultan Barquq who had a distinguished career, rising from Amir Tablakhana (an amir of forty) to governor of Edessa in Syria, to chief dawadar, and finally to Amir Kabir, chief of the armies. In 1451, at the age of seventy-three, he became sultan. He died at eighty after a reign that was just, prosperous, and eventful.

The major distinction of this building is that it is the only one in Cairo representing different ranks in the life of one man. As an amir Inal built the mausoleum, and then as sultan went on to build the khanqah, the madrasa–mosque, a sabil, and a zawiya. Each of its parts was thus conceived and executed separately and successively, and the whole ringed in with a wall. This explains why the dome sits so low along the façade; although by repeating the chevron design of the dome in the mid-section of the minaret there seems to have been an attempt to heighten it visually. Inside, the monument has lost most of its marble facing. The four cenotaphs in the tomb chamber belong to Inal, his only wife Zaynab bint Khassab, and their two children Ahmad and Muhammad.

Complex of the Amir Qurqumas * (No. 162) 1506–07/911–13.
Adjoining Inal's complex on the south is that of Qurqumas, a mamluk of Sultan Qaytbay who was Amir Kabir under Sultan al-Ghuri. The complex as it now stands is what remains of a large number of buildings Qurqumas built in the cemetery—others served as annexes, kitchens, storehouses, lodgings, wells with saqiyas, stables, and ablutions courts. The present building includes a khanqah, a mosque–madrasa, a sabil–kuttab, and private resdential quarters, in addition to the mausoleum. The arrangement of these elements—minaret to the right and sabil–kuttab to the left of the portal, the khanqah façade extending in front of this entrance unit, the mausoleum located behind the madrasa–mosque and projecting slightly in relation to the rest of the building—is exactly the same configuration as that of Sultan Qaytbay's desert complex further on. The three bent supports that extend from the minaret finial were for hanging mosque lamps.

Perhaps the most interesing element of this building are to be found in the living rooms at the southern end of the monu-

Mausoleum of Qurqumas

ment. They can be reached from the main door in the courtyard
or from an internal staircase on the other side of the mausoleum. This unit is called the qasr, the palace. Although the
inclusion of these residential units was common in multifunc-
tional desert complexes, this is the only such example that has
survived. This is where the patron stayed when he visited the
foundation for feast days or on special occasions. At ground
level the arched rooms provided space for storage and stabling.
The area above includes an unroofed courtyard, a large reception room, a sleeping room, and a latrine.

The Polish-Egyptian Group for Restoration of Islamic Monuments worked on the complex between 1984 and 1988. A study
of the more than one hundred skeletons found in underground
crypts noted that in this elite group of Cairenes (amir, harim,
progeny, courtiers), the average life span for men was 53.5

years and for women 43.2 years; there was a high incidence of infectious diseases; and there was a high proportion of children (thirty-seven) to adults (seventy-two).

Qurqumas was the commander-in-chief of the armies, or Amir Kabir, at the time of his death in 1510. The following is Ibn Iyas' account of his funeral:

> The death of Qurqumas the Atabak, Grand Marshal of the Armies of Egypt, occurred on Tuesday the 23rd [of Ramadan]. Cairo went into mourning and his funeral procession was followed by a numerous throng. The four Qadis [judges] were there, and all the officers, junior and senior, the principal civil officials, and the notables. One could say that no one of importance was missing in the funeral cortege. Penitential alms of bread, dates, and sheep were carried before it, but when it arrived at the college of Sultan Hasan, the common people seized these. At various points along the route, pieces of silver [money] were thrown over the bier. Sorrow and weeping were general because Qurqumas was both benevolent and modest. When the procession arrived at the Sabil of al-Mu'mini, the Sultan [Ghuri] left the Hippodrome [below the Citadel] and came on horse to the fountain. He dismounted and entered the oratory. When they placed the bier in front of him, the Sultan kissed the dead man, and then wept bitterly. After the prayer, the Sultan helped carry the coffin for some paces, then the officers took over in relays as they passed in front of the procession. They went to the mausoleum built by the deceased in the desert next to that of al-Ashraf Inal. He was buried under the dome, God have mercy on him. . . . He was over 60 years old and had been ill for four days. He left four young children, boys and girls. His estate was valued at about 70,000 dinars [about $160,000], without counting his movable property. He had manumitted all his slaves, whether Mamluks, blacks, or slave girls.

Complex of Farag ibn Barquq ** (No. 149) 1400–1411/803-13. About two hundred meters southwest of the complex of Qurqumas stands a little tomb in the middle of an intersection.

This is the *Tomb of Asfur* (No. 132) 1507, with a dome pattern of closed tongs and an attractively carved stalactite panel over the entrance. Turn left (east) at this point and you face the Khanqah of Farag ibn Barquq, about one hundred meters away along a sandy road of indeterminate bounds. The original main entrance is at the northwest corner of the building, but it is not used today and entry is through the door at the southwest corner.

This tomb is one of the major monuments of Cairo and one of the three outstanding structures of the Northern Cemetery. The impetus for the development of the Northern Cemetery was initiated by the desire of Sultan Barquq, the first of the Circassian or Burgi Mamluks (ruled 1382–99), that he be buried in the desert next to the tombs of venerated sufi shaykhs, and not in his state monument in the Bayn al-Qasrayn. The complex built for him by his son Farag, at the foot of the Muqattam range, was in reality the first attempt to urbanize the desert. Originally, the complex was planned as the center of a large residential area that was to include, in addition to the main funerary endowment with its kitchens and living units, subsidiary establishments such as baths, bakeries, grain mills, rooms for travelers, alleys, and a market place. With its twin minarets, twin domes, and twin sabil–kuttabs at either end of the long façade, this monument is a good example of the massive Bahri style that was carried into the mid-Burgi period.

The primary designation of this monument is that of khanqah, an institution for Muslim mystics or holy men, but its basic plan of arcades off a central court is not very different from that of a congregational mosque. The recent restorations by the Egyptian Antiquities Organization include a plan of the building at the main entrance. From the vestibule into the corridor that leads to the courtyard one steps over the sill, an ancient pharaonic slab. The shafts that pierce the ceiling of the long corridor are there for both illumination and circulation of air. The cooler air of evening would force out the warm air and create, by convection, a natural cooling system. From the courtyard, stairs in the northwest corner lead to the upper floors—a complex of rooms, passageways, and cubicles that one both passes on the way up and looks down upon from the roof. In these deserted chambers the dervishes once studied, chanted, and slept. On the second floor, the porch of the kuttab over the front entrance is a pleasant place to sit, and it must have been a favorite spot for the senior inhabitants of the complex. Here, one can get a feeling of these tombs as places in which to live. One can climb both minarets, from which there is a splendid view, not only of the necropolis but of the surrounding areas. To the north is Heliopolis, to the west the modern city of Cairo behind the medieval nucleus of al-Qahira, and to the south the complexes of Barsbay, Qaytbay, and the Citadel.

Cross the courtyard toward the sanctuary. The arcades around the sides have shallow domes, which are more common in Syria or Anatolia than in Egypt. Old tombstones rescued from the necropolis at Aswan before the first dam was built are now stored in these arcades. The platform at the edge of the sanctuary is a dikka from which the Quran was chanted. Next to the plain mihrab is a stone minbar that was donated in 1483 by Sultan Qaytbay. It is delicately carved but its most striking feature is how imitative of woodwork it is.

To the north is the tomb chamber in which Sultan Barquq, under the largest tabut, and his son 'Abd al-'Aziz (who reigned briefly from 1405 to 1406), are buried. The other grave-markers are of unknown persons. Sultan Farag was assassinated in Syria, where his remains were left. In the south chamber lie the ladies: Khawand Khariz, a granddaughter of Sultan Barquq, in front of the mihrab; Khawand Shaqra, a daughter of Sultan Farag; and under the limestone tabut in the corner possibly Khawand Qunuqbay, Barquq's wife and mother of 'Abd al-'Aziz, or else the body of a faithful nurse. Across the entrances of both tombs are wooden screens whose geometric patterns resemble the wooden window screens used in Barquq's Bayn al-Qasrayn complex. In the south tomb the screen is original; in the north one it is restored. On entering either chamber one is unprepared for the soaring effect of the interior. These twin domes represent a great development in the technology of stone work. They are the earliest stone domes of this size in Cairo and their enormous span (more than fourteen meters) marks a high point of Mamluk engineering. The exterior decoration of zigzag ribs is the forerunner of the elaborately carved domes of the Qaytbay period. Outside, the increased thickness of the transition zone necessary to support the weight of the dome is

Dome interior of the Mausoleum of Barquq

disguised by a graceful convex–concave molding. Inside, the pendentive formed by shallow niches, which in brick domes was of wood, is now of stone instead. The black and red painted patterns simulate inlaid marble, whose use would have been too heavy for the dome. The new Mamluk window style of one over two bull's-eye windows over three arched openings is evident here.

Outside to the north of Barquq's mausoleum is the tomb of his father Anas, whom he had brought from Circassia and given a position. It was joined to the mausoleum by an arcade, now in ruins.

Farag acceeded to the throne at the age of ten. He was twenty-three when he was deposed and killed in Damascus. His reign was one of continual strife among the amirs and as such was really a history of their rivalries. During this time he went to Syria seven times to quell disturbances. The wonder is that under such circumstances such a magnificent complex was built.

Tombs of Barsbay al-Bagasi 1456/860 and the **Amir Sulayman,** 1544/951 (No. 124). Back on the road, just south of the Tomb of Asfur, is an irregular enclosure within which are two domed tomb chambers. The oldest belongs to Barsbay 'Ali al-Bagasi, who was Sultan Inal's grand chamberlain and master of the horse (amir akhur). He died in Damascus in 1465. The tomb is part of a larger complex, of which the mihrab in the southeast wall is still visible. The design carved in stone over the lintel of the door into the tomb is an elaboration of a Moroccan motif, the *darj wa ktaf* or cheek and shoulder, formed by intersecting lines of arcs, which make a vaguely floral shape resembling a tulip. This is one of the few examples of Maghribi influence in these monuments. Notice also the blue faience roundels at the base of the dome. In the Mamluk period blue ceramic often highlights the loop made in the molding at the apex of an arch. Here it is incorporated into dome decoration.

The other tomb is that of the Amir Sulayman, built ninety years later. Although it was built after the Ottoman conquest, it is essentially a Mamluk building, with its beautiful tapestry dome and the triangular corners of the transition zone. The blue and white tiled inscriptions around the drum and in the lunettes above the windows date it as post-conquest.

Tombs of Barsbay al-Bagasi and Amir Sulayman

Tomb of the Seven Maidens (No. 110) 1450/854. To the south of
Barsbay al-Bagasi's tomb is that of the Seven Maidens (Sab'a
Banat). The identities of its occupants and builder are un-
known.

Qubbat Ma'bad (Dome of the Oratory) of al-Rifa'i (No.
108) mid-15th century. South of the Sab'a Banat, and behind
some apartment buildings, is a squat-domed building. There is
no historic inscription in the building, but it is mentioned, as a
zawiya, in the waqf or endowment deed of the complex of Sultan
Barsbay (see below). This is a curious, but not a unique, piece
of architecture. The door is kept locked, but it is possible to see

that the dome is supported by the arch-over-the-corner window system present in at least two late Mamluk buildings (such as the Qubbat al-Fadawiya, 1480, not described in this book) and in the Mosque of Sinan Pasha in Bulaq (Chapter 15). Ahmad ibn 'Ali Abu al-'Abbas al-Rifa'i, who founded the Rifa'i *tariqa* or order of sufis, died in 1183 in Iraq. His followers do not attribute to him any treatises, and reports about his life are inconsistent; nevertheless, his tariqa became enormously popular in medieval Egypt, where he also became the patron saint of snake charmers. This is presumably the domed room in which the sufis would gather for collective religious ceremonies such as the dhikr.

Tomb of Khadiga Umm al-Ashraf (No. 106) c.1430–40/835–45. To the south, this little tomb is hidden behind a façade of houses. The dome, springing from the square base by a series of steps, is of brick with an interlacing ribbing that appears on several domes (that of the Amir Taghribardi, 1440) and minarets (that of Barsbay, 1425). There is no historic inscription in this tomb but because of its popular identification and its stylistic features it is assumed to belong to Sultan Barsbay's mother.

Tomb of Gani Bak * (No. 122) 1427/830. Return to the street that runs south from Barquq's mausoleum. One hundred meters from the latter you will find the Tomb of Gani Bak, a mamluk of Barsbay. Although Gani Bak had provided for his burial in the complex he built in the city (see Chapter 7), the amir was much beloved by the sultan and his remains were interred in this new tomb. This monument was constructed only sixteen years after Barquq's dome, but the carving on the dome is much more complex. From 1350 to 1490 Cairo was the Islamic world's center of geometric art, and this is a wonderful example of that art applied to domes.

Tomb of Qurqumas (No. 170) 1511/917. This tomb originally stood beside the monumental entrance of the Mosque of al-Hakim on the Qasaba or main street of Fatimid Cairo. When that mosque was restored this tomb was moved to its present site. This is not the same Qurqumas as the one discussed earlier in this chapter—this Turkish name, which might be translated as 'never fear' or 'dread-naught,' was fairly common.

Complex of Sultan al-Ashraf Barsbay ** (No. 121) 1432/835. Some fifty yards to the south of the Tomb of Gani Bak is the Mausoleum of Barsbay. Originally planned as a khanqah or monastery, it is an unusually elongated structure, the appearance of which is marred by an unsightly minaret of later construction. The façade—consisting of mausoleum, mosque–madrasa, two sabils, and sufi lodgings now in ruins—was not only extremely long, but was accentuated by the heavily decorated dome. The chevron decorations on domes that were predominant from 1400 to 1426 are now replaced by a curvilinear interlacing pattern. The unfinished rosette, on the right in the lowest row of the dome, is evidence for the hypothesis that the decoration of such domes was sculpted after the dome was built. In the courtyard in the back there is a small canopy tomb whose dome is one of the first in the series of geometric carved dome surfaces.

The internal decorations of this monument are among the finest of the Northern Cemetery. To the left of the vestibule stretches a long mosque, twenty by fifteen meters, consisting of a center aisle and two raised liwans on either side. The liwans are separated from the center aisle by arched arcades, the pillars of which have classical capitals. The marble mosaic pavements are particularly fine. Ask the attendant to lift the straw mats so they can be seen. The mosque's interior is illuminated by two rows of windows, the upper row of which has modern colored glass set in carved stucco in traditional patterns. The mihrab is in the center of the southeast wall. The mihrabs in the khanqahs of this period seem to run counter to the prevailing trend: while everything else is becoming more and more decorated, the mihrab becomes plainer. Why this is so is a matter of conjecture—perhaps for an ascetic community a plain mihrab was intended to focus on the unadorned life of the spirit. The minbar, a later gift of 1453, is the most beautiful of all Mamluk minbars in Cairo. There is something especially charming and graceful in the way the ivory stars seem to dance across its surface.

At the northern end of the mosque is the tomb chamber, dimly lit by more windows of colored glass set in stucco, again

Mihrab in the Tomb of Sultan Barsbay

not original. The marble cenotaph of Barsbay sits in front of an elaborately-decorated mihrab with marble and mother-of-pearl mosaics and veneer joggling. The mosaics have been restored in places, but much of the original fabric remains. As always, neither the exterior nor the rest of the interior prepares one for the height of the dome, the ceiling of which seems to disappear into infinity.

Barsbay ruled from 1422 to 1438, which was accounted a long reign. He neither drank nor swore. He was noted for milking the economy by a variety of methods, but his reign, according to the historian Taghribirdi, was one of "extreme security and low prices because revolts and expeditions were infrequent."

Takiya of Ahmad Abu Sayf (No. 111) 15th century. This is the next structure on the left after Barsbay's mausoleum, but it is now in ruins.

Complex of Sultan al-Ashraf Qaytbay *** (No. 99) 1472–74/ 877–79. Qaytbay's monument is the jewel of late Mamluk architecture. Here, in a restful oasis, the decorative arts reached their zenith and the result is one of great pleasure to the eye. It is worth the effort to get there.

Continue south down the street that passes by Barquq's and Barsbay's tombs. It meanders slightly but leads eventually to the little square in front of the entrance. To visit this monument directly from the Azhar area or downtown, tell the driver Sharia Salah Salim, al-Qarafa. Have him turn off the main road to the right after dusty domes begin appearing. Then ask the way to Qaytbay.

Stretching north is the façade of Qaytbay's rab' or block of apartments used as lodgings for travelers as part of the waqf or income to support the complex. Between the rab' and the mausoleum on your right is a lovely drinking trough with shallow niches and a roof, also Qaytbay's, where animals were watered. The saqiya or wheel that supplied the water is in back and to the right. These structures were restored in the mid 1980s. The best view of the portal, minaret, and dome is from the small square in front of the entrance. This was the central unit of what was a vast desert establishment and commercial

Mausoleum of Qaytbay (drawing by David Roberts)

center on the main north–south trade route with Syria and the east–west trade route with the Red Sea.

Before going into the madrasa, take a look at these details on the outside: the ablaq or striped masonry, the carving around door and windows, the metal medallion on the door, and the vaulting in the vestibule.

Inside, the plan is that of the modified Cairene urban cruciform madrasa, the qa'a plan, with vestigial liwans on the east and west, and a small covered court. The richness of the decoration is amazing, and yet the total effect is well-proportioned and subdued. Everywhere there is beauty—the marble pavements, the walls, the windows, and the ceiling. The lantern ceiling above the court is a handsome example of a composite decoration using the three primary ornamental forms of Islamic art: calligraphic, geometric, and arabesque. The star is prominent in Islamic art and as a symbol of guidance is often mentioned in the Quran: "He it is Who appointed for you the stars, that you might be guided by them in the darkness of the land and of the sea." (6:97). This is a good place to sit for a while and watch the changing light as the sun moves on.

Beyond the sanctuary liwan is the tomb chamber, one of the most impressive in Cairo. Again, the outside view does not prepare one for the dimensions of the great dome, which seems infinite in its soaring height.

Return to the sanctuary and ask the custodian to let you climb to the roof and up the minaret. You will pass some of the scholars' cells on the way. On the roof there is a splendid view of the delicate carving of the minaret and the dome, which is the apogee of the carved domes of Cairo. On its surface there are two separate designs, complex but clear: one a plain, raised straight-lined star pattern and the other an undulating lacework of floral arabesques that is grooved and recessed. These two patterns provide contrasting surface movements and textures and also refract and reflect the light. As the sun moves and the day progresses, the pattern changes, assuming a fluid nature. In the corners of the transition zone the convex–concave moldings are carved, and the whole cascade is caught by a final fleur-de-lys.

The minaret, both in its total proportions and in the refinement of its decoration, is one of the most beautiful of the

Dome of Qaytbay

Mamluk period. Its outside is also richly inscribed. In addition to the Quranic verses, there are stark little messages such as: "Death, which you try to escape, will catch you;" "Death spares neither father nor son."

Below, to the west, is a smaller, almost equally ornate dome. There is no inscription on this tomb, but since the pattern of the dome is similar to but not as fine as that over Qaytbay's tomb, it is thought that Qaytbay may have built this tomb for himself when he was an amir, and that later it was appropriated by a Turkish sufi named Gulshani, who lived in the mosque during the Turkish period. The building of which it is a part, and the next one to the west, called a maq'ad (a term used to designate a reception area), which has a solid façade and is built over storerooms, were built at the same time by Qaytbay. These are part of the residential area of the complex, for the sultan and guests.

One gets an idea of the size of the total complex when one realizes that all these buildings, including the rab', were enclosed within the same wall. The remains of one of the gates to the enclosure (Bab al-Gindi) is shown on the map, just south of the mausoleum. These large foundations were a way of providing for relatives of the founder, who normally did not succeed or inherit in the Mamluk system. The larger the complex, the more personnel it needed for its running and supervision—posts or jobs most commonly given to members of the Mamluk's own family.

After al-Nasir Muhammad ibn Qalawun, Qaytbay was the most active of the Mamluk builders, a prince of builders. Eighty-five structures built or restored by him are to be found in Syria, Palestine, and Mecca, as well as in and around Cairo and Alexandria. Like al-Nasir Muhammad, he encouraged his amirs to build also. In Cairo there are seventeen monuments from his period, not counting the carved stone pulpit in Barquq's mausoleum. His buildings are noted for their decorative detail and the fineness of the work-manship that went into them. This was a period in which Mamluk style was consolidated and refined.

Qaytbay was one of Barsbay's mamluks, bought originally for fifty dinars. He worked his way up through the ranks to become commander-in-chief of the army and ultimately sultan.

He reigned from 1468 to 1496, a record broken only by al-Nasir Muhammad. Qaytbay was noted for his martial prowess and physical energy, and for his remorseless financial exactions levied on his subjects. The two main preoccupations of his reign were relations with the rising power of the Ottomans and the promotion of trade, especially with the Italians.

Mausoleum of 'Afifi or of Muhammad Tawfiq Pasha *
1894/1312. On leaving the entrance to the complex of Qaytbay turn right and follow the street past the sabil of the mausoleum. Go through the gate and at the end of the street turn left. Continue more or less straight toward the new road to Nasr City and a clump of sycamore trees on the right. This is the garden entrance to the royal family mausoleum built by Fabricius Bey, architect of the khedival palace. The area is also known by the name of a venerable shaykh buried here, Sidi 'Afifi. Many students and shaykhs of al-Azhar are also buried here around his tomb. Except for the main entrance gate, with its garlands and cornucopias in the Ottoman baroque style, the decoration of the building, inside and out, is inspired by the best examples of the medieval period.

The mausoleum contains the tombs of Bamba Khadin, the mother of 'Abbas, who built the beautiful sabil on Sharia Saliba (Chapter 7); of Tawfiq, Isma'il's son, who ruled Egypt from 1879 to 1892; of his wife; and of their sons 'Abbas Hilmi, deposed by the British in 1914, and Muhammad 'Ali, who built Manial Palace. In the far left corner is 'Abd al-Mun'im, son of 'Abbas Hilmi, who acted as regent for Faruq's infant son from 1952 to 1953. In the other corner is a young sister. The wooden inlaid cenotaphs and furniture were made in the school for artisans established by 'Abbas's mother. The chairs were used at the opening of the Suez Canal and brought to the tomb from 'Abdin Palace. The furniture alone is reason enough to visit the tomb, for they are wonderful examples of the work of the period.

Also buried here, in the crypt and in the garden, are the members of Muhammad 'Ali's family who died in Alexandria and were laid to rest in the family tomb in that city. When the tomb, located near the Roman amphitheater, was destroyed in 1954, the bodies were brought to Cairo for reinterment. Muhammad Sa'id Pasha's body (ruled 1854–63) is among them.

Tomb of Tashtimur (No. 192) 1334/735. On passing through Qaytbay's Gate, instead of turning left, turn right. This will lead you back to one of the main arteries of the modern cometery, Sharia Qarafa Bab al-Wazir. Before you get there, about 150 yards down the side street on your right is the Tomb of Tashtimur, a Bahri Mamluk known by the sobriquet of Hummus Akhdar, or 'Green Chickpeas' (for reasons unknown). This tomb has a classic example of the Mamluk jelly-mold or ribbed dome. It is 140 years earlier than Qaytbay's; between the two you see the span of Mamluk dome-building, from its beginning with plastered brick to its ultimate glory in carved stone.

Tomb of Guzal (No. 89) 1403/805. Continue down to the main artery and turn left. About 120 meters from the corner, on your left, is the tomb of Guzal, otherwise known as Sidi Karkar. It is of the same period as Barquq's tomb.

Tomb of Umm Anuk or the Princess Tughay * (No. 81) before 1348/749. At the next intersection after Guzal's tomb there are two tombs on your right. That on the north side of the street is the Tomb of Umm Anuk, favorite wife of Sultan al-Nasir Muhammad and mother of his favorite son, Anuk. She was a great beauty. Al-Maqrizi related that "she saw more happiness than any other of the wives of Turkish [i.e. Mamluk] kings in Egypt." Her tomb was considered one of the most beautiful monuments of Cairo. It can be seen clearly from Salah Salim.

It was originally built as a khanqah with domed mausolea to either side of the vaulted liwan. The tomb on the left was not only smaller but has lost its dome. The dome on the right has a lovely inscription of inlaid tile mosaic in blue, white and green at the base of the ribbing. This is the "Throne Verse" (2:255). The fact that the other faience decorations of merit are also on monuments of al-Nasir's period, such as his minarets in the Citadel and the Mosque of Aslam al-Silahdar near Bab Zuwayla, is evidence of the Tatar influence during this era. Also very fine, and more Persian than Cairene in feeling, are the large stucco roundels and panels that decorate the liwan and the carved stucco arabesque patterns of the mihrab.

Tombs of Princess Tughay and Princess Tulbay

Tomb of the Princess Tulbay (No. 80) 1363–64/765. Across the street is a dome over the tomb of the Princess Tulbay. The exact identity of this princess is disputed. For some Tulbay, a Tatar princess from the Volga, was al-Nasir's principal (as opposed to favorite) wife. For others she is the wife of Sultan Hasan. The inscriptions in the tomb are Quranic. The tomb is locked; later buildings and tombs abut and adjoin the structure, so that it is difficult to form a true idea of its original nature and dimensions.

Tombs of Nasrallah (No. 88) 1441/845 and **Azrumuk** (No. 87) 1503/909. Another hundred yards down the main artery from Umm Anuk's corner are these neighboring tombs. Nasrallah's dome has the same decoration as that of Barsbay al-Bagasi but without the turquoise insets in the chain molding below the zigzag. Nasrallah, like many Mamluks, was nicknamed after something edible. In his case it was a sweet melon, Kuz al-'Asal (meaning literally 'pot of honey').

Azrumuk's dome is nicely carved, and its decoration of blue faience blobs is unique. He was an amir of a thousand under Sultan Qansuh Abu Sa'id.

Other Monuments. At this point you can return to your car and depart satisfied that you have done the City of the Dead, northern half. There are several other monuments worth pointing out, however, even if you do not visit them:

Tomb of Tankizbugha (No. 85) 1362/764. As one drives toward Cairo from Heliopolis on Salah Salim notice off to the left a large desolate structure that sits in isolation some seven hundred meters to the northeast of the Citadel. It is the monument farthest south of any size in the northern cemetery. This is the Tomb of Tankizbugha ('See Bull'), a Bahri amir of Greek origin, who built another tomb in the cemetery to the south of the Citadel (See Chapter 8). Access to the monument is difficult, since there is no road and the site is one of pronounced desolation. Although today only the tomb is apparent, it was originally part of a khanqah establishment.

Tomb of Azrumuk

Cemetery of Bab al-Wazir. As you continue south, Sharia Salah
Salim parallels the ancient access road to the cemetery for part
of its length, but diverges from it and dips down and then curves
around to the left (east) to skirt the Citadel. From that point
there is a classic view of the domes and spires of Cairo, and as
you look to the south you face the site of Bab al-Wazir, one of the
medieval gates leading to the cemetery. The monuments in this
intramuros cemetery are described in Chapter 5. They include
the Mausoleum of Yunus al-Dawadar, whose elongated ribbed
dome is visible from this point, and the Tomb-complex of Nizam
al-Din, a ruined monument on the hill to the left.

14 ◦ Al-Husayniya and the Mosque of Baybars I

Mosque of Baybars I **
Sakakini Palace *

See map 8

Mosque of Baybars I (al-Zahir Baybars al-Bunduqdari) *
(No. 1) 1269/667. This mosque is off the beaten track, not really close to any of the main monuments. It can be visited either as an extension of the monuments listed in Chapter 9 or from the Bab al-Futuh. It is about a mile from the complex of al-Qadi Yahya on Sharia Port Said and just over half a mile from Bab al-Futuh. Beginning at al-Qadi Yahya, follow Sharia al-Gaysh (Army Street) north along the trolley tracks until a trolley kiosk and a diagonal turn-off appear on the left. The corner of the mosque can be seen from here. This is the only medieval monument surviving from the Husayniya quarter, which extended northward from the Northern Walls and flourished until the end of the fourteenth century, when a series of natural disasters and misfortunes caused its decline. The resurgence of this area did not take place until the Muhammad 'Ali period.

This is one of the great arcaded congregational mosques in the tradition of 'Amr, Ibn Tulun, al-Azhar, and al-Hakim. It has suffered a good deal of misuse. In Napoleon's time it was used as a fort, called Fort Sulkowski, subsequently as a soap factory, then a bakehouse. The British turned it into an army store and a slaughterhouse. Under King Fuad the courtyard area was planted as a public garden.

The main entrance was in the center of the northwest wall, directly opposite the sanctuary arcade. With its decoration derived from the Fatimid mosques of al-Aqmar and al-Hakim, it is an impressive gateway. This entrance is locked now, so to look at the original lovely stucco paneling that is above the gate on the inside, enter the enclosure by the gate on the northeast

255

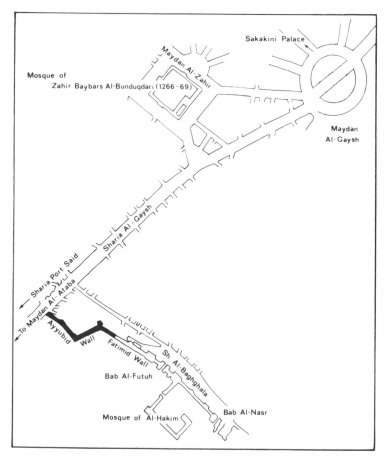

Figure 12: North walls to Mosque of Baybars

Sakakini Palace

on the inside, enter the enclosure by the gate on the northeast wall. This entry to the mosque, now in a state of 'latent restoration,' leads into what was once the original courtyard and later Fuad's garden.

Entry into the mosque proper is through the door on the southeast side. The unusual feature of the interior plan is the large clear space in front of the mihrab, three aisles by three aisles, which was originally covered by an enormous dome. Baybars is said to have made the plan of the mosque himself, and to have ordered stone columns collected from earlier structures throughout Egypt for use in this building. Some of the timbers and marble came from the town of Jaffa, which Baybars seized from the Crusaders in 1268. The marble used in the area of the mihrab was pillaged long ago, but the timbers and the nails for holding the plaster surface covering are still visible in the walls. The windows originally had stucco grills flush with both the inner and outer walls, and some fragments of these grills remain. In some cases the fine bands of Kufic inscription bordering the windows also survive.

Part of the sanctuary arcade has been closed off and set aside as a mosque in modern times. This has made the original plan more difficult to visualize.

Sakakini Palace * 1898. This is a superb *fin de siècle* mansion that lies not far away from the mosque and will well reward the extra effort to see it. From Maydan al-Gaysh four streets go off on the left. Facing north, take the third left off the maydan. The palace, centered in its own maydan, is visible at the end of the street.

The mansion was built by Henri Sakakini Pasha. It rises like a four-tiered wedding cake, embellished with belvederes, balconies, cupolas, spires, urns, garlands, wave-like cornices, and shields. Busts look down from framed insets on the second floor, and at each corner personifications of the seasons emerge from shells. European influences in Cairo were very strong at this time and this is a flamboyant and exuberant expression of West in East.

15 ◊ Bulaq

Dar al-Kutub (The Islamic Book Museum) **
Takiyat al-Rifa'iya
Mosque of Sinan Pasha **
Mosque of al-Qadi Yahya
Mosque of Mustafa Shurbagi Mirza *
Mosque of Abu'l-'Ila *
Palace of Muhammad 'Ali **

See map 12

As is Egypt, so is Cairo the gift of the Nile. The course of the Nile over the centuries has shifted westward, most notably between 1050 and 1350, making available new lands for development. Bulaq, whose name probably derives from the Coptic word for marsh, began modestly in the fourteenth century, by taking over the port city functions of al-Maqs, the Fatimid port, which had dried up as the river bed had shifted. Bulaq at first was a convenient anchorage for boats coming from the Delta, and as a cereals port supplying the markets outside the north walls.

In the fifteenth century, however, when Sultan Barsbay established state monopolies on certain goods and changed the Red Sea trade route, Bulaq became the port of Cairo. Instead of going overland from Qusayr to Qus and then down the Nile to al-Fustat, the new trade route went from Jidda to Qulzum (Suez) and then overland to Cairo. The Suez road led to the northern gates, and thus goods destined for Mediterranean countries were taken to Bulaq to be reloaded. Bulaq became the main port city, the main warehouse for goods coming by boat from neighboring regions for consumption in the capital. It also became an industrial center, with sugar presses and wood and textiles outlets, and a tax collection point.

During the Ottoman period, Bulaq's importance and development accelerated. After 1517 the loss of business Egypt had suffered as a result of the European discovery of the trade route around Africa was offset by her incorporation into the Ottoman

Empire, which until the mid-seventeenth century was the foremost economic and political power of the old world. Bulaq was Cairo's port for trade with the Mediteranean, as well as an important industrial zone.

In the nineteenth century, under Muhammad 'Ali, Bulaq experienced a new renaissance. It became the site of many new ventures established as part of that ruler's plans to modernize the economy, and of his industrial and educational ambitions. These included a textile factory, an iron foundry, a national press, naval installations and riverboat construction, spinning mills, and bleaching plants. Bulaq was more than ever a center of commerce, manufacturing, and transportation. With the building of the Cairo Plaza, Bulaq today has been revitalized as a business and tourist center.

Dar al-Kutub (The Islamic Book Museum) ** 1987. The Egyptian National Library is located on the Nile Corniche north of the 26th July Bridge in the GEBO Building. The ground-floor exhibition gallery is well worth a visit for here are displayed a representative sample of the Library's medieval and modern holdings, from the earliest Arabic inscriptions on bone and bark to the first books printed in Arabic in Europe and by Muhammad 'Ali's nineteenth-century press.

Especially noteworthy are the great illuminated Qurans from the Mamluk period and illustrated scientific and poetic works of the thirteenth to seventeenth centuries. The miniatures done by Bihzad, the great Persian artist, for the poet Sa'di's *Bustan* are among the masterpieces of Islamic painting. Also exhibited are epigraphic novelties such as the grain of wheat upon which are inscribed the names of all the Muslim rulers of Egypt from 639 to 1936.

The following monuments lie in back of the Cairo Plaza, from which they can be seen. The route also offers a vivid impression of liveliness and economic activity—mainly metal and textiles—in this area.

Takiyat al-Rifa'iya (No. 442) 1774/1188. Follow the Corniche north past the Abu'l-'Ila Bridge. Just before reaching the Cairo Plaza the road forks. Bear right onto the old trolley line, a street line, a street called al-Matba' al-Ahliya. Continue past the Cairo Plaza and take the first right. One block further along on the right is this building, which housed the Rifa'i order (See Chapter 13). Containing the tomb of Muhammed 'Ali al-Maghribi, it was also a madrasa–mosque and a hospice. It is currently in service as an elementary school and sewing center.

Mosque of Sinan Pasha ** (No. 349) 1571/979. Just behind the takiya is this hybrid Ottoman–Mamluk building. It dates to the sixteenth century when the great patrons of Bulaq were the Ottoman viceroys, who had the political power, financial means, and personal interest to develop the area. This mosque was originally part of a larger complex that included a wikala and a hammam, and was still chief mosque of the river port at the time of the French expedition.

Sinan Pasha, the conqueror of Yemen, was twice governor of Cairo, five times grand wazir, a very wealthy man, and notable

Mosque of Sinan Pasha

patron of architecture. He was an Albanian recruited for palace service as a boy, who rose to be Sulayman the Magnificent's chief cupbearer. He was then made viceroy of Egypt.

There are several features of this mosque that give it an Ottoman feel. It is free-standing in a garden and surrounded on three sides by an open verandah-like gallery roofed with flat cupolas. Bulaq at the time was a newly-developed area of the city, so this kind of large-scale rectangular planning was possible. Three doors, one in each face (except the qibla wall), lead into a large-domed room. A central dome is a feature also favored by the Ottomans, but the squinch system (a tri-lobed arch spanning two windows in each corner) is unusual and goes back to an instance in the Mamluk period (the Qubbat al-Fadawiya 1479–81/884–86). The name of God appears above the muqarnas decoration in the squinches in the mihrab wall; but the double chevron pattern that appears in the opposite squinches dates back to Mamluk mihrab hoods.

Apart from the mihrab of polychrome marble, the only touch of color and perhaps the real focus of attention are the windows—eight in the transition zone and sixteen in the dome—whose S-curved shapes originate in the Fatimid period. The windows are inset with colored rounds of glass, and the effect is decorative and restful. Over the northwest entrance there is a gallery, to serve as either the viceregal box or a platform for reading the Quran. The ablutions fountains and minaret are in the back. The mosque was restored in 1983.

The wikala of which this mosque was a part is unrecognizable, but the hammam is still in operation. Leave the enclosure by the gate near the ablutions area. Turn right. At the very end of the block, through a rather ornate entrance on the right, is the bath, for men only. Nearer the mosque just a few doors beyond the minaret is the *mustawrad*, where the water was heated and piped to the bath. Traditionally garbage was used for fuel. The extra heat was used to cook *ful mudammas* (baked broad beans), and the ash to make mortar—a neat example of Egyptian recycling.

Mosque of al-Qadi Yahya (No. 344) 1448–49/852–53. Halfway down the block along the back of Sinan's mosque, Sharia Qolongi leads off to the left and into this mid-Burgi period monument, the earliest of three mosques that this qadi or judge built in Cairo. The top half of the minaret is missing. The mosque, plain and unadorned, is of the congregational court-yard plan. It was restored in 1983.

Mosque of Mustafa Shurbagi Mirza * (No. 343) 1698/1110. Leave the mosque of the qadi by the southern entrance (on your right as you face the mihrab) and walk half a block forward until you reach Haret al-Saber on the left. This small street will lead straight to the façade of the mosque in Sharia Mirza. Turn right for the entrance. The mosque was built by a man of considerable power and influence, a mustahfizan or member of the military corps instituted by the Ottoman sultan Selim I to police the city. He lived nearby in a large and attractive house. The shops, at ground level below the mosque, were part of its supporting endowment.

The plan is that of a congregational mosque, with a covered courtyard. There is a gallery or loggia over the northwest side for Quran reading. On the roof there are three malqafs that once provided ventilation, but are now closed up. The poly-chrome inlaid marble paving of the entrance aisle and court-yard and the decoration of the mihrab and of the lower half of the walls are derived from the Mamluk period. The use of surface tiles is Ottoman. Although the tiles are late and not of the best quality, the effect of the whole, with the large panels of colored glass in the windows, is very pleasing. The atmosphere is cool, quiet, and restful—in marked contrast to the hurly-burly of the streets outside.

On leaving the mosque turn left, and at the corner turn right onto Sharia Ish al-Nakhla. At the corner, the remains of a sabil endowed by Shurbagi Mirza is all but hidden by billowing scarves and gauzy fabrics. One is now in the thick of a very lively textile bazaar, in which the narrow streets are lined with shops and carts selling material by the yard and by the piece, and full of men and women buying and selling and looking. Turn left at the end of the street, and almost immediately right again. This is Sharia Wikalat al-Balah ('date-merchants' hostel' street), which will lead to Sharia al-Matba' al-Ahliya, with the tram tracks to the rear of the Cairo Plaza.

Mosque of Abu'l-'Ila * (No. 340) c.1485/890. This monument is visible about one block on the right off 26 July Street as it continues east from the Abu'l-'Ila Bridge. The mosque was constructed by Ibn al-Qanish al-Burullusi and dedicated to Shaykh al-Husayn Abu'Ali, of which Abu'l-'Ila is a corruption. The shaykh died and was buried in the mausoleum shortly after 1485. Extensive alterations were made to the building in the nineteenth century; of the Mamluk monument only the mausoleum, entrance bay, east wall, and minaret are original. Still it is an interesting place to visit because it is a spacious and well-tended shrine. The local population continue to visit the saint, whose *baraka* or 'blessing' and intercession are still very important in their lives.

The Royal Stables. A few yards further on the right there is a double-winged building. From the middle of each wing a model of the head of a horse protrudes; between them there is a gateway. Except for the perimeters, there is not much to be seen of the royal stables from the late nineteenth century that once occupied a very large piece of land on this site. The Carriage Museum has been transferred to the Citadel.

Façade of nineteenth-century house. One block before the Mosque of Abu'l-'Ila, on the left side of the 26 July, is this house on the corner of an alley (Sharia Sidi al-Khatiri). It is worth looking at, since it offers a wonderful façade of mashrabiya windows and balconies, elaborate moldings, and geometric frames.

Palace of Muhammad 'Ali ** (No. 602) 1808. Muhammad 'Ali built several palaces in Cairo. Part of the summer palace of Shubra, begun in 1808 and elaborated in 1826, survives. It consisted of several pavilions and kiosks set amid fabulous and extensive gardens. Today the 'Fountain Kiosk,' which is perhaps the most sybaritic, is on view as the Muhammad 'Ali Museum. To get there follow the Corniche north about six and a half kilometers from the Cairo Plaza to the first right turn after the overpass over the Isma'iliya Canal. At the turn there will be a sign for Crystal Asfur, Shubra al-Khayma. Proceed for one long block; at the end the wall on your left will be pierced by a gate leading into the grounds of the Department of Agriculture, Ain Shams University, where the Museum stands.

Marble basin of Muhammad 'Ali

The pavilion is a charming mixutre of oriental fantasy and European luxury. A continuous gallery, six meters wide and supported by thin marble columns, encloses a vast marble basin. Various fountains supply the basin with water: four lions spout water over cascades in each corner and twenty-four crocodiles support the octagonal platform in the middle, with its own splashing fountain. The basin is only four feet deep but it is wide enough for several boats. The platform provided a stage for musicians and dancers. It was here that Muhammad 'Ali came to pass an hour or two during the heat of summer evenings, while the ladies of the harim rowed in the basin.

At the corners of the pavilion are four rooms: a billiard room (northwest, or far left as one stands in the entrance), whose table and complete set of balls and cues were a gift from King Louis-Philippe of France; a small dining room (southwest, or near left), a reception room (southeast, near right), and a resting room (northeast, far right). All are high-ceilinged and decorated with *trompe l'oeil* scenes of landscapes, palaces, and colonnades. The most ornate is the reception room, with its beautiful marquetry floor, large mirrors on wood-paneled walls, and ceilings of sculpted wood, gilded and painted in startling, fresh colors. Descriptions speak of the magnificent Persian carpets that covered the floors, the silken hangings and tapestries on walls, chandeliers for illumination, and divans for reclining.

The Shubra palace was the first in a new viceregal domain. From 1810 to 1880 the Nile banks became the setting for elaborate mansions centered in vast gardens of flowers, grottoes, and terraces that constituted one of the great attractions of Cairo for the foreign visitor. A few vestiges of these palaces remain, such as the reception area of the Marriott Hotel on the Gezira Island (part of the palace the Khedive Isma'il built to accommodate the Empress Eugénie when she came to Egypt in 1869 to open the Suez Canal) and the site of the Club Med on Roda Island, which was a family hunting lodge. Otherwise it is only names that remain: Qasr al-Nil (the area of the Nile Hilton and the Egyptian Museum); Qasr al-Dubara (the area around the U.S. and British embassies); and Qasr al-'Ali and Qasr al-'Aini (the area of Garden City from the Nile Hotel to the Mamluk aqueduct).

Glossary of Architectural Terms

Ablaq—striped; different courses of colored masonry.

Arabesque—ornament based on vegetal forms in which leaves and stems form a reciprocal, continuous, interlacing pattern.

Bab—gate or door.

Baraka—'blessing,' luck, grace, charisma, usually associated with a holy person or site.

Bayt—house.

Caravansarai—a rectangular structure that provided lodgings for merchants and space for commercial transcations.

Clerestory—the upper part of a central aisle, pierced by windows.

Dar—house, mansion.

Darb—path, way.

Dhikr—Sufi litany or prayer service.

Dikka—raised platform or gallery used for Quranic recitations, chants, and calls to prayer.

Finial—A formal ornament at the top of a canopy, minaret.

Funduq—inn, temporary lodgings where out-of-town merchants could stay.

Hammam—a bath, private or public.

Haramlik—literally the 'forbidden' area, the private or women's apartments.

Hod or hawd—a drinking trough for animals.

Hosh or hawsh—courtyard.

Joggled—interlocking.

Khan—place where goods are produced, sold, and stored, which also provided accommodations for travelers, merchants.

Khanqah—residential institution specially endowed for Sufis, Muslim ascetics, bound to lead a communal life of prayer and poverty.

Kufic—earliest style of Arabic script, angular and unpointed.

Kursi—wooden dais from which a reader could read large Qurans.

Kuttab—Quranic school, usually for young boys or orphans.

Lintel—a horizontal beam or stone bridging an opening.

Liwan or iwan—originally a sitting-room with a raised floor opening on to a covered court. Used here to describe the vaulted spaces surrounding the central courtyard of a madrasa.

Mabkhara—literally 'incense pot,' referring to the shape of early Ayyubid and Mamluk minaret finials.

Madhhab—a school or rite of Islamic jurisprudence or law. In Sunni Islam there are four rites: the Shafi'i, Hanafi, Maliki, and Hanbali.

Madrasa—literally 'a place of study' or school. Used in this book to designate theological schools, in which the madhhabs were taught.

Manzil—residence.

Malqaf—wind scoop, which in Egypt always faces north.

Maq'ad—literally a 'sitting-place' or seat. An open, arch-fronted area, on the second floor, overlooking the courtyard.

Maqsura—a railed and/or elevated enclosure in a mosque.

Maristan or bimaristan—a hospital.

Mashhad—literally a 'place of martyrdom or witness,' tomb-sanctuary, shrine.

Mashrabiya—literally a 'drinking-place-thing,' the alcove in wooden lattice windows where water in porous earthen bottles exposed to air currents was cooled by evaporation, and extended to designate projecting window or screen with a lattice-work grill. It is a typical feature of Cairene domestic architecture, which also appears in religious architecture.

Mastaba—stone bench at the entrance to buildings for sitting.

Maydan or midan—originally a polo ground, an open space or square in the city.

Merlon—A parapet with alternating raised portions and indentations, usually leaf-form.

Mihrab—niche that indicated the direction of Mecca and prayer.

Minaret—literally 'beacon,' tower from which the call to prayer is given five times daily.

Minbar—pulpit from which the address at the Friday noon prayer is given.

Mulid—brithday of saint, or religious fair.

Muqarnas—an ornamental arrangement of multi-tiered niches found in domes, squinches, portals. Also called stalactite, honeycomb.

Naskhi—cursive script, or one that is written with a running hand.

Pendentive—triangular area formed by cutting away corners at the internal angles of a square building to accommodate a dome.

Pier—a solid masonry support, usually square or rectangular.

Qa'a—a large hall or reception room.

Qasr—castle or palace.

Qibla—direction in which Muslims face to pray, i.e. toward Mecca, which in Egypt is approximately southeast. The qibla or sanctuary arcade or liwan is the one in which the mihrab is located.

Qubba—dome, or domed tomb chamber.

Rab'—apartment building or tenement for middle- and lower-class tenants.

Riwaq—an arcaded aisle hall.

Sabil—a public drinking fountain or dispensary for free distribution of water.

Sahn—the central courtyard of a mosque.

Saqiya—a waterwheel.

Salamlik—literally the 'greeting' area, the public or men's apartments.

Salsabil—carved marble panel over which water flowed.

Spandrel—area just inside or outside of an arch.

Squinch—an arch or system of arches placed at internal angles of a square structure so as to accomodate a dome.

Suffa—an elegant marble console where ewers and precious vases were stored in a house.

Sufi—Muslim ascetic, mystic, dervish.

Tabut—wooden cenotaph or grave marker.

Tahtabush—receiving area off the courtyard in a house.

Takiya or tekke—the Ottoman word for a khanqah, or Sufi hostel.

Tiraz—a band of historic inscription on the façade of a monument.

Thuluth—literally 'third,' denoting a monumental script in which the vertical strokes are three times taller than the horizontal ones.

Turba—tomb, usually a domed cube.

Voussoirs—wedge-shaped stones used in arch construction.

Waqf (pl. awqaf)—an assignment of revenue in perpetuity to some religious, educational, or charitable purposes; a religious endowment that cannot be alienated. The Western legal equivalent to the concept of waqf (literally 'stop') is mortmain.

Wikala—bonded warehouse for storage of goods, with upper floors for rent.

Ziyada—literally 'an addition,' which refers to the outer courtyards or areas that separated early mosques from the urban scene.

Zawiya—a residence for Muslim Sufis centered around a shaykh and a particular personal *tariqa* or path, order.

ℐslamic ℂalendar and ℐrincipal ℱeasts

The Islamic calendar is a lunar calendar and moves forward approximately eleven days each year. The year 1414 begins June 21, 1993.

Islamic Months and Festivals

Muharram
  1   New Year's Day
  10   Commemoration of the Battle of Karbala
Safar
Rabi' al-Awal
  12   Mulid al-Nabi (birth of Prophet Muhammad)
Rabi' al-Akhir
  25   Mulid (birth) of al-Husayn
Jumada al-Ula
Jumada al-Ukhra
Rajab
  15   Special day for visiting cemeteries
  20   Mulid of Sayyida Zaynab
  27   Lailat al-Isra' wa-l-Mi'rag (ascent of Prophet to heaven)
Sha'ban
  4   Mulid of Imam al-Shafi'i

271

Ramadan
  1   Beginning of month of fasting
  27   Lailat al-Qadr ('The Night of Power')
Shawwal
  1   'Id al-Fitr (Little Bairam), 3 days
Dhu al-Qa'da
Dhu al-Hijja
  10   'Id al-Adha (Feast of Sacrifice, Great Bairam), 4 days

Times of Afternoon Prayer
Summer: ca. 1:00 p.m., 4:30 p.m.
Winter: ca. 12:00 noon, 3:30 p.m.

Arabic Numerals
١   ٢   ٣   ٤   ٥   ٦   ٧   ٨   ٩   ٠
1   2   3   4   5   6   7   8   9   0

Bibliography

These books are recommended for additional information or color:

Abu Lughod, J. *Cairo: 1001 Years City Victorious.* Princeton, 1974.

Aldredge, J. *Cairo: A Biography of a City.* Boston, 1969.

Atil, E. *Renaissance of Islam: The Art of the Mamluks.* Washington, 1981.

Behrens-Abouseif, D. *The Minarets of Cairo.* Cairo, 1985.

Blue Guide Egypt. London and New York, 1983.

Creswell, K.A.C. *Early Muslim Architecture, Vol. 2.* Oxford, 1932–40.

—. *Architecture of Muslim Egypt.* 2 vols. Oxford, 1952–59.

—. *A Bibliography of the Architecture, Arts and Crafts of Islam.* Cairo, 1961.

—. *A Bibliography of the Architecture, Arts and Crafts of Islam, Supplements I and II.* Cairo, 1973 and 1984.

Devonshire, H. *Rambles in Cairo.* Cairo, 1931.

Dodge, B. *El-Azhar: A Millenium of Muslim Learning.* Washington, 1974.

Encyclopaedia of Islam. New Edition. ("Al-Qahira," "Ayyubid," "Fatimid," "Mamluk," etc.). Leiden.

Gayer-Anderson, R.G. *Legends of the Bayt al-Kritliya.* London, 1951.

Grabar, O., ed. *Muqarnas, Vol. 2: The Art of the Mamluks.* New Haven, 1984.

Glubb, J. *Soldiers of Fortune: The Story of the Mamluks.* London, 1973.

Holt, P.M. *Egypt and the Fertile Crescent 1516–1922.* Cornell, 1966.

Husayn, T. *A Stream of Days.* Trans. H. Wayment. London, 1948.

Ibn Iyas. *Journal d'un bourgeois du Caire.* Trans. G. Wiet. Paris, 1955.

Kessler, C. *The Carved Domes of Mamluk Cairo.* Cairo, 1976.

Kubiak, W.B. *Al-Fustat: Its Foundation and Early Urban Development.* Cairo, 1987.

Lane, E.W. *The 1001 Nights.* London, 1838.

—. *Manners and Customs of the Modern Egyptians.* London,1836.

Lyster, W. *The Citadel of Cairo.* Cairo, 1990.

Mahfouz, N. *Midaq Alley.* Trans. Trevor Le Gassick. Cairo, 1985.

—. *Palace Walk.* Trans. William M. Hutchins, Olive Kenny. Cairo, 1990.

Ministry of Culture. *Cairo: The Life Story of 1,000 Years.* Cairo, 1969.

Ministry of Waqfs. *The Mosques of Egypt.* Cairo, 1949.

Marlowe, J. *The Making of the Suez Canal.* London, 1964

—. *Cromer in Egypt.* New York, 1970.

Marsot:, A.L.S. *A Short History of Modern Egypt.* Cambridge, 1985

Lane-Poole, S. *Medieval Towns: The Story of Cairo.* London, 1906; 1924.

—. *Cairo: Fifty Years Ago.* London, 1896.

—. *Cairo: History, Monuments and Social Life.* London, 1898.

—. *A History of Egypt in the Middle Ages.* London, 1914.

Raymond, A. *The Great Arab Cities in the 16th and 18th Centuries.* New York, 1984.

Russell, Lady Dorothea. *Medieval Cairo.* London, 1963.

Ruthven, M. *Cairo.* Time–Life "Great Cities" Series, 1981.

Society for the Preservation of the Architectural Resources of Egypt: *Maps* 1, 2 and 3. Cairo.

Stewart, D. *Great Cairo: Mother of the World.* Cairo, 1981.

Wiet, G. *Cairo: City of Art and Commerce*. Oklahoma, 1972.

—. *Mosques of Cairo*. Trans. John Hardman. Beirut, 1966.

—. "L'Egypte arabe: 642–1517." Vol IV of G. Hanotaux (ed.): *Histoire de la nation égyptienne*. Paris, 1937.

Volkoff, O.V. *Le Caire 969–1969*. Cairo, 1971.

Index

This index includes all monuments that appear in the text or on maps. Additionally, it presents chronological and typological arrangements of materials that in the text are arranged geographically. References to maps are in bold type. Asterisks draw attention to important monuments.

Ahmad Effendi Salim, sabil–kuttab of, **2**; 58
Ahmad ibn Tulun, 9, 51–52
  aqueduct of, 9
  mosque of***, fig. 1, 3, 4; **2, 5**; 9, 27, 51–56
  Nilometer, addition to, 9, 36
Ahmad Katkhuda al-Karbutli, 160
Ahmad Katkhuda al-Razzaz, bayt of**, **4**; 90
Ahmad al-Mihmandar, mosque of*, **4**; 99–100
Ahmad Pasha, sabil–kuttab of*, **10**; 217
Ahmad Pasha Tahir, mausoleum of, **2**; 59
Ahmad al-Qazid, mausoleum of, **10**; 209
'Aisha, Sayyida, mosque of, **5, 6**; 132
Akhur, Amir, mosque of*, **3, 4**; 73, 74
alabaster, 223, 224
'Alam al-Din Sangar, Amir, 53, 122
'Ali (fourth khalif), 9, 121, 216
  name on monuments, 122, 138, 139, 198, 224, 228
'Ali Bey al-Kabir, 159, 171
  tomb of*, **7**; 141–42
  restoration to mausoleum of Imam al-Shafi'i, 136
'Ali Agha Dar al-Sa'ada, sabil–kuttab of, **2**;116
'Ali Badr al-Din al-Qarafi, tomb of, **6**; 128
'Ali Effendi Habib, manzil of, **3**; 73, 74
'Ali al-Rifa'i, Shaykh, 71
Alin Aq, palace of*, **4**; 84, 86
Alti Barmaq, mosque of*, **4**; 96
Altinbugha. *See* al-Maridani
Amna bint Salim al-Gazzar, 56
'Amr ibn al-'As, 7, 9, 43
  mosque of*, fig. 3; **1**; 20, 40–42
Anas, tomb of, **11**; 79, 239
Anatolia, Anatolian, 67, 127, 211, 237
al-Aqmar Mosque***, **10**; 107, 122, 138, 197–99
Aqsunqur, mosque of**, **4**; 86-88
aqueduct, fig 3; 22, 226
  of Ahmad ibn Tulun, 9
  of al-Ghuri, 44–45
  Mamluk*, **1, 5**; 7, 44–45
  of al-Nasir Muhammad, **5**; 44–45
arabesque decoration, 44, 49, 50, 73, 79, 105, 111, 113, 132, 158,
    160, 163, 170, 204, 213, 217, 229, 246, 250, 267
arches, fig. 5; 54, 87, 163, 184, 225
  blind, 136
  flat, 137
  keel, fig. 5; 27, 77, 91, 98, 100, 105, 107, 114, 122, 124, 137,
    169, 180, 197, 199, 211
  pointed, 27, 36, 52, 54
  relieving, 210

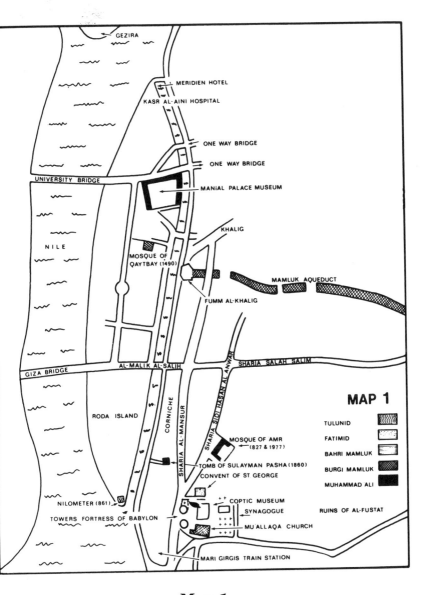

Map 1
The Island of Roda and South Cairo
(Ch. 3)

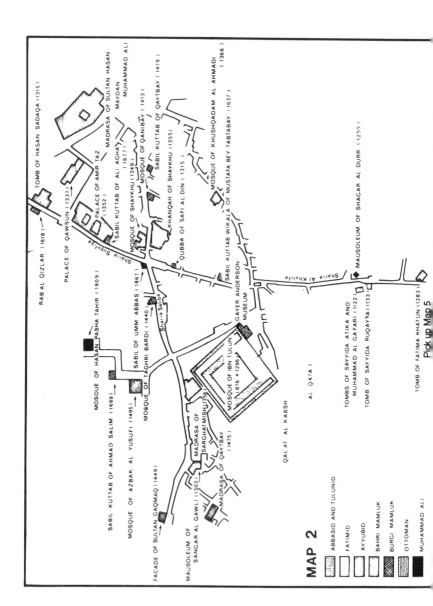

Map 2

Ibn Tulun and Sharia Saliba

(Ch. 4, 5, 8)

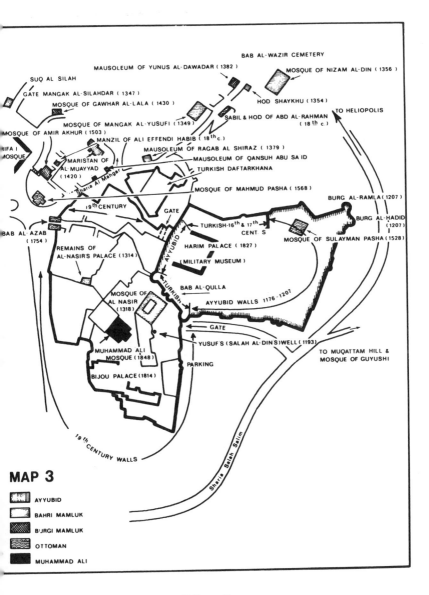

Map 3
The Citadel and Bab al-Wazir
(Ch. 5, 12)

303

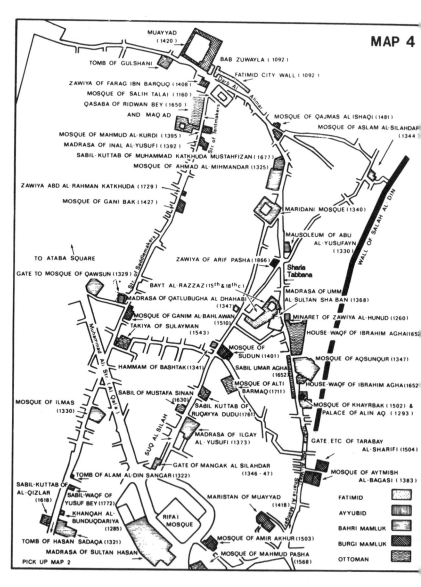

MAP 4

MUAYYAD (1420)

BAB ZUWAYLA (1092)

TOMB OF GULSHANI

FATIMID CITY WALL (1092)

Darb Al... Ahmar

ZAWIYA OF FARAG IBN BARQUQ (1408)
MOSQUE OF SALIH TALAI (1160)
QASABA OF RIDWAN BEY (1650)
AND MAQ AD

Str. of tentmakers

MOSQUE OF QAJMAS AL ISHAQI (1481)
MOSQUE OF ASLAM AL-SILAHDAR (1344)

MOSQUE OF MAHMUD AL-KURDI (1395)
MADRASA OF INAL AL-YUSUFI (1392)
SABIL-KUTTAB OF MUHAMMAD KATKHUDA MUSTAHFIZAN (1677)
MOSQUE OF AHMAD AL-MIHMANDAR (1325)

ZAWIYA ABD AL-RAHMAN KATKHUDA (1729)

MOSQUE OF GANI BAK (1427)

MARIDANI MOSQUE (1340)

MAUSOLEUM OF ABU AL-YUSUFAYN (1330)

WALL OF SALAH AL-DIN

TO ATABA SQUARE

Str. of Saddlemakers

ZAWIYA OF ARIF PASHA (1866)

Sharia Tabbana

GATE TO MOSQUE OF QAWSUN (1329)

BAYT AL-RAZZAZ (15th & 18th c.)
MADRASA OF QATLUBUGHA AL DHAHABI (1347)

MADRASA OF UMM AL-SULTAN SHA BAN (1368)

MOSQUE OF GANIM AL-BAHLAWAN (1510)
TAKIYA OF SULAYMAN (1543)

MINARET OF ZAWIYA AL-HUNUD (1260)
HOUSE-WAQF OF IBRAHIM AGHA (1652)

MOSQUE OF SUDUN (1401)

MOSQUE OF AQSUNQUR (1347)

Muhammad Ali Str. (Al Qala)

HAMMAM OF BASHTAK (1341)

SABIL UMAR AGHA (1652)

MOSQUE OF ALTI BARMAQ (1711)

HOUSE-WAQF OF IBRAHIM AGHA (1652)

SABIL OF MUSTAFA SINAN (1630)

SUQ AL SILAH

SABIL KUTTAB OF RUQAYYA DUDU (1761)

MOSQUE OF KHAYRBAK (1502) & PALACE OF ALIN AQ (1293)

MOSQUE OF ILMAS (1330)

MADRASA OF ILGAY AL-YUSUFI (1373)

GATE ETC OF TARABAY AL-SHARIFI (1504)

GATE OF MANGAK AL SILAHDAR (1346-47)

MOSQUE OF AYTMISH AL-BAGASI (1383)

TOMB OF ALAM AL-DIN SANGAR (1322)

SABIL-KUTTAB OF AL-QIZLAR (1618)

SABIL-WAQF OF YUSUF BEY (1772)

MARISTAN OF MUAYYAD (1418)

FATIMID

AYYUBID

KHANQAH AL-BUNDUQDARIYA (1285)

RIFA'I MOSQUE

BAHRI MAMLUK

BURGI MAMLUK

TOMB OF HASAN SADAQA (1321)

MADRASA OF SULTAN HASAN

PICK UP MAP 2

MOSQUE OF AMIR AKHUR (1503)

MOSQUE OF MAHMUD PASHA (1568)

OTTOMAN

Map 4
Sultan Hasan to Bab Zuwayla
(Ch. 5, 6, 7)

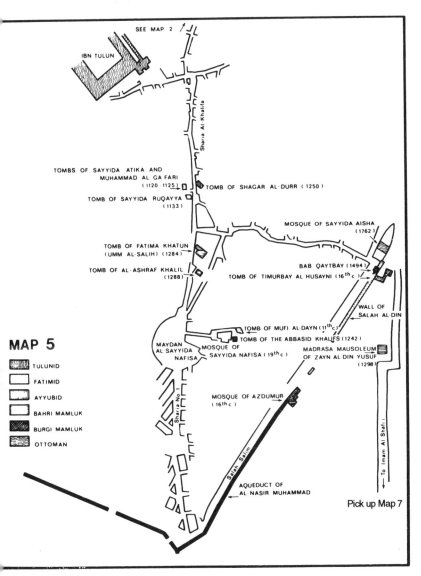

SEE MAP 2

IBN TULUN

Sharia Al Khalifa

TOMBS OF SAYYIDA ATIKA AND
MUHAMMAD AL GA FARI
(1120 - 1125)

TOMB OF SHAGAR AL-DURR (1250)

TOMB OF SAYYIDA RUQAYYA
(1133)

MOSQUE OF SAYYIDA AISHA
(1762)

TOMB OF FATIMA KHATUN
(UMM AL-SALIH) (1284)

BAB QAYTBAY (1494)

TOMB OF AL-ASHRAF KHALIL
(1288)

TOMB OF TIMURBAY AL HUSAYNI (16th c)

WALL OF
SALAH AL-DIN

TOMB OF MUFI AL-DAYN (11th c)

TOMB OF THE ABBASID KHALIFS (1242)

MAYDAN
AL-SAYYIDA
NAFISA

MOSQUE OF
SAYYIDA NAFISA (19th c)

MADRASA MAUSOLEUM
OF ZAYN AL-DIN YUSUF
(1298)

MAP 5

TULUNID

FATIMID

AYYUBID

BAHRI MAMLUK

BURGI MAMLUK

OTTOMAN

Sharia No 1

MOSQUE OF AZDUMUR
(16th c)

Salah Salim

To Imam Al Shafi'i

AQUEDUCT OF
AL-NASIR MUHAMMAD

Pick up Map 7

Map 5
Southern Cemetery: A)
Sharia Saliba to Maydan Sayyida Nafisa
(Ch. 8)

305

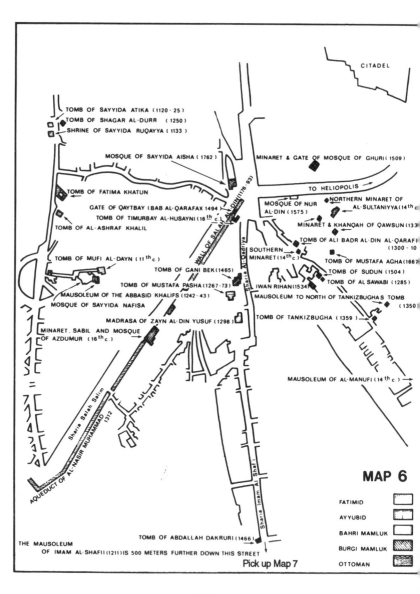

CITADEL

TOMB OF SAYYIDA ATIKA (1120 - 25)
TOMB OF SHAGAR AL-DURR (1250)
SHRINE OF SAYYIDA RUQAYYA (1133)

MOSQUE OF SAYYIDA AISHA (1762)

MINARET & GATE OF MOSQUE OF GHURI (1509)

TO HELIOPOLIS

TOMB OF FATIMA KHATUN

GATE OF QAYTBAY (BAB AL-QARAFA X 1494)
TOMB OF TIMURBAY AL-HUSAYNI (16 th c.)
TOMB OF AL-ASHRAF KHALIL

MOSQUE OF NUR
AL-DIN (1575)

NORTHERN MINARET OF
AL-SULTANIYYA (14 th c)

MINARET & KHANQAH OF QAWSUN (133

TOMB OF ALI BADR AL-DIN AL-QARAFI
(1300 - 10

WALL OF SALAH AL-DIN (1176 - 93)

SOUTHERN
MINARET (14 th c.)

TOMB OF MUSTAFA AGHA (1667

TOMB OF MUFI AL-DAYN (11 th c.)

TOMB OF GANI BEK (1465)

TOMB OF SUDUN (1504)
TOMB OF AL SAWABI (1285)

TOMB OF MUSTAFA PASHA (1267-73)

IWAN RIHAN (1534)

MAUSOLEUM OF THE ABBASID KHALIFS (1242 - 43)

MAUSOLEUM TO NORTH OF TANKIZBUGHAS TOMB

MOSQUE OF SAYYIDA NAFISA

(1350

MADRASA OF ZAYN AL-DIN YUSUF (1298)

TOMB OF TANKIZBUGHA (1359)

MINARET, SABIL AND MOSQUE
OF AZDUMUR (16 th c.)

Sharia Al-Qadiriya

MAUSOLEUM OF AL-MANUFI (14 th c.)

Sharia Salah Salim

AQUEDUCT OF AL-NASIR MUHAMMAD (1312

Sharia Imam Al-Shafi

MAP 6

FATIMID
AYYUBID
BAHRI MAMLUK
BURGI MAMLUK
OTTOMAN

THE MAUSOLEUM
OF IMAM AL-SHAFII (1211) IS 500 METERS FURTHER DOWN THIS STREET

TOMB OF ABDALLAH DAKRURI (1466)

Pick up Map 7

Map 6
Southern Cemetery: B) Middle Area—South of the Cita
(Ch. 8)

306

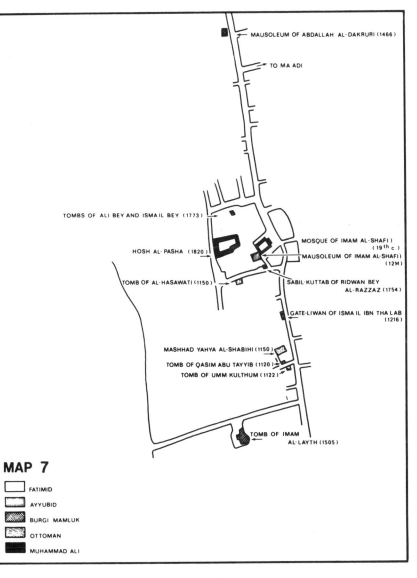

← MAUSOLEUM OF ABDALLAH AL-DAKRURI (1466)

← TO MA ADI

TOMBS OF ALI BEY AND ISMAIL BEY (1773)

MOSQUE OF IMAM AL-SHAFI'I
(19ᵗʰ c.)

HOSH AL-PASHA (1820)

MAUSOLEUM OF IMAM AL-SHAFI'I
(12M)

TOMB OF AL-HASAWATI (1150)

SABIL-KUTTAB OF RIDWAN BEY
AL-RAZZAZ (1754)

GATE-LIWAN OF ISMA IL IBN THA LAB
(1216)

MASHHAD YAHYA AL-SHABIHI (1150)

TOMB OF QASIM ABU TAYYIB (1120)

TOMB OF UMM KULTHUM (1122)

TOMB OF IMAM
AL-LAYTH (1505)

MAP 7

☐ FATIMID

▨ AYYUBID

▨ BURGI MAMLUK

▨ OTTOMAN

■ MUHAMMAD ALI

Map 7
Southern Cemetery: C) The Lesser Qarafa
(Ch. 8)

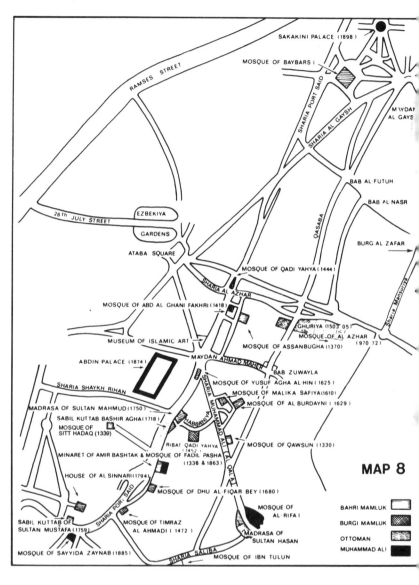

SAKAKINI PALACE (1898)

MOSQUE OF BAYBARS I

RAMSES STREET

SHARIA PORT SAID

SHARIA AL GAYSH

MAYDAN AL GAYSH

BAB AL FUTUH

BAB AL NASR

26th JULY STREET

EZBEKIYA

GARDENS

QASABA

BURG AL ZAFAR

ATABA SQUARE

MOSQUE OF QADI YAHYA (1444)

SHARIA AL AZHAR

MOSQUE OF ABD AL GHANI FAKHRI (1418)

GHURIYA (1503-05)

MOSQUE OF AL AZHAR (970-72)

MUSEUM OF ISLAMIC ART

MOSQUE OF ASSANBUGHA (1370)

SHARIA MANSUR

ABDIN PALACE (1874)

MAYDAN AHMAD MAHER

BAB ZUWAYLA

MOSQUE OF YUSUF AGHA AL-HIN (1625)

SHARIA SHAYKH RIHAN

MOSQUE OF MALIKA SAFIYA (1610)

MADRASA OF SULTAN MAHMUD (1750)

MOSQUE OF AL BURDAYNI (1629)

SABIL KUTTAB BASHIR AGHA (1718)

MOSQUE OF SITT HADAQ (1339)

HABBANIYA

SHARIA MUHAMMAD ALI

RIBAT QADI YAHYA (1452)

MOSQUE OF QAWSUN (1330)

MINARET OF AMIR BASHTAK & MOSQUE OF FADIL PASHA (1336 & 1863)

HOUSE OF AL SINNARI (1794)

MAP 8

MOSQUE OF DHU AL-FIQAR BEY (1680)

SHARIA PORT SAID

MOSQUE OF AL-RIFA'I

BAHRI MAMLUK

SABIL KUTTAB OF SULTAN MUSTAFA (1759)

MOSQUE OF TIMRAZ AL AHMADI (1472)

MADRASA OF SULTAN HASAN

BURGI MAMLUK

OTTOMAN

MUHAMMAD ALI

MOSQUE OF SAYYIDA ZAYNAB (1885)

SHARIA SALIBA

MOSQUE OF IBN TULUN

Map 8
Sharia Port Said
(Ch. 9, 14)

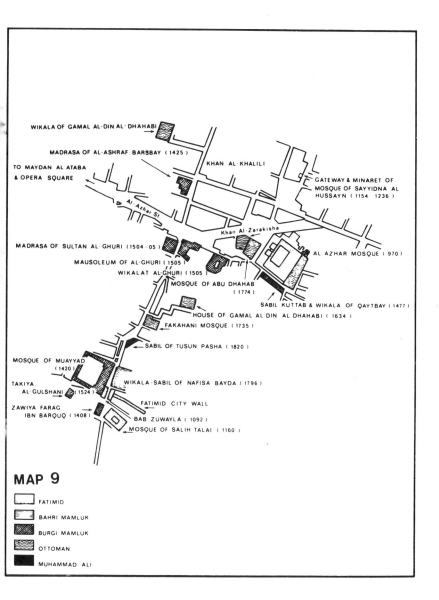

WIKALA OF GAMAL AL-DIN AL-DHAHABI

MADRASA OF AL-ASHRAF BARSBAY (1425)

KHAN AL-KHALILI

TO MAYDAN AL ATABA
& OPERA SQUARE

GATEWAY & MINARET OF
MOSQUE OF SAYYIDNA AL
HUSSAYN (1154 1236)

Al-Azhar St.

Khan Al-Zarakisha

MADRASA OF SULTAN AL-GHURI (1504-05)

AL AZHAR MOSQUE (970)

MAUSOLEUM OF AL-GHURI (1505)

WIKALAT AL-GHURI (1505)

MOSQUE OF ABU DHAHAB
(1774)

SABIL KUTTAB & WIKALA OF QAYTBAY (1477)

HOUSE OF GAMAL AL DIN AL DHAHABI (1634)

FAKAHANI MOSQUE (1735)

SABIL OF TUSUN PASHA (1820)

MOSQUE OF MUAYYAD
(1420)

WIKALA-SABIL OF NAFISA BAYDA (1796)

TAKIYA
AL-GULSHANI (1524)

FATIMID CITY WALL

ZAWIYA FARAG
IBN BARQUQ (1408)

BAB ZUWAYLA (1092)

MOSQUE OF SALIH TALAI (1160)

MAP 9

FATIMID

BAHRI MAMLUK

BURGI MAMLUK

OTTOMAN

MUHAMMAD ALI

Map 9
Bab Zuwayla to al-Azhar
(Ch. 10)

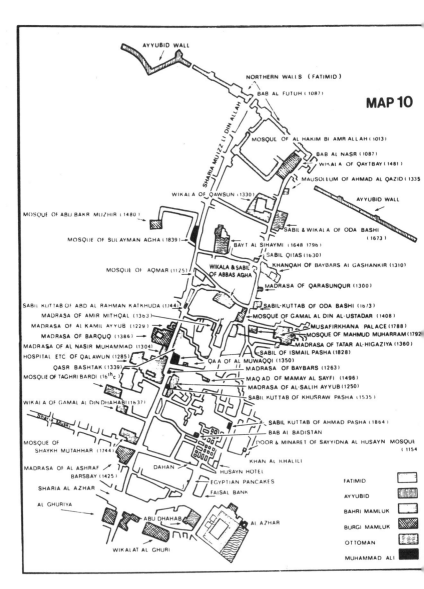

MAP 10

AYYUBID WALL

NORTHERN WALLS (FATIMID)

BAB AL FUTUH (1087)

MOSQUE OF AL HAKIM BI AMR ALLAH (1013)

BAB AL NASR (1087)

WIKALA OF QAYTBAY (1481)

MAUSOLEUM OF AHMAD AL QAZID (1335

SHARIA MUIZZ LI DIN ALLAH

WIKALA OF QAWSUN (1330)

AYYUBID WALL

MOSQUE OF ABU BAKR MUZHIR (1480)

SABIL & WIKALA OF ODA BASHI

MOSQUE OF SULAYMAN AGHA (1839)
(1673)

BAYT AL SIHAYMI (1648 1796)

SABIL QITAS (1630)

MOSQUE OF AQMAR (1125)

WIKALA & SABIL
OF ABBAS AGHA

KHANQAH OF BAYBARS AL GASHANKIR (1310)

MADRASA OF QARASUNQUR (1300)

SABIL KUTTAB OF ABD AL RAHMAN KATKHUDA (1744)

SABIL-KUTTAB OF ODA BASHI (1673)

MADRASA OF AMIR MITHQAL (1363)

MOSQUE OF GAMAL AL DIN AL-USTADAR (1408)

MADRASA OF AL KAMIL AYYUB (1229)

MUSAFIRKHANA PALACE (1788)

MADRASA OF BARQUQ (1386)

MOSQUE OF MAHMUD MUHARRAM (1792

MADRASA OF AL NASIR MUHAMMAD (1304)

MADRASA OF TATAR AL-HIGAZIYA (1360)

HOSPITAL ETC OF QALAWUN (1285)

SABIL OF ISMAIL PASHA (1828)

QAA OF AL MUWAQQI (1350)

QASR BASHTAK (1339)

MADRASA OF BAYBARS (1263)

MOSQUE OF TAGHRI BARDI (16th c)

MAQAD OF MAMAY AL SAYFI (1496)

MADRASA OF AL-SALIH AYYUB (1250)

SABIL KUTTAB OF KHUSRAW PASHA (1535)

WIKALA OF GAMAL AL DIN DHAHABI (1637)

SABIL KUTTAB OF AHMAD PASHA (1864)

Sharia Muizz

BAB AL BADISTAN

DOOR & MINARET OF SAYYIDNA AL HUSAYN MOSQUE
(1154

MOSQUE OF
SHAYKH MUTAHHAR (1744)

KHAN AL KHALILI

MADRASA OF AL ASHRAF
BARSBAY (1425)

DAHAN

HUSAYN HOTEL

EGYPTIAN PANCAKES

SHARIA AL AZHAR

FAISAL BANK

AL GHURIYA

FATIMID

AYYUBID

BAHRI MAMLUK

ABU DHAHAB

BURGI MAMLUK

AL AZHAR

OTTOMAN

MUHAMMAD ALI

WIKALAT AL GHURI

Map 10
Al-Azhar Square to Bab al-Futuh
(Ch. 11)

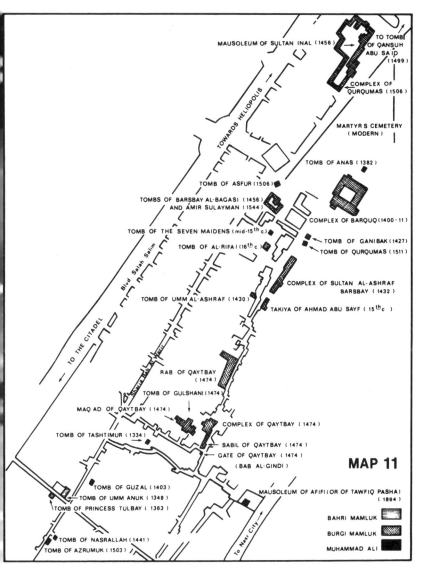

MAUSOLEUM OF SULTAN INAL (1456)

TO TOMB OF QANSUH ABU SA'ID (1499)

COMPLEX OF QURQUMAS (1506)

MARTYRS CEMETERY (MODERN)

TOWARDS HELIOPOLIS

TOMB OF ANAS (1382)

TOMB OF ASFUR (1506)

TOMBS OF BARSBAY AL-BAGASI (1456) AND AMIR SULAYMAN (1544)

COMPLEX OF BARQUQ (1400-11)

TOMB OF THE SEVEN MAIDENS (mid-15th c.)

TOMB OF GANIBAK (1427)

TOMB OF AL-RIFAI (16th c.)

TOMB OF QURQUMAS (1511)

Blvd Salah Salim

COMPLEX OF SULTAN AL-ASHRAF BARSBAY (1432)

TOMB OF UMM AL-ASHRAF (1430)

TAKIYA OF AHMAD ABU SAYF (15th c.)

TO THE CITADEL

RAB OF QAYTBAY (1474)

TOMB OF GULSHANI (1474)

MAQ'AD OF QAYTBAY (1474)

COMPLEX OF QAYTBAY (1474)

TOMB OF TASHTIMUR (1334)

SABIL OF QAYTBAY (1474)

GATE OF QAYTBAY (1474) (BAB AL-GINDI)

MAP 11

TOMB OF GUZAL (1403)

MAUSOLEUM OF AFIFI (OR OF TAWFIQ PASHA) (1894)

TOMB OF UMM ANUK (1348)

TOMB OF PRINCESS TULBAY (1363)

BAHRI MAMLUK

BURGI MAMLUK

MUHAMMAD ALI

TOMB OF NASRALLAH (1441)

TOMB OF AZRUMUK (1503)

To Near City

Map 11
Northern Cemetery
(Ch. 13)

311

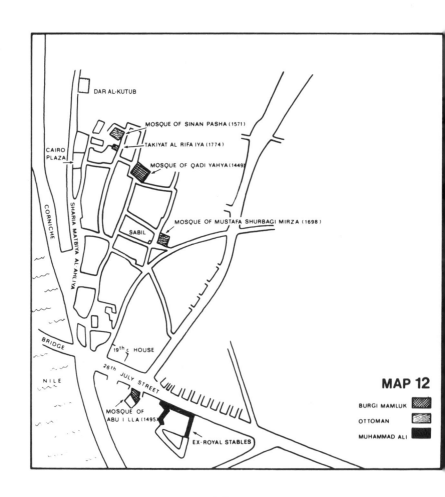

Map 12
Bulaq
(Ch.15)

312